The History of English FREEMASONRY

LEWIS MASONIC
Books

The History of English FREEMASONRY

JOHN HAMILL

Librarian and Curator of the United Grand Lodge of England

LEWIS MASONIC

Books

First published in England in 1994

Published by LEWIS MASONIC
Ian Allan Regalia Ltd, Coombelands House, Coombelands Lane
Addlestone, Surrey KT15 1HY, who are members of the Ian Allan Group.

ISBN 085318 205 1

British Library Cataloguing in Publication Data.

A Catalogue record for this book is available from the British Library

Typeset, printed and bound in Great Britain by
Latimer Trend & Company Ltd, Plymouth

For my Mother and to the memory of my late Father

CONTENTS

LIST OF COLOUR ILLUSTRATIONS

between pages 160 and 161

12 HRH Albert Edward, Prince of Wales (Edward VII), being welcomed as a Past Grand Master, 1870. Painting by S. Rosenthal.

13 Third Degree Tracing Board by Josiah Bowring (1757–1831), dated 1819.

14 Wedgwood jug, 20 inches high, inscribed 1803 and decorated with transfers referring to all the then known Masonic degrees.

15 John Hervey, Grand Secretary 1868–80. Portrait in oils by H. Tettenborn, 1870.

16 James Asperne in his regalia as a Grand Steward, 1813. Portrait in oils by Samuel Drummond.

17 HRH The Duke of Kent, KG, Grand Master, opening the public exhibition at Freemasons' Hall, 4 July 1986.

18 Grand Lodge meeting at Earls Court, London, on 10 June 1992 to celebrate the 275th Anniversary of the Grand Lodge and the 25th Anniversary of the Grand Mastership of HRH The Duke of Kent, KG.

19 Members of Quatuor Coronati Lodge No. 2076, the premier Lodge of Masonic Research, November 1993.

20 HRH The Duke of Kent, KG, Grand Master since 1967. Portrait by Derek Hill commissioned by Grand Lodge in 1986.

LIST OF MONOCHROME ILLUSTRATIONS

between pages 96 and 97

FOREWORD

My name is Michael Higham and I am the Grand Secretary of the United Grand Lodge of England. If we want to understand Freemasonry and be able to explain it to our families and friends and colleagues, it is important that we should know something of its origins and be able to reply on what is written about it.

Over the last 250 years many books have been written about Freemasonry, both by Masons and by commentators who are not members of the Craft. Some of the books are highly speculative; some are inaccurate, and some are deliberately misleading. A few, by long-dead Brethren of some Masonic eminence, contain embarrassingly fanciful ideas of what Freemasonry is about. It is therefore not surprising if both Freemasons and the general public do not know what to accept as true—and it is a pleasure to introduce a book written by a sensible Freemason who is master of his subject. He uses simple terms to explain the history of the English Craft and how it works; its relations with the Royal Arch and other degrees; its charitable activities, and its defences against the 'attacks of the insidious'—ill-informed critics and incredulous opponents of Freemasonry.

What we might in short form call Masonic education, and what the Grand Master describes as stimulating and satisfying natural curiosity about Freemasonry, is becoming more and more to be seen as important to our work, both in Lodge and outside. This will be a useful part of the Masonic educational process, and I recommend it—both to Brethren and to those who are not Masons.

GRAND SECRETARY

United Grand Lodge of England

INTRODUCTION TO THE REVISED EDITION

My original publisher having declined to bring out a revised edition of this book, or to go on printing the original edition, I was delighted when Chris Beach said that he would be interested in reprinting it. The original edition was written and printed at speed and a number of minor factual and printing errors crept in, which have now been corrected.

Writing in 1985 for publication in 1986 the final chapter—Attacks on the Craft—was literally 'hot news' and very quickly overtaken by later events. The chapter has now been rewritten to take into account the many problems which public misconceptions of Freemasonry have caused the Craft since 1986. The last eight years have also seen major changes in the Craft and Royal Arch—the penalties debate and the revision of the Royal Arch ritual—as well as the major celebrations of 1992. The relevant sections of the original text have been extended to take note of those events.

Those who have read the original edition will not find any major changes in the arguments put forward in that text. The reaction of a number of brethren to the Chapter on the origins was 'like many historians you have demolished the various theories but you have not given us your theory'. My answer was quite simple: I do not have a theory for our origins. For the reasons argued in this book I lean towards the theory of an indirect link with operative masonry, that being, on the evidence we have, the most sustainable. I have often been asked if I would welcome discoveries which would provide the origins of our Institution. The historian in me says YES!, because historians like to find answers, but the human says no because the discovery of our origins would deprive me and my colleagues in Masonic research of many happy and harmless hours of argument over what the answer to that great question is.

John Hamill
London 1994

INTRODUCTION TO THE FIRST EDITION

FREEMASONRY has been much in the news over the last few years and many of the reports, and the resultant correspondence, have shown how little is known about the subject and how much nonsense has been built upon that lack of knowledge. Part of the problem is due to poor research by those making comments and part to Freemasonry itself, which in a world in which privacy has become almost a dirty word has been perhaps too protective of its privacy. This book is an attempt to provide a simple and, it is hoped, readable account of the origins and development of Freemasonry in England. It has not been written in any sense as a direct rebuttal of any criticism which has appeared in the press nor is it in any sense an official publication, despite the author being an official of the United Grand Lodge of England. Unless otherwise stated, any opinions expressed are the personal opinions of the author.

As there is a fairly extensive literature of the subject the question may be asked, why another book on Freemasonry? The answers are simple. Firstly, although much has been written on the subject much of it is out of print or privately printed and now available only in reference libraries. As with many specialised subjects, books on Freemasonry tend to be printed in short runs and are rarely reprinted.

Secondly, Masonic books have tended to have been written by Freemasons for other Freemasons and presuppose a certain basic knowledge of the workings of Freemasonry and its terminology. This book has been written principally for non-Masons who do not have that basic knowledge but it is hoped that members of the Order will also find much in it to interest them. Thirdly, Freemasonry has suffered from a small number of its own members who have published their own decidedly odd interpretations of the nature of Freemasonry—interpretations that are unacceptable to the majority of Freemasons and at variance with officially published statements. It is hoped that the present work will dispel some of the erroneous impressions given by such writers.

To attempt to define Freemasonry succinctly is an almost impossible task; in many ways it is easier to say what is is not. As there is no official dogma, and because an individual Freemason's response to his Freemasonry is an intensely personal one, it is almost certain that if six members were asked to define what Freemasonry was to them six differing answers would result. To assist members in answering questions as a result of the intense interest sparked off by media attention the Board of General Purpose in 1984 published a leaflet entitled *What is Freemasonry* in which it is defined as:

> One of the world's oldest secular fraternal societies . . . a society of men concerned with spiritual values. Its members are taught its precepts by a series of ritual dramas, which follow ancient forms and use stonemason's customs and tools as allegorical guides. The essential qualification for admission and continuing membership is a belief in a Supreme Being. Membership is open to men of any race or religion who can fulfil this essential qualification and are of good repute . . .

As will be seen in Chapter Ten, what freemasonry is *not* is a secret society; a religion or substitute for religion; a self-help group; a quasi-political pressure group; a shadowy conspiracy manipulating government at all levels, the law in all its branches, industry or commerce, the government of the various churches, or the education system.

The candidate for initiation learns very early in his masonic career that the basic principles of Freemasonry are Brotherly Love, Relief, and Truth. *Brotherly Love* in its sense of promotion of tolerance and respect for the beliefs and ideals of others, and the building of a world in which that tolerance and respect, together with kindness and understanding, can flourish. *Relief* not in the limited sense of monetary giving but in the widest sense of charitable giving of money, time, and effort to assist the community as a whole. *Truth* in the sense of striving for high moral standards and in conducting one's life—in all its aspects—in as honest a manner as possible. In simple terms, a Freemason is taught his duties to his God, his fellow man, and the laws of his country.

Like all other institutions Freemasonry has developed its own terminology and phraseology which are instantly understood by its members but may appear strange to others. As a number of terms will have to be regularly used in this book a few definitions will be necessary.

Freemasonry is both a general and a specific term. In its general sense it covers the whole subject in all its diverse aspects. It is also used in a specific sense in the Craft to mean simply the three degrees of Craft Freemasonry. It is often shortened to Masonry and when used as an adjective the word *Masonic* is used in preference to *Freemasonic*.

The Craft means simply the first three degrees of Entered Apprentice, Fellowcraft, and Master Mason practised in a lodge of Freemasons, what might be termed basic Freemasonry. All other Masonic degrees are additional to the Craft and a Master Mason is not required to take them, though it is essential to be a member of the Craft should he wish to go into any of these branches of Freemasonry. A Freemason who remains solely a member of the Craft will not in any way regard himself as being incomplete.

The terms *Operative* and *Speculative* are used to differentiate between the old operative stonemasons and the newer free and accepted or speculative masons. Speculative is used in its original sense of one who engages in thought or reflection upon and meditation on or enquiries into a particular subject.

Degree is used in Freemasonry in its sense of a step or stage in a process. Thus the three Craft degrees are the steps or stages by which a candidate becomes a Freemason.

Freemasonry is a living organisation and has developed over a long period, imperceptibly changing and adapting itself to the periods in which it has existed, on occasions deliberately altering its ceremonies or rules but without changing its basic principles and tenets. As such it is not always possible to pin-point accurately when a particular practice was introduced or modified. As will be seen, the major questions of why and when Freemasonry came into existence have still to be answered. But exist it does, and on a scale that could not have been foreseen by its originators. In a relatively small publication it is only possible to give an outline of Freemasonry's development, but it is hoped that what has been written will prove of sufficient interest to lead at least some of its readers to further study of an institution which has survived over such a long period and has attracted to it men from a very wide cross-section of society holding widely differing religious and political views but able to meet in harmony and equality.

Having worked in the Grand Lodge Library and Museum for over fourteen years I have been in a privileged position without which it would have been difficult to write this book. My position has given me daily access to the collections now under my care and has given me the opportunity of 'making a daily advancement in Masonic knowledge' through the many queries that have to be answered. It has also afforded me the opportunity of meeting, assisting, and discussing problems with the major Masonic scholars of today.

My fellow members of Quatuor Coronati Lodge No. 2076, internationally recognised as the premier Lodge of Research, will I hope forgive my having directed the book to a general audience rather than specifically to them. For a hundred years the Lodge has provided those interested in Masonic history and research with an unrivalled storehouse of knowledge in its transactions *Ars Quatuor Coronatorum* (AQC). To its members present and past we all owe a great debt of gratitude. It would be invidious for me to single out individuals, with one exception. Terence Haunch, my immediate predecessor as Librarian and Curator, possesses an encyclopaedic knowledge of the history, traditions, and working of Freemasonry which I had the pleasure of sharing during twelve years of working closely with him. I could not have wished for a more knowledgeable or courteous mentor and friend.

The present Grand Secretary, Cdr. M.B.S. Higham RN, and his predecessor, Sir James Stubbs KCVO, have, perhaps unwittingly been of great assistance by leading me to consider aspects of Freemasonry which would not normally have come within my professional duties. To the Board of General Purposes I am grateful for permission to have access to and to quote from both the archives at Freemasons' Hall and from current publications as well as for permission to reproduce the illustrations.

To my parents I owe a great deal. My late father gave me my love of history and tradition and was my introduction to the Craft. Neither of us realised where that step would lead. I hope that he would have enjoyed reading this book.

JOHN HAMILL
January 1986

1

THEORIES OF ORIGIN

WHEN, Why, and Where did Freemasonry originate?

There is one answer to these questions: we do not know, despite all the paper and ink that has been expended in examining them. Indeed, the issues have been greatly clouded by well-meaning but ill-informed Masonic historians themselves. It is only slightly more than a century ago that British masonic historians began critically to examine the traditional history of the Craft passed down to them over the preceding century and a half. Finding that 'history' wanting, they began to search out actual documented evidence of speculative Freemasonry prior to the formation of the premier Grand Lodge of England in 1717. Their research and writing did not put a halt to the writings of what may be termed the *mystical* or *romantic* (in the true sense of that word) school of Masonic historians, which had led to even more confusion. Thus there are two main approaches to Masonic history: the *authentic* or *scientific* approach, in which theory is built upon or developed, out of verifiable facts and documentation; and the *non-authentic* approach in which attempts are made to place Freemasonry in the context of the Mystery tradition by a correlation of the teachings, allegory, and symbolism of the Craft with those of the various esoteric traditions. To further complicate matters, there are divisions of opinion within the two main schools.

The average Freemason derives his initial knowledge of the history of the Craft from the ritual itself. As he progresses through the ceremonies he learns that at the building of King Solomon's Temple at Jerusalem the skilled masons were divided into two classes, Apprentices and Fellow; that they were presided over by three Grand Masters (King Solomon, Hiram King of Tyre, and Hiram Abiff) who shared certain secrets known only to them. That these secrets were lost by the murder of Hiram Abiff—a result of his refusal to divulge the secrets—and that certain substituted secrets were adopted 'until time or circumstance should restore the former'. The implication in the ritual is that Freemasonry was already established in Solomon's time and has continued as an unchanged system since then. The ritual, however, as the candidate quickly realises, is not literal or historical truth but a dramatic allegory by means of which the principles and tenets of the Craft are handed down.

The first history of the Craft appeared, with official sanction, as part of the first *Constitutions*,[1] compiled and published on behalf of the premier Grand Lodge by the Revd Dr James Anderson in 1723. Anderson's work is largely a legendary history of the builder's craft from Adam in the Garden of Eden down to the formation of the premier Grand Lodge of England in 1717. Anderson makes no distinction between operative and speculative Masonry, implying that the one was a continuation of the other. Anderson has often been harshly criticised for his history, but this is unfair to him. He was not writing a history as we would term it today but producing an *apologia* to give a relatively new institution an honourable descent. He did not even claim to have written an original work but, as he explained in the second edition (1738) of the *Constitutions*, had simply digested the old Gothic Constitutions (see p. 33). It was from these that he derived the traditions of Freemasons' lodges having existed from ancient times; of various promoters, or Grand Masters of the Craft; and of a Prince Edwin having called a great assembly of masons at York in AD 926[2] at which he had granted them a Constitution and ordered them to meet in Quarterly Communications to regulate their lodges. The impression is given that the Grand Lodge or Assembly had continued from that date down to 1717. Had Anderson not produced a revised and much expanded version of his history for the second edition of the *Constitutions* the 1723 version would have been accepted for what it was: an *apologia* constructed from legend, folklore and tradition.

For the 1738 edition Anderson appears, unfortunately, to have given full reign to his imagination, constructing a detailed 'history' of English Masonry from the supposed Assembly at York down to the revival of the Grand Lodge in 1717 and continuing it from thence to 1738. To Anderson the terms Geometry, Architecture and Masonry were synonymous. Any English monarch or historical personality who had in any manner patronized architects or masons was listed either as a Grand Master or, at least, a Grand Warden of Freemasonry. To 'prove' the ancient and unbroken lineage of the Institution he claimed that the coming together of the four London lodges as a Grand Lodge in 1717 was not the creation of a new organisation but a *revival*[3] of an ancient organisation which had been allowed to fall into 'decay' by the neglect of its Grand Master, Sir Christopher Wren. A startling claim, and one for which no evidence exists, particularly as in the 1723 version no mention of a revival is made and Sir Christopher Wren appears only in a footnote, as the Architect of the Sheldonian Theatre at Oxford. Strangely, Wren was still living when the 1723 version appeared but was safely dead by the time Anderson began his revisions.

Because Anderson's history was published with the sanction of the Grand Lodge it took on the guise of holy writ, the more so as its contents were not challenged by those who had taken part in the events of 1717. So acceptable did his work prove that it continued to be reprinted without alteration, simply being brought up to date, in all subsequent editions of the premier Grand Lodge's *Constitutions* down to the final edition of 1784. It was plagiarised by the various editors of the eighteenth-century *Freemasons' Pocket Companions*[4] and formed the basis of the historical section of William Preston's *Illustrations of Masonry* down to the posthumous seventeenth edition of 1861, edited by the Revd Dr George Oliver. There were plans to incorporate it in the 1815, 1819 and 1827 editions of the *Book of Constitutions* of the United Grand Lodge of England, the published portions of which are entitled *Part the Second*, announcements being made that *Part the First* would be a history of Freemasonry. Fortunately, it never appeared. As the premier Grand Lodge *Constitutions* and Preston's *Illustrations* were exported to North America, and the early editions were translated into French and German, Anderson's misinformation was given wide circulation and was to have a profound effect on the Craft's conception of, and attitude towards, its history well into the nineteenth century.

Indeed Anderson's lack of differentiation between operative and speculative Masonry was to colour attitudes to the Craft's history for generations and could be said to have given rise to the desire to establish a direct link once the authentic school began its critical approach to the accepted history of the Craft. Whilst the approach of writers of the authentic school has the appearance of scientific research their methods were not what we would accept as scientific today. Though they carefully examined and tested each fragment of evidence that came to light, their areas of research were limited to architectural, building and guild records; their work, in fact, gives the appearance of a search for evidence to fit a preconceived theory. Intent on proving a direct descent from operative to speculative masonry through a transitional phase, they assembled fragments of information from various parts of the British Isles which appeared to forge links in their chain of descent. In doing so they often took such evidence out of its context and made assumptions for which only tenuous substantiation existed. In particular they assumed a parity of conditions and activities in England, Ireland and Scotland, and thus ignored the crucial social, cultural, political, legal and religious circumstances in each country. They did not take into account, for instance, that until the Act of Union of 1707 England and Scotland, although linked through the crown in 1603, were separate countries with a common border and that events occurring in one country were not necessarily paralleled in the other. So persuasive, however, so ably written, and so often published was their theory of an operative-transitional-speculative development that it has become dangerously near to being accepted as unquestionable fact. It is still necessary to emphasise that it is only a theory.

In Scotland they found undeniable evidence of the existence of lodges of operative stonemasons, lodges which were geographically-defined units controlling the operative trade with the backing of statute law. They also traced undeniable evidence that these Scottish operative lodges began in the seventeenth-century to admit non-operative members as *accepted* or *gentlemen* masons and that by the early eighteenth-century in some lodges the accepted or gentleman masons had gained the ascendancy: those lodges became, in turn, speculative lodges, whilst others continued their purely operative nature. The speculative lodges eventually combined to form the Grand Lodge of Scotland in 1736. Researchers of the authentic school also discovered references to the Scottish operative lodges having a *Mason word*[5] and secret modes of recognition to enable *bona fide* operative masons to gain work or sustenance when they removed to the area of another lodge. Assembling these facts they had a case for a gradual transition from operative to speculative. Or did they? The flaw in their argument was the assumption that because the accepted or gentlemen masons received into Scottish operative lodges were non-operatives, then they must have been speculative masons, or at least there must have been a speculative implication in their acceptance. No evidence has yet come to light to support such assumptions. Indeed, the evidence would seem to point to the non-operatives simply being honorary members of the lodges in the same way that prominent personalities today are made honorary members of clubs, societies, or institutions with which they have no professional or vocational connections.

When the authentic school came to examine the English records they could find no evidence at all of the existence of operative lodges. In medieval times the operatives' lodge had simply been a hut or lean-to on the site in which they stored their tools and took their refreshment and ease. By the 1600s the guild system, with the exception of the London Livery Companies, was virtually moribund. Nor was there any evidence of an English Mason word or of the English operatives having had secret modes of recognition. Such evidence as they found of non-operative or accepted masonry was all in purely non-operative, context, and where names occurred which could be checked very few of them had even the most tenuous connection with building or architecture. Accepted masonry (there are still doubts as to whether it can truly be called speculative in the seventeenth century) simply seems to have appeared in England as a new organisation without any prior connections with the operative craft. Despite this lack of substantiation the authentic school put together the Scottish and English gleanings and constructed the operative-transitional-speculative theory of the origins of Freemasonry,[6] ignoring the differences and discrepancies between the two sets of evidence. Above all they overlooked, or ignored, the fact that non-operative masonry was developing in England when the Scottish operative lodges began to *accept* non-operatives. If the Scottish operative lodges formed the medium of transition, how could purely non-operative masonry already have existed in England?

The search for a direct link was not confined to the British Isles, nor only dated from the period of the so-called Assembly at York. Attempts were made to give it a classical parentage as a descendant of the Roman *Collegia Fabrorum* or Schools of Masons, implying that 'School' meant the existence of a philosophical or 'mystery' cult attached to the Roman builders. The legend of the *Commacine Masters* appeared to give a religious foundation to the Craft. It was stated that the masons of the Como area of Northern Italy were so renowned and had such recondite secrets to impart to other operatives that they were formed into an Order by a non-existent Papal Bull and ordered to travel Europe sharing their skills and 'mystery'. Evidence of their actual existence is singularly lacking. The traditions and records of the German *Steinmezen* and French *Compagnonage* were diligently searched for traces of a speculative element, but none was found. The evidence comes back all the time to the appearance of non-operative masonry in England in the seventeenth century.

The theory of a direct descent from operative masonry continues to have its supporters, notably the late and much revered Harry Carr; but some current researchers working in the tradition of the authentic school are looking now at the probability of indirect links with the operatives.[7] Rather than seeking to prove a direct descent they are exploring the possibility that the originators of speculative masonry clothed themselves in the appearance of an operative organisation or guild to cloak activities and ideas which, at that time, it was impossible to practise openly. The period in which Freemasonry is believed to have evolved, the late 1500s and 1600s was one in which politics and religion were inextricably linked and in which differences of opinion could split families, and eventually led to civil war. Particularly in regard to religion, legal sanctions operated against those who chose not to follow the dictates of the State. Two possible ideas for the origin of Freemasonry in this period therefore suggest themselves. First, that the originators were a group opposed to the intolerance of State politics and religion who wished to bring together men of differing political and religious views with the common aim of social improvement. Since they found themselves in a situation where such views would be considered subversive there was a total restriction on the discussion of these subjects to outsiders. This feature appears to have existed since Freemasonry originated. Second, that the originators were a group, probably Nonconformist in character, opposed to State domination of religion who did not seek the overthrow of the established religion but rather the promotion of tolerance and the creation of a society in which men were free to follow their consciences in matters of religion. There is a common aim in both groups: the promotion of toleration and the consequent creation of a better society. The use of allegory at this time was a common didactic technique: what more appropriate allegory for a creation of a better society could be devised than the erection of an actual building? There was even a biblical metaphor to hand—the building of

King Solomon's Temple. Once such an allegorical framework had been established it was a logical step to adopt the guise of a builders' organisation or guild. Thus meetings became lodges, the principal officers became a Master and Wardens, and the working tools of the stonemason were utilized both for their practical uses and as symbols.

An alternative indirect theory has recently been put forward which approaches the origins from the charitable rather than the philosophical aspect.[8] This sees Freemasonry as a development of the growing self-help movement in the seventeenth-century. With no State Welfare system, those who fell sick or on hard times had to rely on local charity and the rigid working of the Poor Law. Different groups of trades began to make their own arrangements. Meeting convivially in inns and taverns, they kept a box into which members paid 'dues' at each meeting and from which members could draw money in times of need. From this practice they became known as Box Clubs. Initially they were reserved to members of a particular trade, and there is evidence that they used primitive initiatory rites. It also seems that, like Scottish operatives lodges, the Box Clubs began to admit members not connected with their particular trade. The possibility has been raised that Freemasonry originated as just such a Box Club for operative masons which later began to admit members of other trades. The possibility that Freemasonry was still basically a trade-orientated society at the time of the formation of the premier Grand Lodge in 1717 was raised by Henry Sadler.[9] He suggested that a struggle for control took place in the early 1720s between the original trade-orientated members and those brought into the lodges under the influence of Dr. John Theophilus Desaguliers and others and that truly speculative Freemasonry did not emerge until the latter group had won control and had begun to transform Freemasonry from a benefit Society into a 'system of morality, veiled in allegory and illustrated by symbols'.

The origins of Freemasonry have also been sought in other organisations. A long-standing, though now discarded, theory saw Freemasonry as the direct descendant of the medieval Knights Templars. It was claimed that after the suppression of the Templars and the death of Jacques de Molay, that last Grand Master, in 1314 a number of Knights escaped to Scotland. There they gathered at the mysterious Mount Heredom (or Heredon) near Kilwinning and, fearful of further persecution, transformed themselves into Freemasons, turning the supposed secrets of the Templars into those of Freemasonry. Unfortunately for supporters of this theory the mysterious Mount Heredom (which was to become a central feature of many additional degrees invented in eighteenth-century France) did not exist. Nor were the Templars persecuted in Scotland. Indeed they formed a part of Scottish religious and political life up to the Reformation, the Prior of Torpichen (the Senior Templar Priory in Scotland) being by right of office one of the Lords Spiritual in Scottish government. The Templar legend continued to have a romantic appeal. The Revd Dr. George Oliver claimed to have an eighteenth-century manuscript of what he called the *Rite de Bouillon*, a ritual of the Craft degrees in which the candidates were informed of their descent from the Templars. Oliver's manuscript is known only in nineteenth-century copies and an examination of their content shows a highly developed ritual for the three Craft degrees incorporating many of the ritual changes and additions made *after* the Union of the two English Grand Lodges in 1813.

Some have sought the origins of Freemasonry in Rosicrucianism, either as a British manifestation of the Rosicrucian Brotherhood or as a breakaway group from the mainstream of Rosicrucianism.[10] This is not the place to discuss the existence or non-existence of a Rosicrucian Brotherhood. Whatever the truth of that is, the Rosicrucian idea has continued to weave its way in and out of European thought since its emergence in the early 1600s. The only factors common to both Rosicrucianism and Freemasonry are the central idea of the creation of an ideal society and the use of allegory and symbolism to impart this ideal to initiates. There the similarity ends. There is no common pool of symbolism and both developed along different paths. There is no evidence to show a common origin or the development of one out of the other. Much has been made of the fact that Elias Ashmole, the first recorded non-operative initiate, was also interested in Rosicrucianism; but nothing is said about the other known accepted Masons who had no Rosicrucian connections (real or imagined), or about the claimed Rosicrucians who had no links with accepted Masonry.

The non-authentic school has four main approaches, which might be categorised as the *esoteric*, the *mystical*, the *symbolist*, and the *romantic*. All four approaches have two factors in common: a belief that Freemasonry has existed 'time immemorial' and an apparent inability to distinguish between historical fact and legend. The esoteric and mystical schools are in fact concerned with the transmission of ideas and esoteric traditions, in itself a valid line of research; but in doing so they convert similarities between groups widely separated in time into evidence of a continuing tradition handed down from one group to another, a sort of esoteric apostolic succession. They also tend to have unorthodox ideas on the nature and purpose of Freemasonry endowing it with mystical, religious and even occult implications which it has never possessed.

Those who follow the esoteric approach take the principles, rituals, forms, symbols and language of Freemasonry, trace similarities in other groups (ignoring the fact that the principles and many of the symbols are universal and not peculiar to Freemasonry), and assume that these similarities are not fortuitous but deliberate and are therefore evidence of a linked tradition. They place great emphasis on the additional degrees, investing them with a spurious antiquity, and read a great deal more into their esoteric content and symbolism than was ever intended.

Viewing Freemasonry in all its diverse branches as a coherent initiatory rite, which it is not, the esoteric school compares it with other initiatory rites, finds similarities, actual or imposed, and assumes an intercommunication. John Yarker is probably the major figure of this school. His *magnum opus, The Arcane Schools* (Belfast, 1909) is a monument to misapplied scholarship. It reveals not only the breadth of his reading but also his inability to digest, or in some cases understand, what he had read. On the surface he appears to be working in the authentic school and makes much use of 'documentary' evidence. Close examination shows that he was uncritical in his use of sources, accepting tradition, folklore, and legend as fact yet denying actual documented facts. Yarker was firmly convinced that Freemasonry had existed amongst the medieval operative stonemasons and that they had had a complex series of degrees embracing the Craft and many of the additional degrees. He believed that their system had declined and that its 're-emergence' in the eighteenth-century was a revival but in a perverted form. To accept Yarker's thesis we would have to accept that the medieval stonemasons were men of great intellectual prescience, comprehending ideas which did not enter Western philosophy until after the Renaissance. Yarker saw Freemasonry as the culmination or *summum bonum* of all esoteric systems. Having failed to 'purify' the existing system, Yarker introduced, from America, the Antient and Primitive Rite of Freemasonry. A combination and reduction of the ninety-seven degrees of the Rite of Misraim and ninety-five degrees of the Rite of Memphis, the Antient and Primitive rite was a pot-pourri of Egyptology, Gnosticism, Rosicrucianism, Cabala, Alchemy, Eastern Mysticism and Christianity. It perfectly sums up the eclectic and uncritical mind of its chief promoter in England. The Rite barely survived Yarker's death.

The mystical school is perhaps best represented by the Revd George Oliver and A. E. Waite. Oliver was a fervent pre-Darwinian fundamentalist who firmly believed that Freemasonry was Christian and had existed in one form or another since the beginning of time. In some ways he could have been the progenitor of the authentic school. He avidly read any Masonic book available to him, collected whatever scraps of evidence he could; but like Yarker, he was uncritical in his reading and prone to invention where evidence was lacking. Waite, like Oliver, believed that Freemasonry was essentially Christian in origin and character. He believed that Freemasonry had its origins in the guild system but that it had been transformed into a mystical system, its rituals, particularly of the additional degrees, conveying secret knowledge in the tradition of the Mysteries. His disorganised *New Encyclopaedia of Freemasonry*, with its heavy emphasis on existing and defunct additional degrees, was critically savaged by the authentic school when it was published in 1921.

The *symbolist* school seeks the origins of Freemasonry in a comparison and correlation of symbolism and ritual language and tries to link in a lineal descent various religions, cults, mysteries and societies with Freemasonry. Like the esoteric school, this line of research has a certain validity, but as the anthropology of symbolism not as the search for the origins of Freemasonry. The incidence of certain symbols, gestures and terminologies had led this school to compare Freemasonry with Indian religions, Mayan ceremonies, Mithraic and Aboriginal rituals, Egyptian temple paintings, Indian castemarks. . . . The problem is that Masonic symbols are not peculiar to Freemasonry but are in many instances universal. Included in the symbolist school are those who have sought the origin and authors of Masonic ritual by combing the works of well-known writers to find examples of 'Masonic language'. The most outlandish was probably Alfred Dodd, who convinced himself that Shakespeare (be he Shakespeare, Bacon or Marlowe) composed the Craft ritual![11]

The *romantic* school are in one sense following the Andersonian tradition, implicitly believing in the direct connection between operative and speculative Masonry, whether it goes back to Adam, Solomon, or the medieval builders. They differ from the authentic school by the refusal to acknowledge, or possibly their ignorance of, the many ways in which Freemasonry has altered and developed during the period for which records exist. They are quite ready to believe that the ritual, either its basics or its complete detail, has been practised *time immemorial.*

The lack of knowledge of, and variety of approaches to, the origins of Freemasonry perhaps explain the strength and continual appeal it still has. The lack of any official dogma, and even—in England—of any standard, centrally controlled ritual or interpretation of the ritual which all lodges must accept, means that the individual member can make as little or as much meaning as he wishes. Whether we shall ever discover the true origins of Freemasonry is open to question. The records of medieval buildings have been fully scoured but religious, local and family archives are largely untapped. If Anderson is correct in claiming that many manuscript records were deliberately burnt in 1720 'by some scrupulcus Brothers that those papers might not fall in to strange hands' it may be that the vital evidence we seek has already been lost.

2

THE PRE-1717 ENGLISH EVIDENCE

It is necessary to state why the evidence in this chapter is limited to England. With others, I firmly believe that Free and Accepted or speculative Masonry had its origin in England. No evidence has yet come to light of any operative organisation capable of going through a transitional stage, leading to speculative Masonry, having existed in England. All the English evidence appears in a non-operative context.

In Scotland there is a wealth of evidence for the existence of operative lodges organised on a geographical basis and backed up by statute law.[1] From the early 1600s there are also many documented examples of the introduction of non-operatives into Scottish operative lodges. There is not, however, any evidence that these non-operative members in any way altered the nature or workings of Scottish operative lodges until very late in the seventeenth-century, by which time accepted Masonry was well established in England. All the evidence suggests that accepted Masonry emerged in England and spread from there to Scotland.

The late appearance of two purely operative lodges in England—at Alnwick in Northumberland (1701) and Swalwell in County Durham (1725)—is a red herring.[2] Their closeness to the Scottish border and method of working indicate Scottish influence rather than evidence of an indigenous growth. It is singularly unlikely that no record of operative lodges in England have survived whilst so many other documents for the same period have come down to us.

This lack of evidence has led many Masonic researchers to seize upon the medieval and later usage of the word freemason not only as evidence for operative lodges but also for the existence of speculative Masonry in medieval times. However, the word 'freemason' was a technical term describing a specialist stonemason: one who worked in freestone—usually limestone—capable of being immediately carved for decorative purposes. It has been demonstrated that freemason—in an operative context—is a contraction of 'freestone mason'. When the term begins to appear in print it is clear that it is being used as a technical term describing a particular type of operative mason, since it is generally to be found on the title pages of works devoted to the Orders of Architecture or architectural design and decoration compiled for the use of various trades, including free[stone] masons. The earliest printed use so far traced comes in *The Pilgramage of Perfection*—usually attributed to William Bonde—printed in 1526 by Wynkyn de Worde. The author states:

> The freemason setteth his prentyss first long tyme to learn to hewe stones and whan he can do that perfectly he admytteth him to be a freemason and choseth hym as a conynge man to be master of the Craft.

When used on tombstones and monuments—especially when they are decorated with stonemasons' tools—the word freemason has been seized upon as evidence for the existence of both operative lodges and early speculative freemasonry.

In early non-operative contexts references are usually to Accepted or Adopted Masons, Freed Masons, Free and Accepted Masons, Free-Masons, or Free Masons. Anderson in his 1723 *Constitutions* makes 126 references to Masons, 12 to Free Masons, 10 to Free and Accepted Masons, 9 to Free-Masons, 4 to Accepted Masons, and 1 to Accepted Free Masons. The usual convention in early printed works on speculative Freemasonry was to use Free-Mason or Free Mason and the contraction to Freemason (or Freemasonry) was not used until the early nineteenth-century. To point this out may appear to be simply semantic nit-picking; but the use of Free-Mason and Free Mason may have been a conscious usage to distinguish between the operative and speculative crafts, for freemason as an operative technical term continued in use for many years after the formation of the premier Grand Lodge in 1717.[3]

Attempts have been made to explain a freemason in the operative context as one who had been made free of his craft or, in a town, had been made a Freeman. Where guild records exist there is no evidence to support this suggestion. The granting of the Freedom of a city or town was a civic and not a trade prerogative. The 'free' in Freemason in its speculative use is generally held to mean one who is a Mason without being tied to the operative craft, one analogy being the Free House—a public house not tied to a particular brewery.

Another red herring is the stonemason's custom of 'signing' his work with a distinctive mark. Much has been made of the existence of these marks—particularly those which resemble later masonic symbols. The present-day existence of a Mark Degree—during the ceremony of which the candidate chooses a mark—has given a spurious importance to operative masons' marks. The collecting and collating of such marks may reveal much to the architectural historian but tells us nothing of the origins of Freemasonry.

There exists a collection of documents which has been called up as evidence both for the operative and non-operative origins of Freemasonry. Described by Anderson as the Gothic Constitutions, and now known collectively as the Old Charges, some 127 versions have been traced of which 113 are still in existence, the remainder having either been lost or known only from passing manuscript or printed references. Much work has been done in collating, dating, and textually comparing the various texts of the Old Charges. All have a common form:

a. an opening pray
b. a legendary history of the mason craft tracing it from biblical origins to its establishment in England
c. a code of regulations for Masters, Fellows and Apprentices covering both craft practices and morals
d. arrangements for large-scale 'territorial' assemblies at which attendance was obligatory
e. procedures for the trial and punishment of offenders
f. admission procedures 'for new men that were never charged before', including an oath of fidelity

Textual analysis has revealed certain major differences between versions which have led to them being divided into groups or families, it has also been established that the documents are of English origin, the few versions with a completely Scottish provenance are later copies of the English originals.

Historically, the Old Charges fall into three groups. The first comprises the two earliest versions, the Regius MS of *c*.1390 and the Cooke MS of *c*.1420. The former is in verse and a 'family' of its own. The latter gave its name to a family of three versions. The second, and largest, group begins with the Grand Lodge No. 1 MS, dated 25 December 1583, and covers all the versions datable before the formation of the premier Grand Lodge in 1717. The third group comprises manuscript and printed versions produced after 1717, the majority of which appear to have been produced as antiquarian curiosities. Whilst much work has been done in classifying, dating and collating the various versions little has been done in comparing the content and meaning of the differing texts.[4] Nor has much research been carried out into *why* the documents were produced; it has been assumed that they were produced for operative lodges, for the existence of which there is no evidence.

Of the three historical groups the second is the most important, and raises a number of interesting questions. Unless a number of fifteenth- and sixteenth-century versions have been lost, or have not yet been discovered, why should a new version appear in 1583 which has little similarity to the Regius MS and more differences than similarities to the Cooke MS?[5] If the two earliest versions had some trade or guild connection, why should there have been such a revival in their production after 1583, when the guild system was virtually extinct and no operative lodges existed? If, as has been claimed, the manuscripts were prepared for operative lodges, why have these documents survived and not others that might provide evidence of operative lodges? These questions have led one researcher to propose the theory that the post-1583 versions of the Old Charges were not produced for operative purposes but are the first evidence of non-operative Freemasonry.[6]

Internal evidence from the Old Charges shows them to have been used at the 'making of masons'. Other evidence shows them to have been used at the 'making' of accepted masons. They clearly had an importance for the early members of the premier Grand Lodge, for copies are known to have been produced at early meetings of the Grand Lodge and Anderson 'digested' them when preparing the 1723 *Constitutions*. The actual Charges were certainly important, for Anderson codified them to form the *Ancient Charges* with which he prefaced the Grand Lodge *Regulations* in the 1723 *Constitutions*. These *Ancient Charges* have prefaced the *Book of Constitutions* ever since, slightly altered in later versions of Anderson but reaching their present form in 1815.

One version of the Old Charges—Sloane MS No. 3438 (British Library)—was very probably written for the 'making' of the earliest accepted mason of which we have documentary evidence. Elias Ashmole, the Antiquary and founder of Oxfords' Ashmolean Museum recorded his 'making' in his *Diary* as follows:

1646 Oct.4H.30 P.M. I was made a Free-Mason at Warrington in Lancashire wth Coll. Henry Mainwaring of Karincham in Cheshire. The Names of those that were of the Lodge, Mr. Rich: Penkett Warden. Mr. James Collier, Mr. Rich: Sanchey, Henry Littler, John Ellam, Rich: Ellam, Hugh Brewer.

Sloane MS No. 3438 is signed and dated 'ffinis p. me Edu. Sankey decimo sexto die Octobris Anno Domini 1646'. Sankey is known to have been a relative of the 'Rich: Sanchey' who was one of those who formed a lodge for Ashmole's initiation.

Obviously Ashmole and Mainwaring, his father-in-law, were not the first 'Free-Masons'; the seven who formed the lodge must have been 'made' at some stage. What is important about the lodge is that, with one possible exception, none of those who formed it had any connection with the operative mason's craft. In 1646 Warrington was a Parliamentary stronghold. Ashmole had been a Royalist, was captured by the Parliamentarians, and at the time of his 'making' was on parole in the care of his father-in-law. Whilst under Col. Mainwaring's charge he changed sides and as a Parliamentary supporter was able to return to London. Much research has gone into tracing Ashmole's 'lodge', both in trying to identify those present and to trace other records of its activities. Such evidence as we have points not to the existence of continuing lodges holding regular meetings but to what have become termed *occasional lodges*, i.e. the calling together of sufficient masons to hold a lodge for the purpose of making a new mason, the 'lodge' existing only as long as the occasion for which it was called.

The only other references to Freemasonry in Ashmole's diary come some thirty-six years after his 'making':

10. About 5H:PM I recd. a Summons to appear at a Lodge to be held the next day, at Masons Hall, London

11. Accordingly I went, & About Noone were admitted into the Fellowship of Free Masons, Sir William Wilson Knight, Capt. Rich: Borchwick, Mr. Will: Woodman, Mr. Wm Grey, Mr. Samuell Taylour and Mr. William Wise. I was the senior Fellow among them (it being 35 years since I was admitted). There were present beside my selfe the Fellowes after named. Mr. Thos: Wise Mr. of the Masons Company this present yeare. Mr. Thomas Shorthose, Mr. Thomas Shadbolt, Wainsford Esq., Mr. Nich: Young, Mr. John Shorthose, Mr. William Hamon, Mr. John Thompson, & Mr. Will: Stanton.

We all dyned at the Halfe Moone Taverne in Cheapside, at a Noble Dinner prepared at the charge of the New-accepted Masons.

This long gap between the 1646 and 1682 entries in his *Diary* has led many to claim that Ashmole did not greatly care for his Free-Masonry. This claim presupposes two factors. First, that Ashmole's admittedly voluminous *Diary* was a complete record of all his activities (it was not).[7] In it he recorded some, but not all, of the major events of the period covered by the *Diary*, as well as a great deal of trivia. Nor does it contain entries for every day. Second, such a claim would imply the existence of continuing lodges meeting with regularity; but as has already been stated, the evidence points only to the existence of 'occasional lodges'. What the 1682 entries *do* reveal is that Ashmole was known to be a Free-Mason, for he was *summoned* to the meeting at Masons' Hall. Nor do those entries give any indication that this was the first occasion since his own 'making' that Ashmole had attended a lodge or that this was the first time he had been summoned to Masons' Hall.

Mention of Masons' Hall brings us to a consideration of the London Masons' Company. Now one of the Livery Companies of the City of London, the Masons' Company had its origins as the operative masons' guild controlling the London trade. In this it had a purely operative function, with no speculative connotation whatsoever. In the seventeenth century, however, it had within it a curious phenomenon now known as the Acception.[8] All records of the Masons' Company before 1620 have been lost, but an Accounts Book begun on 1 July 1619—and kept in meticulous detail—has some interesting entries upon which much has been built. An entry for 1621 begins 'At the making of

Masons . . .' and at first sight would appear to be an entry concerning the registering of Liverymen of the Company. The fees recorded as being paid for these 'makings', however, were in excess of those paid for the Livery, and three of those recorded as having paid them had already paid their Livery fees the previous year. Many of the later entries also show persons paying for their 'making' who had previously paid the Livery fine. Others paid for 'making' and had no connection whatsoever with the Livery. It would seem therefore that the 'making of Masons' was something completely separate from the trade function of the Masons' Company and that the 'Acception' was an inner circle within the Company. There is also reference to what was possibly a version of the Old Charges and to a framed parchment listing all those who had been Accepted; both items are unfortunately now lost.

In his *Hole Craft and Fellowship of Masonry* (London, 1894) Edward Conder jun. theorized that the Acception was a speculative lodge working within the Masons' Company. However, Conder can hardly be called an unbiased writer, for he was not only a Freemason but also Master of the Masons' Company at the time his study was published. Harry Carr[9] firmly believed that the Acception was further evidence of a transitional stage from operative to speculative and that the Acception was a transitional lodge on the Scottish model with operative and non-operative members. Others might require more evidence than a few entries in an Accounts Book before they accept the Acception as evidence for speculative Masonry. The evidence of Ashmole visiting a lodge at Masons' Hall has also been used to show an operative-transitional-speculative development. But there is nothing to link the Acception with the lodge which Ashmole visited. Though it is often assumed that they were one and the same, records of the Acception in the Masons' Company Accounts Book cease in the 1650s, thirty years before Ashmole attended. As some of those Ashmole lists as having been present were also member of the Masons' Company, it *may* have been a meeting of the Acception; but it could also have been an occasional lodge summoned to meet at the Masons' Hall because of the Company connections of some of those present.

Ashmole's initiation had been preceded by what is, so far, the earliest printed reference to the Mason word. Adamson's *The Muses Threnodie* had been published in Edinburgh in 1638 and on folio 32 the following couplet appears:

For we be brethren of the Rosie Cross
We have the Mason word and second sight

Adamson being a Scot, it can be argued that what he is referring to is the Scottish operative Mason and his secret mode of recognition rather than to non-operative or Accepted Masonry. The linking of 'Rosie Cross' and 'Mason word' have often been cited as evidence for a connection between Freemasonry and Rosicrucianism. A similar reference to the Mason word appeared in England in 1672 in Marvell's *The Rehearsal Transposed*, in which one character states '. . . and as those that have the Mason word, secretly discern one another. . .'. Again it is arguable whether Marvell was referring to Scottish operative practice or had knowledge of the existence of Accepted Masonry in England.

Randle Holme the Third (1627–99) provides us with information of a lodge meeting in Chester. An antiquary, Herald and Deputy for Garter King of Arms in Cheshire, Holme in his *Academie of Armoury* (1688) writes: 'I cannot but honour the Fellowship of the Masons because of its antiquity; and the more as being [myself] a member of that Society called Free-Masons'. It is argued that here Holme is dealing with two separate organisations: the Fellowship of Masons—i.e. the operative, trade governing guild—and the Society of Free-Masons—of which he and other non-operatives were members. In the British Library is what is now known as the Harleian MS No. 2054 of the Old Charges written out by Holme *c.* 1650. Preserved with it are two important scraps of paper, again in Holme's hand. The first contains the earliest traced reference to signs and words:

> There is seu^{r}all wordes and signes of a free Mason to be revailed to ye wch as ye will answ: before God at the Great & terrible day of Judgm^{t} ye keep Secret & not to revaile the same to any in the heares of any pson w but to the M^{r} and fellows of the said Society of free Masons so helpe me God, xt.

Note the reference at the beginning and end to 'free Masons'. The second scrap is a list of twenty-six names, including Randle Holme, against which certain sums of money are set. Much investigation has been done into the names, leading to the belief that the list is of members of Holme's lodge *c.*1672. It has been shown that the trades of those listed break down into six operative masons, six bricklayers, three carpenters three slaters and plaisterers, two glaziers, one painter, one tanner, one tailor, one bootseller, one gentleman and one name which has not been identified. Twenty-one of those listed have been shown to have been leading building trade employers in the rebuilding of Chester after the siege which destroyed much of it during the Civil War. Many of them were known to have held high civic office as well as office in the trade guilds of Chester, and at least eight were armigerous. The preponderance of building-orientated members with the addition of non-trade members has led to Holme's lodge being claimed as definitive evidence of a transitional lodge. The existence, however, of a guild controlling trade affairs and Holme's distinction between the 'Fellowship of Masons' and that 'Society called Free-Masons' would seem to contradict this. Apart from the Old Charges, fragment of obligation, and list of members, no other records of the lodge at Cheser appear to have survived.[10]

That Accepted Masonry was sufficiently known to the public by 1676 is shown by a lampooning advertisement printed in that year. *Poor Robin's Intelligence* was a scurrilous sheet printed in 1676–7 which included a series of divertisements, facetious burlesques of advertisements. One ran as follows:

> These are to give notice, that the Modern Green-ribbon'd Caball, together with the Ancient Brother-hood of the Rosy-Cross; the Hermetick Adepti and the Company of Accepted Masons, intend all to dine together on the 31st November next, at the Flying-Bull in Windmill-Crown-Street . . . .

Once again we have linked in the public eye the Accepted Mason and the Brotherhood of the Rosie Cross, this time with the added dimension of Hermeticism.

Dr. Robert Plot, though not himself a Free-Mason claimed, in his *Natural History of Staffordshire (1686)* that Accepted Masonry was widespread. He states:

> [85] To these add the *Customs* relating to the *County* whereof they have one, of admitting Men into the *Society of Free-Masons*, that in the *moorlands* of the *County* seems to be of greater request than anywhere else, though I find the *Custom* spread more or less all over the *Nation*; for here I found persons of the most

eminent quality, that did not disdain to be of this *fellowship*. [Plot then proceeds to criticise what was obviously a copy of the Old Charges, the section now being referred to as the Plot Extracts.]

Plot, unfortunately, was both gullible and prone to exaggeration. His work, however, is important in that it gives us the earliest traced indication of what was involved at a 'making':

[86] Into which *Society* when they are admitted they call a *meeting* (or *Lodge* as they term it in some places), which must consist at least of 5 or 6 of the *Ancients* of the Order, whom the candidates present with *gloves*, and so likewise to their *wives*, and entertain with a *collation* according to the Custom of the plan: This ended, they proceed to the *administration* of them, which chiefly consists in the communication of certain *secret signs*, whereby they are known to one another all over the *Nation*, by which means they have maintenance wither ever they travel . . . .

Plot, again, has been called up as evidence for transitional lodges—i.e. his reference to 'persons of the most eminent quality', but he could equally be describing a Box Club.[11]

The diarist John Aubrey (1626–7), a contemporary of Plot, published his *Natural History of Wiltshire* in 1686. The manuscript is now in the Bodleian Library and on folio 73 he writes:

Sir William Dugdale told me many years since, that about Henry the third's time, the Pope gave a Bull or diploma (Patents) to a Company of Italian Architects to travell up and downe all over Europe to build Churches. From those are derived the *Fraternity* of Adopted-Masons. They are known to one another by certayn Signes & Marks and Watch-words: it continues to this day. They have Severall Lodges in severall counties for their reception: and when any of them fall into decay, the brotherhood is to relieve him &c. The manner of Adoption is very formall, and with an oath of secrecy.

This passage confirms what Plot had stated in more extravagant terms, that Free-Masonry was known in several Counties. Aubrey's reference to the Comacine Masters and their reputed Papal Bull led to the legend of Freemasonry descending from the travelling masons from the Como area of North Italy.

The manuscript of Aubrey's *Natural History of Wiltshire* has an Addendum on the verso of folio 72, facing the above quoted passage, which has added confusion to an already muddled subject: the question of whether or not Sir Christopher Wren was an Accepted or Free Mason. The Addendum is in Aubrey's hand:

This day [18 May 1691, being Monday after Rogation Sunday] is a great convention at St. Paul's Church of the Fraternity of the Accepted Masons: where Sr Christopher Wren is to be adopted a Brother: and Sr Henry Goodrie . . . of ye Tower & divers others—There have been kings that have been of this Sodalitie.

Aubrey's is the only record of the 'great convention'; the Addendum is certainly in his hand and there would seem to be no reason for his having invented the incident.

Sir Christopher Wren is treated rather curiously in the 1723 and 1738 editions of the *Constitutions*. In the first edition he is mentioned only twice: as 'the ingenious Architect Sir Christopher Wren' and, in a footnote, as the Architect of the Sheldonian Theatre in Oxford. There is no mention of his having been a Freemason or having held high office and neglected his charge. By the 1738 edition this has all changed. Now Anderson states that Wren was a member of the Craft, had been Grand Warden (1663), Deputy Grand Master (1669, 1673–85, and 1695–8), and Grand Master (1685–95, 1698–?). This raises two problems. First, there is conflict between Aubrey and Anderson, the former stating Wren was *accepted* in 1691, the latter claiming he had been Grand Warden in 1663, some twenty-eight years earlier. The second problem is why Anderson only mentions Wren in passing in 1723 but by 1738 (Wren having died in 1723) has remembered such an exact catalogue of his high ranks. The only conclusion we can draw is that Anderson needed a major figure to bolster his claim that the formation of Grand Lodge in 1717 was a revival. The best that can be said of Wren's connection with Freemasonry is that it is not proven.

From the early 1690s onwards we begin to get more evidence of non-operative lodges. The York No. 4 MS of the Old Charges was written in 1693 by one Mark Kipling and ends with the following note:

The names of the Lodg

William Simpson Christopher Thompson

Antony Horsman Christopher Gill
Mr. Isaac Brent Lodge War[den]

Harry Carr concluded that with such a small membership the lodge could not have been operative.

Anderson, in the second edition (1738) of the *Constitutions*, in a paragraph dealing with the year 1693, claimed that at least eight lodges were working in London:

an occasional lodge headed by Sir Robert Clayton;
a *stated lodge* near St. Thomas's Hospital, Southwark;
the *old* lodge at St. Paul's;
one in Piccadilly over against St. James's' Church;
one near Westminster Abbey;
another near Covent Garden;
one in Holborn;
one on Tower Hill;
'and some more that assembled statedly'.

It is not clear how much credence can be put in Anderson's statement. It is believed that 'the old lodge at St. Paul's' later became one of the founding lodges of Grand Lodge in 1717 and is now the Lodge of Antiquity No. 2; they have in their possession a version of the Old Charges dated 1686 which there is every reason to believe has always been in the possession of the lodge. What is interesting is Anderson's differentiation between an 'occasional' and a 'stated' lodge, the latter being the first implication of lodges meeting on a regular basis.

Free Masonry appears to have been well enough known in London by 1698 to warrant the publication of an anti-Masonic leaflet, the only known copy being in the Grand Lodge Library:

TO ALL GODLY PEOPLE IN THE CITIE OF LONDON

Having thought it needful to warn you of the Mischiefs and Evils practised in the sight of God by those called Freed Masons, I say take care lest their Ceremonies and secret swearings take hold of you: and be wary that none cause you to err from Godliness. For this devlish Sect of Men are Meeters in Secret which swear against all without their following. They are the Anti-Christ which was to come leading Men from their Fear of God. For how should Men meet in Secret Places and with secret Signes taking Care that none observe them to do the Work of God: are not these the ways of Evildoers? Knowing how that God observest privilly them that sit in Darkness they shall be smitten and the Secrets of their Hearts layed bare. Mingle not among this corrupt People lest you be found so at the World's Conflagration.

Another version of the Old Charges, the Scarbrough MS,[12] has an endorsement, of 1705, as follows:

M[emoran]dum: Thatt at A private Lodge held at Scarborough in the County of York the tenth daty of July 1705 before William Thopson Esq p'sident of the said Lodge and several others brethren ffree Masons the several psons whose names are hereunto Subscribed were then admitted into the Said ffraternity[:]

Ed: Thompson
Jo: Tempest
Robt: Johnson
Tho: Lister
Samuel W. Duck
Richard Hudson

In the same year, 1705, more evidence comes from Yorkshire: the records of a non-operative lodge in York which later became the Grand Lodge of All England.[13] The earliest records of this York lodge are known only from a letter of 29 August 1778 from the Grand Secretary of the York Grand Lodge, Bro. Jacob Bussey, to the Secretary of the Lodge of Antiquity in London. Bussey states: '. . . I have inspected an original Minute Book of this Grand Lodge beginning at 1705 and ending in 1734 from which I have extracted the names of the Grand Masters during that period.' There is still in existence a parchment roll, York Roll No. 7, labelled 'A Parchment Roll containing the manual Subscriptions etc of Persons made macons in the Gr. Lodge'. Begun on 19 March 1712, the roll contains minutes of meetings and signatures of members down to 1730. From 1705 to 1725 the presiding officer was referred to as the President or Deputy President, the pre-1717 holders being Sir George Tempest (1705), Rt. Hon. Robert Benson (later Lord Bingley, 1707), Sir William Robinson Bt. (1708), Sir Walter Hawksworth Bt. (1711), and Sir George Tempest again (1713).

The Minutes included in the Roll give a few clues as to what occurred in the lodge. Most meetings are headed 'private lodge' but those held on the Feasts of St. John the Evangelist and St. John the Baptist are headed 'general lodge'. Only one ceremony appears to have been used, in which the candidate was 'Admitted and sworne into the Ancient and Honble. Society and Fraternity of Free Masons'. The lodge is referred to variously as the 'Society and Fraternity of Free Masons', the 'Company of Free Masons' and 'the Society of Free and Accepted Masons'. From the names of the presiding officers and some of the candidates as well as the evidence of the Minutes it is clear that the York Lodge was not an operative lodge but one of accepted masons. Among the membership were two peers, three baronets, eight esquires, and fifteen 'Gentlemen'.

Meetings of the York lodge do not appear to have been confined to York itself. In 1713 it held an 'occasional' lodge in Bradford at which '18 Gentlemen of the first families in that neighbourhood were made Masons'. George Grey of Southwich recorded in his *Diary*: '1710 Feb. 20 I was made a Free Mason at Beedall [Bedale]', which may have been a meeting of an 'occasional' lodge or a visit by members of the York lodge.

Public references to Free Masons' modes of recognition appear in *The Tatler* in 1709 and 1710. In No. 26 for 7–9 June 1709 the following appears:

[9 June 1709] But my Reason for troubling you at this present is, to put a Stop, if it may be, in an insinuating, increasing Set of People, who sticking to the Letter of your Treatise, and not to the Spirit of it, do assume the Name of Pretty Fellows; nay, and even get new Names, as you very well hint. . . . They have their Signs and Tokens like Free-Masons. . . .

The subject was referred to again in issue No. 166 for 29 April to 2 May 1710:

[2 May 1710] . . . You may see them at first Sight grow acquainted by Sympathy, insomuch that one who had not studied Nature, and did not know the true Cause of their suddent Familiarities, would think, That they had some secret Intimitation of each other, like the Free-Masons.

Claims that many lodges sprang up in London—operative in character—as a result of the need to rebuild the City after the Great Fire of 1666 are not substantiated by hard evidence. We have Anderson's statement that there were at least eight lodges in London in 1693, but with the possible exception of 'the old lodge at St. Paul's' we have no other evidence for them. What we do know is that there were certainly four lodges in existence in London in 1717, the four which came together to form the Grand Lodge. They were:

(1) the lodge at the Goose and Gridiron, St. Paul's Churchyard, now the Lodge of Antiquity No. 2. Described as a time immemorial lodge, it is believed to be Anderson's 'old lodge at St. Pauls' of 1693. According to the engraved *List of Lodges* for 1729 it came into existence in 1691.
(2) the lodge at the Crown, Parker's Lane, Lincoln's Inn Fields, which went out of existence in 1736. According to the engraved *List of Lodges* for 1729 it came into existence in 1712.
(3) the lodge at the Rummer and Grapes, Channel Row, Westminster, now the Royal Somerset House and Inverness Lodge No. 4 with time immemorial status. Its date of origin is not known.
(4) the lodge at the Apple Tree Tavern, Charles Street, Covent Garden, now the Lodge of Fortitude and Old Cumberland No. 12 with time immemorial status. Its date of origin is not known.

No early records of these four lodges have survived, so we have no indication as to their membership or work.

3

THE GRAND LODGE SYSTEM

THE GRAND LODGE is the governing body of Craft Freemasonry controlling subordinate lodges which work only the three degrees of Entered Apprentice, Fellowcraft, and Master Mason. It is composed of the Grand Officers for the year with the actual Masters and Wardens of every lodge and Past Grand Officers and Past Masters of lodges who remain subscribing members of a lodge under the Grand Lodge. None of the members of Grand Lodge are elected or selected in any way; all are members by virtue of their status within the Craft and all have the right to attend and vote on all matters raised at each Quarterly Communication. The present United Grand Lodge of England was formed as the result of a Union between the premier and Antients Grand Lodges of England, which took place on 27 December 1813 and ended sixty-two years of opposition. Although only two were involved in 1813 there had at one point in the eighteenth-century been five Grand Lodges claiming jurisdiction over all or part of England. The Union itself was to cause the creation of a further, though short-lived, Grand Lodge.

The Grand Lodge of England was formed on 24 June 1717 in London, as the first Grand Lodge in the world, by the four lodges referred to at the end of the previous chapter. The event was completely ignored by the press of the day and no minutes for it, or for the first six years of theGrand Lodge's existence, appear to have been kept. As a result we have to rely largely on Anderson's 1738 edition of the *Constitutions* for our knowledge of the early days of the Grand Lodge. According to Anderson representatives of the four London lodges met in 1716 and resolved to meet the following year to *revive* the Annual Assembly and Feast, at which they would 'chuse a Grand Master from among themselves till they should have the Honour of a *Noble Brother* at their Head'. Accordingly they met at the Goose and Gridiron Ale House in St. Paul's Churchyard, placed the oldest Master Mason present in the Chair, and proceeded to elect one Anthony Sayer,[1] Gentleman, as the first Grand Master. Sayer, of whom little is known, was duly installed and invested and 'commanded the Master and Wardens of Lodges to meet the Grand Officers every Quarter in Communication'.

Despite the new Grand Master's command the Grand Lodge, from the evidence of Anderson, appears to have met only for the Annual Assembly and Feast in the first four years of its existence. The only business transacted was the election of the new Grand Master and Grand Wardens and their subsequent installation. There seems little doubt that initially the Grand Lodge was simply an opportunity for members of the London lodges to meet together socially. No evidence has come to light to show the Grand Lodge acting in any way as a regulatory body until late in 1720. Nor is there any evidence that it was concerned with lodges outside the Cities of London and Westminster.

In 1720 a change begins to be discernible. The catalysts for this change are believed to have been George Payne (Grand Master 1718 and 1720), and the Revd Dr John Theophilus Desaguliers (Grand Master 1719 and Deputy Grand Master 1722–3 and 1726). Payne was an official of the Commission for Taxes and is credited with compiling the first Grand Lodge regulations in 1720. Desaguliers was a Huguenot minister and lecturer and experimenter in physics and is credited with introducing the aristocracy and men of intellect[2] into the Craft. Certainly they both persuaded John, 2nd Duke of Montagu to accept the nomination as Grand Master in 1721. From Montagu's installation the Grand Lodge began to meet more regularly and to exercise powers as a regulatory body. The presence of a nobleman as Grand Master brought Freemasonry to the notice of the general public and reports of Grand Lodge meetings and those of private lodges, particularly when someone of note was initiated, began to appear frequently in the press.

Why the Grand Lodge came into existence in 1717 has never been answered satisfactorily. Anderson's claim that it was a *revival*[3] is not regarded as tenable, there being no evidence of either a Grand Lodge or any similar governing body having existed before 1717. Sadler in his *Masonic Facts and Fictions*[4] puts forward his belief that the Grand Lodge was formed by remnants of the old operative craft as a purely social meeting but that the non-operatives began to take it over and influenced its development as a regulatory body. Sadler believed that the curious events surrounding the installation of Philip, Duke of Wharton as Grand Master in succession to Montagu were the last attempts of the old operative element to keep control of the Craft.

According to Anderson, who was not uninvolved in the matter, Montagu had proved so popular as Grand Master that the brethren wished him to continue in office, but Wharton 'being ambitious of the Chair' persuaded a number of brethren to meet him at Stationers' Hall on 24 June 1722, and despite there being no Grand Officers present, and the facts that Wharton had not been Master of a lodge or properly nominated and proposed as Grand Master, he was duly proclaimed and installed. Anderson goes on to state that 'the *Noble Brothers* and all those that would not countenence irregularities, disowned Wharton's authority'. To heal the breach Montagu summoned a Grand Lodge on 17 January 1723, at which Wharton was officially proclaimed Grand Lodge Master.[5]

The year 1723 was the first watershed in the Grand Lodge's history. William Cowper, Clerk of the Parliaments, was elected the first Secretary *to* Grand Lodge[6] and official Minutes began to be kept from June 1723. Anderson's first edition of the *Constitutions* was officially sanctioned and published. The first lists of lodge members were recorded in the Minute Book[7] and the first engraved *List of Lodges*[8] was issued containing the sign of the tavern at which each lodge met and their days of meeting. From a purely social gathering in 1717 the Grand Lodge by 1730 had established itself as a governing body in London and had begun to extend its authority into the provinces and to export the Craft abroad by issuing 'deputations' to constitute lodges in Spain and India. It had begun to organise a Provincial system by the appointment of Provincial Grand Masters[9] to act for the Grand Master in the farther counties and a central Charity Fund had been established, to which all lodges were invited to contribute. The number of lodges had risen from four to over seventy by existing independent lodges agreeing to come under the control of Grand Lodge and by the constituting of new lodges by authority of the Grand Master.

The Grand Lodge had also introduced a concept that was to become fundamental and was to affect its relations with other Grand Lodges as they came into existence: the concept of regular and irregular Freemasonry.

According to the 1723 *Constitutions*, a new lodge could only be considered regular and its members accepted as regular made Masons if it had been created by permission of the Grand Master and had been personally constituted by him or his Deputy or, in the case of the Provincial lodges, by a suitably qualified local brother who had been officially deputed by the Grand Master for that purpose. Once a new lodge had been constituted a certificate of constitution had to be returned to the Grand Secretary so that the new lodge could be both entered on the 'books of Grand Lodge'; and in the next issue of the engraved *List of Lodges*, thereby publishing its regularity to all lodges under Grand Lodge's control. Any lodge which had not gone through this process was considered to be irregular until it submitted to Grand Lodge, and its members were branded as clandestine and not to be countenanced as visitors to regular lodges.[10]

The 1730s was a period of consolidation but also brought a serious problem for the Grand Lodge which was to have far reaching consequences. For much of the 1720s the Grand Lodge had not been a truly separate entity but had functioned as a representative meeting of the Masters and Wardens of London lodges. With the expansion into the provinces the Grand Lodge began, in the late 1720s, to initiate regulations rather than simply acting as a forum for the discussion of problems arising in London lodges. In addition to regulations covering the manner of conducting the Grand Lodge and the setting up of new lodges it began to rule on matters of regalia, admission of candidates and visitors, the number of lodges to which a London Mason could belong, the administration of the Charity Fund, and many other matters. It also began to exercise a judicial function, hearing Masonic complaints from lodges and individual brethren and ruling on them.

Anderson in the 1738 *Constitutions* shows how steadily the Craft was growing at home and abroad. As an appendix to the *Constitutions* he printed lists of 'deputations' issued to form lodges outside London and abroad, as well as patents issued to permit Provincial Grand Masters to function both at home and abroad. Those appointed were given wide powers and were authorised to constitute new lodges in the name of the Grand Master. These locally constituted lodges were supposed to be registered with the Grand Lodge so that they could be entered on the *List*, but due to the problems of travel and communication many of these locally constituted lodges outside England and Wales went out of existence before they could be registered, or else the papers concerning their formation were lost at sea, and so they did not appear in the *List* until many years after their formation.

One of the more notable events of the 1730s was the initiation of the first English Royal Freemason. Frederick Lewis, Prince of Wales, was the eldest son and heir to George II but predeceased his father and so never came to the throne. On 5 March 1737 an *occasional lodge* was held at the Prince's palace at Kew, presided over by Dr. Desaguliers, and the Prince of Wales was made an Entered Apprentice and Fellowcraft on the same evening. The lodge was reconvened on another date and he was made a Master Mason. In 1738 he appears to have become Master of a Lodge for Anderson dedicated the second edition of the *Constitutions* to him in that capacity. Frederick Lewis does not appear to have taken a very active part in Masonic affairs but his example appears to have influenced his brothers and sons and began the long association between the Royal House and the Craft which continues to this day.[11]

A much less happy series of events began in 1730. As we shall see in Chapter 5, the Craft had a very public face in the 1720s and 1730s. In some ways Grand Lodge had courted publicity by advertising its meetings in the daily press. Not unnaturally this made the public curious as to the nature of Freemasonry and that curiosity was to be answered, from 1723 onwards, by the printing of so-called exposures of the ritual and 'secrets' of the Craft both in the press and in pamphlet form.[12] As the early exposures were rather scrappy and uninformative, or else deliberately misleading, they were ignored by Grand Lodge. In 1730, however, one Samuel Prichard, describing himself as a 'late Member of a Constituted Lodge', published a pamphlet entitled *Masonry Dissect'd*[13] which purported to be the full ceremonies and catechisms for the three Craft degrees. So popular was Prichard's pamphlet that it went through three 'regular' and at least two pirated editions in a few weeks. It would appear that Prichard had been correct in his exposure for Grand Lodge was greatly concerned and warned its lodges of the necessity of carefully checking unknown visitors to ensure that they were regular Masons and not readers of Prichard's pamphlet. Their warning appears to have been necessary but does not seem to have had the desired effect for at some time in the late 1730s they took the drastic step of altering the recognition words in the first two degrees to prevent imposters gaining entry to their lodges. As we shall see, this action was to be one of the reasons for the setting up of a rival Grand Lodge.

The 1740s saw a considerable change in the fortunes of the Grand Lodge. Although the Masters and Wardens of all lodges were members of Grand Lodge, because of the problems of travel in the eighteenth century the Grand Lodge meetings were largely attended by members of London lodges. London Masonry went into a decline in the 1740s—probably because it had been allowed to expand too rapidly. Petitions for new lodges in London began to be rejected and the 1724 regulation restricting London Masons to membership of only one lodge was reactivated in an attempt to prevent the demise of London lodges. All this led to a further decline in attendances at Grand Lodge, compounded by a seeming lack of interest on the part of the Grand Officers. To a certain extent their absence can be explained by many of them being involved in military duties resulting from the War of the Austrian Succession and the abortive Jacobite Rising of 1745. Unfortunately the problems were increased in 1747 by the election to the Grand Mastership of the 5th Lord Byron (great-uncle of the poet). Despite his promise to work 'to the utmost of his power to promote the benefit of the Craft' he attended his installation on 30 April 1747 and was never seen again until he appeared on 16 March 1752 to nominate his successor. As a result of Byron's neglect of his duties only seven meetings of Grand Lodge were held between 1747 and 1752; no Grand Feast was held, the Grand Officers remained in office for the whole period and were similarly lax in their attendances, and dissatisfaction began to spread amongst the lodges. It was only by the swift action and tact of Dr. Thomas Manningham, a Past Grand Steward, that open rebellion and the deposition of Byron were prevented. Manningham was rewarded by Byron's successor with appointment as Deputy Grand Master and began to put the Grand Lodge's affairs into order.

Horace Walpole, himself a Mason, writing to a friend in 1743 had said: 'The Free Masons are in so low a repute now in England that . . . I believe that nothing but a persecution could bring them into vogue here again. . . .'[14] It was not, however, a persecution but the advent of a rival in 1751 that eventually led to the revitalising of the premier Grand Lodge. Until the publication of Sadler's *Masonic Facts and Fictions*, in 1887, it was believed that the rival Antients Grand Lodge had been formed by schismatics from the premier Grand Lodge. Sadler showed that there was no evidence at all for the schism theory and that the majority of founders of the Antients were not English but Irish Masons. Having been unable to gain access to English lodges they formed their own and it was perhaps inevitable that they should then have formed a Grand Lodge.

Initially the formation of the Antients Grand Lodge had no effect on the premier Minutes until 1755, when the Antients were declared irregular and therefore not admissible in premier lodges. Lord Byron's successors as Grand Master may have been more regular in their attendance at Grand Lodge but they took little action to halt the decline in London Masonry. When a renumbering of the lodges was ordered in 1755, the first since 1740,[15] it was discovered that of the 271 lodges on the *List* 72 had ceased to exist, the majority of them in London. A turning point came in 1764 with the installation of Cadwallader, 9th Lord Blayney as Grand Master. He revived the practice of the Grand Master officially visiting London lodges and berated a number of them for the poor quality of their ritual. He formed and presided over an *occasional lodge* at the Horn Tavern to initiate HRH Henry, Duke of Gloucester on 16 February 1766 and on hearing that the Dukes of York and Cumberland had become Masons persuaded the Grand Lodge to elect all three Princes as Past Grand Masters. The presence of the three Royal Princes attracted many of the nobility and gentry back to the Craft.

Blayney's successor Henry, 5th Duke of Beaufort continued the work of revitalisation. Attempts had been made as early as 1762 to persuade the premier Grand Lodge to seek a Charter of Incorporation[16] and Beaufort took the cause up, reasoning that if a Charter was procured the Grand Lodge would at last be able to purchase property and establish a permanent headquarters. What was not stated, but was quickly grasped by the rival Antients Grand Lodge, was that Incorporation would enable the premier Grand Lodge to have recourse to the Courts over anyone claiming to practice Freemasonry outside the control of an Incorporated Grand Lodge. A Bill of Incorporation was duly presented to Parliament in 1768 and was given two readings. So intense, however, was the feeling of the Craft *against* the Bill—it being feared that it was a legal method of 'misappropriating' the Charity Funds for other purposes—that the debate on the Bill was adjourned *sine die* at the start of its third reading.

Beaufort was more successful in his plans for providing a central home for the premier Grand Lodge. In 1768 he put forward a scheme for financing the provision of a Hall and furniture and regalia for the Grand Lodge. The Grand Lodge had, since its formation in 1717, met in various City taverns and held the Annual Feast in the Hall of one of the City Livery Companies. The Grand Secretaries, many of whom were lawyers, had usually worked from their home or office, receiving no salary but receiving a portion of the various fees received and out-of-pocket expenses. The scheme was approved with some minor changes and not only resulted in the building of a Hall but completely altered the administration of the Grand Lodge. Up to 1768 lodges had paid a fee for their 'constitution' and for Grand Lodge certificates if they required them and had sent a few guineas to the Charity Fund whenever they could afford it. Under the new scheme the fees for constitution, lodge warrants and certificates, and fees of honour for those appointed Grand Officers were raised and compulsory registration of members was introduced. All lodges had to register their members in 1768 and for the future had to register, and pay a fee for, all initiates and joining members, resulting in the setting-up of Grand Lodge membership registers. The project met with great support in London but a number of the Provincial lodges objected to having to finance a Hall which they had little chance of seeing, let alone using; nor did they see why they should now have to pay registration fees.

Their opposition met with no success and the plan went ahead. Beaufort's successor in 1772, Robert, 9th Lord Petre, did much to finalise the project. In 1774 premises were acquired in Great Queen Street comprising two houses and a garden, purchased for £3,150. An architectural competition was held, won by Thomas Sandby, and tenders were put out for the conversion work and building of the Grand Hall over the garden. The original estimates were for £5,000 but inflation is no new thing and by the end of the century over £20,000 had been spent on the Hall and the Freemasons' Tavern which fronted it on Great Queen Street. Lord Petre laid the foundation stone of the Hall on 1 May 1775 and dedicated the completed structure on 23 May 1776. Petre was the leading Roman Catholic of his day and, despite the Papal Bulls against Freemasonry in 1738 and 1751, did much to strengthen the Grand Lodge and continue the revival of fortunes of the London lodges. He was greatly assisted by James Heseltine who served Grand Lodge for thirty-five years as Grand Secretary 1769–83 and Grand Treasurer 1785–1804. Once the new scheme for administration had been accepted he ensured that it was carried through and made to work for the benefit of the Craft.

The revival of the premier Grand Lodge was crowned in 1782 by the election as Grand Master of HRH Henry Frederick, Duke of Cumberland. His election set the precedent of appointing an Acting Grand Master—now termed Pro Grand Master—whenever a Royal Prince was elected Grand Master. Under Royal patronage the Grand Lodge went from strength to strength with new lodges being constituted in London, the provinces, and abroad. Much of the revival in the provinces was due to Thomas Dunckerley, one of the major figures in eighteenth-century Freemasonry.[17] A natural son of King George II, Dunckerley retired from the sea in 1767 and having been granted a pension by the King, as well as grace and favour apartments at Hampton Court, devoted the rest of his life to Freemasonry. In the mid-1760s the office of Provincial Grand Master was revived and between 1767 and 1786 Dunckerley was appointed Provincial Grand Master for Hampshire, Essex, Isle of Wight, Dorset, Wiltshire, Bristol, Gloucestershire, Somerset and Herefordshire. He regularly visited his charges, held Provincial Grand Lodges, constituted new lodges, and ensured that they remained in contact with the Grand Lodge and properly registered their members.

The death of the Duke of Cumberland in 1790 was a blow to the Grand Lodge but moves were soon made to provide an even more exalted successor. The Duke had interested three of his nephews in Freemasonry: the Duke of Clarence (later King William IV), the Duke of York, and the Prince of Wales (later Prince Regent and King George IV). To the great pleasure of the Craft the Prince of Wales agreed to accept nomination as Grand Master. He had been initiated at a special lodge on 6 February 1787 and founded the Prince of Wales's Lodge (now No. 259) in the same year. He showed a great interest in the Craft but like his uncle appointed an Acting Grand Master, Francis Rawdon (later 2nd Earl of Moira and 1st Marquess of Hastings[18]), who acted as liaison between the Prince and the Grand Lodge. Moira, as he is best known in Masonic circles, proved an excellent choice. A proven soldier, statesman and administrator he guided the premier Grand Lodge through a very difficult period.

The French Revolution had caused panic throughout Europe. In England suspicion was cast upon Freemasonry by the publication of two French books claiming that the Jacobins and the Revolution had been guided by French Masonic lodges.[19] Prompt action by Moira in assuring the Crown and the government that far from plotting revolution English

Freemasonry supported the Crown and enjoyed the patronage of the King's sons prevented any action being taken against Freemasons in England. The Industrial Revolution, the growth of manufacturing towns, and the limited franchise in England prompted the formation of political Corresponding Societies and proto-trade unions. Fears of such groups and the example of the French Revolution led in the 1790s to a number of Acts being passed in Parliament against oath taking and secret societies. An Unlawful Societies Act was passed in 1799[20] which could have closed down all lodges in England and Wales. Moira requested an interview with the Prime Minister, William Pitt, to whom he gave an explanation of the nature of Freemasonry, its patronage by Royalty and the nobility, and its support of lawfully constituted authority. His explanations impressed Pitt and resulted in Freemasonry being specifically exempted from the terms of the Act, provided that every lodge secretary made an annual return of members with their addresses and occupations to the local Clerk of the Peace.

The history of the premier Grand Lodge after 1800 is so bound up with that of the Antients that we should now consider its development. Until it was chosen by C. N. Batham as the subject for his Prestonian Lecture[21] in 1981 the Antients Grand Lodge had been ignored by most Masonic historians and was usually dismissed as an artisan organisation of little importance. Despite claims that the Antients had had their origins in a schismatic group of the premier Grand Lodge and that they had been in existence in the late 1730s there seems little doubt that they had had no formal organisation before 1751. The Grand Committee which met for the first time in June 1751 at the Turk's Head in Greek Street, Soho, represented no more than a hundred Masons who formed themselves into six lodges. The majority of these Masons had been made in lodges in Ireland but had been refused entry to London lodges either on grounds of their class or because their ritual did not conform with the changes that had been made in England in the late 1730s. Artisans and tradesmen they may have been but they were good organisers and administrators. The first task which the Grand Committee set itself was the drawing up of a set of regulations for the government of the Grand Lodge and its subordinate lodges.

There is no doubt that the success of the Antients was greatly due to Laurence Dermott, their Grand Secretary from 1752–71 and Deputy Grand

Master 1771–7 and 1783–7. Born in Ireland and initiated in a Dublin lodge in 1741—of which he was Master in 1746—Dermott was a journeyman painter when he came to London but soon made a successful living as a wine merchant. A forceful character, a master politician, and a very able administrator he cajoled, bullied and moulded the Antients into an equal to the premier Grand Lodge so that when the movement towards Union began the Antients were able to treat with the premier Grand Lodge without any sense of inferiority and to insist on certain conditions before they would agree to the Union.

The original intinerant Irish members of the Antients soon departed and were replaced by English artisans, tradesmen, and minor professionals. They brought their business skills into Freemasonry and from the start established a firm administration. All lodge members had to be registered with the Grand Lodge from the beginning of its existence and quarterly dues were collected and entered in the Registers. A central Charity Fund was established and a Stewards Lodge set up to advise on petitions for relief. Like its opposite in the premier Grand Lodge it soon received the status of a general committee reporting, investigating and commenting on matters referred to it by the Grand Lodge.

In 1756 Dermott published the first Constitutions of the Antients, to which he gave the title *Ahiman Rezon*[22]—the meaning of which had caused much discussion. It is generally construed to mean 'a help to a brother'. The regulations contained a mixture of plagiarisms of Anderson's *Constitutions* and Irish regulations which Dermott had learned in Dublin. It also included an historical essay by Dermott which was largely a vituperative diatribe against the premier Grand Lodge, which he claimed had departed from the Ancient Landmarks and perverted pure ancient Masonry. *His* Grand Lodge, he claimed, was working according to the Old Institutions. Hence the two rivals became known as the Antients and the Moderns, although the latter was by far the senior of the two.

Possibly because of its members' social backgrounds the Antients was a much more democratic organisation. The Grand Master had no independent authority; any decision he made had to be ratified by the Grand Lodge. Authority to constitute new lodges lay not with the Grand Master alone but with him acting with the *approbation* of the Grand Lodge. All Grand Officers were elected by the Grand Lodge, elections occasionally being hotly contested. Provincial Grand Masters were not appointed in their own right but as Masters of Provincial Grand Lodges, which were warranted in the same manner as private lodges, numbered on the Register, and empowered to elect successor Provincial Grand Masters and Provincial Officers in the same manner as a lodge elected its Master and officers. Nothing could be done without the full agreement of the Grand Lodge.

Like the premier Grand Lodge the Antients were initially a London-based organisation, but they soon spread into the country and had a much greater success abroad than their rivals. Much of this success was due to the many travelling warrants they issued to regiments in the British Army, forming lodges that travelled with and met wherever the regiment was stationed. Although not constitutionally empowered to do so, these travelling military lodges would admit local civilians who, when the regiment moved on, would apply to the Antients for a warrant for a stationary lodge. The Provincial Grand Lodges established abroad by the Antients were given authority to constitute new lodges within their areas, which lodges were supposed to be registered in London with the Grand Lodge but, as with the premier Grand Lodge, many were out of existence before this could happen, or else the Provincial Grand Lodge did not maintain contact with London and began to act almost as an independent Grand Lodge.

Rivalry between the two Grand Lodges was intense and often bitter in London, but the further removed from London the friendlier the relations between lodges of the two obediences, despite the regular commands from their Grand Lodges to discountenance each other as irregular. This rivalry does not seem to have spread to the other three Grand Lodges which appeared for short periods in the eighteenth-century and which seem to have been allowed to function without any comment or interference from either the premier or the Antients Grand Lodges.

In Chapter 2 mention was made of the lodge at York whose records dated back to 1705. In 1725 it declared itself the Grand Lodge of All England but does not appear to have exercised any of the functions of a Grand Lodge from that date until it became dormant in 1741. It reappeared again in 1761 but as a true Grand Lodge electing Grand Masters and constituting at least thirteen subordinate lodges before it suddenly disappeared forever in 1792. Like the Antients it did not concern itself solely with the Craft but had its own Grand Chapter for the Royal Arch and a governing body for its Knights Templar groups. This York Grand Lodge itself added to the number of Grand Lodges by warranting a fourth which, being centred on London, was styled the Grand Lodge South of the River Trent. This had its origins in a breakaway group from the time immemorial Lodge of Antiquity, one of the Founding Lodges of the premier Grand Lodge, led by William Preston, the foremost Masonic teacher of his day.[23] After a major row with the premier Grand Lodge in 1779 over an alleged 'public procession of Masons cloathed in the badges of the Order' Preston and his followers seceded from the Lodge of Antiquity and operated as an independent lodge in London. They applied to York for a warrant as a Grand Lodge, which was granted, and for some ten years worked in London with at least two subordinate lodges before they begged pardon of the premier Grand Lodge and once again became part of the Lodge of Antiquity.

The fifth Grand Lodge is very shadowy and was only brought to the attention of Masonic scholars by Henry Sadler in 1905. It would appear from Sadler's researches that it had its origins in Scottish members of two Antients lodges in London who broke away and formed their own lodges and a Grand Lodge in London in 1770. Sadler believed it had five subordinate lodges but was unable to trace any records of it after 1772.[24]

After the disappearance of the York Grand Lodge in 1792 only the premier and Antients Grand Lodges remained. Whilst they managed to exist together in England, neither recognising each other nor regarding each other's members as regularly made Masons, problems were beginning to arise in dealing with the Grand Lodges of Ireland and Scotland and the Grand Lodges appearing in Europe and the newly created United States of America, none of which appeared willing to recognise both Grand Lodges in England. There were those on both sides who began to see that some sort of Union between the two could only strengthen Freemasonry and end the almost farcical situation of having two completely separate organisations that, though they were administered and worked on the same lines, claimed that each other was irregular.

Attempts began to be made in the late 1790s to lead towards a Union but met with little success. In 1802 the Thomas Harper affair offered an opportunity but was badly bungled.[25] Harper was the Deputy Grand Master of the Antients and a former Grand Steward of the premier Grand Lodge and well known as an active member of both Grand Lodges. Out of personal jealousy a complaint was laid against him and he was hauled before the Committee of Charity to answer the question of his 'alleged' membership of an irregular Grand Lodge. Quite how the Committee could have sat with a straight face to ask the question knowing full well Harper's position in the Antients is a mystery. Harper refused to give up his membership of the Antients and suggested that instead of the premier Grand Lodge expelling him they should consider opening discussions on a possible union with the Antients. His suggestion was agreed to but a time limit was placed on it. The records are silent on the Antients' reaction but it cannot have been favourable for Harper did not reappear before the Committee of Charity and was summarily expelled.

The next move towards Union came in 1809 when the premier Grand Lodge ordered its lodges to reverse the ritual changes made in the late 1730s and warranted a special Lodge of Promulgation to look into the differences between its rituals and those of other Grand Lodges. The work of the Lodge of Promulgation resulted in various changes which paved the way ritualistically for a Union. As a result, Committees of both Grand Lodges were set up in 1810 to negotiate an equitable Union. The premier Grand Lodge negotiators, led by the Earl of Moira, were given full authority to work out the basis for a Union but those of the Antients were given no authority at all and had to refer every decision, major or minor, back to their Grand Lodge for approval. Not surprisingly this dragged out the negotiations, to such an extent that in 1811 Lord Moira wrote to them that unless they were given authority to negotiate there was little point in continuing the discussions. It was not until 1813 and the arrival of HRH the Duke of Sussex as Grand Master of the premier and HRH the Duke of Kent as Grand Master of the Antients Grand Lodge that matters were speeded up. In a matter of six weeks they had concluded the negotiations, drawn up Articles of Union which were agreed by their Grand Lodges, and arranged the great Union meeting on 27 December 1813 at which the United Grand Lodge came into existence as the sole Craft authority for England and Wales and English lodges abroad.

Whilst the basic principles for Union had been agreed few of those involved in the negotiations could have realised the changes it would bring about. The Grand Mastership was easily settled by the Duke of Kent standing down and gracefully proposing his brother the Duke of Sussex as Grand Master.[26] A happier choice could not have been made. A forceful character with abundant energy, and a great enthusiasm for Freemasonry were the ideal characteristics for the monumental task of ensuring that the Union held together with the minimum of fuss and opposition. The Duke of Sussex proved equal to the task, personally directing the reorganisation of Grand Lodge, and was to keep a firm control over it for thirty years until his death in 1843.

The present and past Grand Officers of the two former Grand Lodges retained their status in the United Grand Lodge and a standardised list of Grand Officers was introduced. The office of Grand Secretary was made a joint one with W. H. White from the premier and Edwards Harper from the Antients, though there was no doubt that White considered himself the senior of the two. A small problem arose over the precedence of lodges and the amalgamation of the two previous registers. Almost on the toss of a coin the Antients' Grand Master's Lodge No. 1 became No. 1 of the United Grand Lodge and the premier Grand Lodge's Lodge of Antiquity No. 1 became No. 2, although much the senior lodge in terms of age. The remaining lodges filled in alternately.

Constitutional changes took rather longer.[27] Unbound sheets of the new *Book of Constitutions* were issued in 1815 as a discussion document but were not finally settled until 1819. Amongst the major changes it brought about were an increase in the number of Grand Officers, with precise definitions of their duties; the definition of the powers of a Provincial Grand Master and the introduction of mandatory annual meetings of his Provincial Grand Lodge; the introduction of four Boards to take over the functions of the former Committee of Charity and the Stewards Lodge; the necessity for a new lodge to be sponsored by another lodge in the locality and, in the case of the Provinces, to have the active support of the Provincial Grand Master; regulations limiting the holding of the Mastership of a lodge to a maximum of two consecutive years; detailed regulations concerning regalia and jewels; the mandatory issue of a Grand Lodge certificate to every initiate once he had taken all three degrees; the introduction of a Board of Benevolence to take over the administration of the former charity funds. As we shall see in the next chapter, there were also great changes in the ritual.

Despite all the changes there was little opposition to the amount of work undertaken by the Duke of Sussex and his aides. Opposition, however, did briefly flare up in Lancashire.[28] In 1818 what might appear at first to have been a trivial incident resulted in open rebellion. The question arose as to the minimum number of members required for a lodge to function, a question not covered by the *Book of Constitutions*. Largely as a result of an ineffectual and absentee Provincial Grand Master and a certain abruptness on the part of the Grand Lodge, the simple question was allowed to develop into a major argument over the ritual changes, the new *Book of Constitutions*, and even the legality of the United Grand Lodge itself. As a result of the acrimony several lodges in the Lancashire area were struck off the Register and many of their members were expelled from the Craft. They immediately formed themselves into a separate Grand Lodge centred on Wigan, now known as the Wigan Grand Lodge,[29] and reverted to their pre-Union practices. Their rebellion was short lived and the new Grand Lodge was soon reduced to one lodge—Sincerity—meeting in Wigan which, however, managed to work along and independently from the United Grand Lodge until 1913 when its members petitioned Grand Lodge to be regularised and the lodge became No. 3677 on the Register.

The four Boards set up at the Union covered General Purposes, Finance, Works, and Schools. It was soon realised that the work of all four overlapped and by 1838 all had been absorbed into the Board of General Purposes, which continues to be the policy-making body of the Craft. In 1838 it consisted of a President and ten Grand Officers appointed by the Grand Master and fourteen Masters and Past Masters elected by Grand Lodge. The Board soon adopted a committee system whereby the details of particular matters were worked out in committee and the full Board dealt only with matters of policy and actual decisions and recommendations to be reported to Grand Lodge. All matters, however, including disciplinary proceedings and appeals, were discussed in full in Grand Lodge, even down to the matter of the salaries of the Grand Secretary and his clerks.

The Duke of Sussex's firm hand and attention to detail over the thirty years of his Grand Mastership—1813 to 1843—ensured that the Union of the two Grand Lodges was a success and that the necessary changes were brought about and accepted with a minimum of fuss. His successor, Thomas, 2nd Earl of Zetland, does not appear to have had the same firm grasp and by the mid-1850s Grand Lodge and its affairs were virtually being run by the Grand Secretary William White, who had been in office since 1809, and the Grand Registrar and President of the Board of General

Purposes. Dissatisfaction was expressed in Grand Lodge. The position of the Mark degree had been mishandled; the Canadian question had been exacerbated rather than ameliorated by the triumvirates' actions; the Grand Master seemed unhappy about having to select one brother over another to make Grand Officers, who remained in office over too long a period; and provincial brethren felt that they had no say in the workings of the government of the Craft. Not only did a vociferous 'anti-dais' party emerge at Grand Lodge meetings but a quarterly newsletter[30] was published shortly after each Grand Lodge meeting giving verbatim reports on the proceedings with an acerbic commentary. In 1856 and 1857 the unprecendented step was taken of proposing an alternative candidate when the Grand Master's name was proposed for re-election. Many of the problems appear to have subsided after the forced retirement of the octogenarian Grand Secretary in 1857. Despite the problems Lord Zetland presided over a period of expansion in the Craft. Many new lodges were formed, resulting in Grand Lodge finances being almost trebled and enabling Freemasons' Hall to be greatly extended in the 1860s, though still preserving Sandby's Hall of 1776.

The election of a new Grand Master in 1870, the Earl de Grey and Ripon (soon to be 1st Marquess of Ripon), should have signalled a rejuvenation of Grand Lodge's status, but his rule was short lived. Having converted to Roman Catholicism he felt it essential that he should resign his office in 1874 as his Church was so implacably opposed to Freemasonry. His successor was Albert Edward, Prince of Wales (later King Edward VII), who readily accepted nomination as Grand Master in December 1874, and continued in office until his accession to the throne in 1901. He took great interest and delight in Freemasonry and did much to publicise the Craft by attending meetings wherever he went at home or abroad and publicly laying the foundation stones of many public buildings with Masonic ceremonial—all of which events were widely reported in the press. In the words of P. R. James[31] 'By his devotion and enthusiasm the Prince of Wales had enlarged the fraternity and improved its general conduct and social status.' He it was who introduced the practice of conferring Past Grand Rank as an honour for service to the Craft. Although he limited it to occasions on which major anniversaries—Masonic or civil—were celebrated he set a precedent which became annual after the First World War and enabled many brethren, particularly in the provinces, to achieve Grand Rank.

In accordance with the precedent set by George IV, the Prince of Wales resigned from active participation in Freemasonry on ascending the throne in 1901 and took the title of Protector of the Order. He had presided over what was probably the most peaceful twenty-six years in the history of Grand Lodge and was succeeded by his brother the Duke of Connaught, who was in turn to preside as Grand Master for thirty-eight years during which both Grand Lodge and the country as a whole went through great changes.

Two problems arose, both of which were brought to a halt by the outbreak of war in 1914. Despite the rebuilding of Freemasons' Hall in the 1860s it quickly became apparent that a new central meeting place was required capable of catering both to the needs of Grand Lodge and its administrative functions and those of the growing number of lodges meeting in London. It was planned to further extend the existing Hall as a memorial to Edward VII after his death in 1910 and some preparatory work was undertaken before the contractors were taken off for essential war work. At the same time dissatisfaction was being voiced at the manner in which Grand Lodge was being governed. It was argued by the Provinces that they had very little say in the working of Grand Lodge or the Board of General Purposes and that because of problems of travel both were heavily biased towards London lodges. A committee of enquiry was set up under the Chairmanship of the then Pro Grand Master, Lord Ampthill, and produced a most complex plan for a complete reorganisation of the government of the Craft, involving various levels of representation, which in practice would have been almost unworkable. Again the war intervened and the plan was quietly shelved, but a major change was made in the composition of the Board of General Purpose in 1916 when it was agreed that for the future the elected members of the Board should be nominated equally by London lodges and the Provinces, which is still the situation today.

The major event of Connaught's Grand Mastership was the building of the present Freemasons' Hall, which occupied fourteen years.[32] It was at the Grand Master's request that consideration was given in 1919 to the building of a new Hall as a permanent memorial to all those members who had given their lives during the war. Although alternative sites were discussed the acquisition of property to the west of the existing Hall meant that a substantial building could be raised on the original site. An international architectural competition was held, the panel of judges being chaired by Sir Edwin Lutyens (a non-Mason), the winning entry being that of Messrs. H. V. Ashley and Winton Newman. The foundation stone was laid in 1927 and within six years the building was complete and ready for occupation. The formal dedication was carried out by the Grand Master assisted by the then Prince of Wales (later King Edward VIII and Duke of Windsor), the Duke of York (later King George VI), and Prince George (later Duke of Kent).[33] The Hall, in addition to the Grand Temple, provided nineteen lodge rooms, committee and conference rooms, a Library and Museum, administrative offices for the Grand Secretary and his staff, and complete maintenance workshops.

The Duke of Connaught resigned in 1939 and was succeeded by his grand-nephew HRH The Duke of Kent. Tragically the Duke's rule was cut short by his death on active service with the Royal Air Force in 1942. He was in turn succeeded by his brother-in-law the Earl of Harewood, who guided the Craft through the difficulties of war as, first, Pro Grand Master and Grand Master. Despite the problems of the war and the London Blitz the Grand Lodge continued to function, moving its meetings to day times and dispensing with the usual Grand Officer's Mess. The end of the war brought another period of great expansion in the number of candidates and new lodges and a gradual return to normality with much time being spent on the problems of the revival of regular Freemasonry in the recently liberated countries of Europe. The Earl of Harewood died in 1947 and was succeeded by the Duke of Devonshire, who continued the normalisation of work after the effects of war. The Craft, however, suffered a double blow in 1951–2 by his death and that of King George VI. The King had been a very active Freemason but in accordance with custom had retired from active participation on coming to the throne after the Abdication Crisis of 1936. However, he had continued his interest in Freemasonry and had broken with tradition by not only attending but actually installing as Grand Master his brother the Duke of Kent, his brother-in-law the Earl of Harewood, and the Duke of Devonshire. He was to have installed the Earl of Scarbrough in 1952 but what proved to be his final illness prevented his attendance.

The installation of the 11th Earl of Scarbrough as Grand Master in 1952 began another period of stability and continuity in the life of Grand Lodge. Much of the fifteen years of his Grand Mastership was taken up with foreign relations but a number of domestic matters required attention. Grand Lodge time was still much taken up with disciplinary matters and resultant appeals, making for very long Grand Lodge meetings. In 1957 an *ad hoc* appeals committee was instituted, later formalised into a Commission for Appeals which heard all such matters and then reported its findings to Grand Lodge for a final decision. The publication of Walton Hannah's *Darkness Visible* in 1951 led Grand Lodge to a serious consideration of the relationship between religion and Freemasonry resulting eventually in Grand Lodge issuing an official statement in 1962 and again in 1985 (see Chapter 10).

In 1964 Grand Lodge was the scene of one of the most important debates in its history: the question of the physical penalties in the obligations of the three degrees. The debate had been started by a group led by Bishop Herbert, who had a great distaste for taking or administering an obligation during which the candidate, with his hand on the Volume of the Sacred Law, had to uphold certain barbaric penalties which were contrary not only to the law but were illogical in the context of the obligation he was taking. The matter was argued at all levels of the Craft before it reached debate in Grand Lodge, resulting in what was termed a 'permissive' variation being introduced by which the penalties became referred to as traditional and historical, the amended obligation only reminding the candidate that they had formerly existed. Grand Lodge did not, however, rule on the matter but left it to each lodge to decide whether or not they adopted the variation.[34]

The culmination of Lord Scarbrough's Grand Mastership was the celebration of the 250th Anniversary of the formation of Grand Lodge in 1967. He had expressed his wish to step down as Grand Master and suggested that a fitting means of celebrating so notable an anniversary would be to once more have the pleasure of a Royal Grand Master. HRH the Duke of Kent, having been initiated some years previously, was approached and readily consented to his name being put forward for election by Grand Lodge. To the great pleasure of the Craft he was installed at the Royal Albert Hall in June 1967 and requested Lord Scarborough to remain as Pro Grand Master, the duties of which office he carried out until his death in 1969.

After that notable occasion the Grand Lodge continued imperceptibly to adapt itself to a changing world without departing from its principles or traditions. The present Grand Master, HRH the Duke of Kent, although not able to attend as many meetings as his Royal predecessors, is by no means a figurehead. He insists on being fully briefed about what is happening in Grand Lodge, gives wise advice, and suggests changes and new ideas for the consideration of Grand Lodge. It was at his instigation that the major review of the funding and operation of Masonic charity took place in the 1970s (see Chapter 9) and that the question of the physical penalties in the obligations was again raised in 1978 and 1985, resulting in the great debate in Grand Lodge in 1986 and the removal of the physical penalties from the obligations. It was also at his suggestion, in 1984, that Grand Lodge began to reconsider its traditional policy of 'no comment' on questions about Freemasonry from outside, instituting a new policy of limited comment and the provision of more basic information to the non-Masonic world so that non-Masons could better judge for themselves the accuracy, or otherwise, of reports appearing in the media.[35] Having begun the process he has supported it throughout and became the first Grand Master of England to be interviewed about Freemasonry live on radio.

The high regard in which the Grand Master is held was clearly shown in 1992 when Grand Lodge was held at Earls Court on 10 June to celebrate the 25th Anniversary of his Installation to that high office, the 275th Anniversary of the Grand Lodge of England and to commemorate the 40th Anniversary of the accession to the throne of Her Majesty the Queen. Over twelve thousand, five hundred brethren and their guests—including ladies and the full panoply of the media—attended the Quarterly Communication of Grand Lodge during which the Grand Master dedicated the foundation stone of a community for handicapped adults to be built at Rowde, Wiltshire, for the building and equipping of which the Grand Charity and the Masonic Trust for Girls and Boys had provided £1,750,000. In addition to representatives of English lodges the meeting was attended by deputations from eighty four foreign and Commonwealth Grand Lodges.

Had the representatives of those four London lodges who came together to form the Grand Lodge in 1717 looked down on Earls Court that day they would have been amazed at what had resulted from their desire to come together in fellowship. From that simple social gathering in 1717 Grand Lodge has grown to an organisation of over 8500 lodges, mainly in England and Wales but still with some in former colonial territories and in the new countries of the Commonwealth. By an almost paradoxical process of adaptation and resistance to change it has safeguarded its authority without in any way losing its original democratic nature. It may at times appear to be acting dictatorially or in an authoritarian manner, but its members know that they are safeguarded by their position as members of their own governing body and by their inalienable right to approve or disapprove of any actions taken.

4

THE DEVELOPMENT OF THE LODGE

OUR KNOWLEDGE of the development of the lodge is hampered by lack of records. It is generally believed that until at least the 1660s lodges were not permanent but were simply groups of Freemasons brought together for the purposes of initiating a candidate, what has become known as an *occasional lodge*. From the little evidence we have it would seem that it was thought essential to have a copy of the Old Charges present at an initiation and that at least the Charges, if not the whole document, were read. Why people were initiated and what being a Freemason at that date meant are questions which still have to be answered. Anderson suggested that lodges had been established in London during the rebuilding caused by the Great Fire of 1666, but whether he was correct and whether they were operative or speculative lodges cannot be established due to lack of evidence. It is possible that Randle Holmes's lodge at Chester may have met on a regular basis but no minutes have survived to substantiate this. The present time immemorial Lodge of Antiquity is believed to be the 'old lodge at St. Paul's' mentioned by Anderson as meeting in 1693, but again no early minutes survive although the *Antiquity MS* of the Old Charges is dated 1683 and has always been in the lodge's possession. As we have seen in Chapter 2, the old lodge at York had minutes from 1705 showing that it met regularly to make Freemasons.

It is not until 1726 that we have extant minutes of a lodge which was purely speculative. These belonged to a lodge constituted at the Swan and Rummer Tavern, Finch Lane, London, on 2 February 1726.[1] Sadly, the minutes reveal very little, being mainly a list of dates on which the lodge met with details of the meeting place and lists of those present. A few of the minutes show the lodge balloting for candidates and working ceremonies. The Entered Apprentice and Fellowcraft degrees were often worked on the same evening but the Master Mason's degree was rarely worked. Meetings were held fortnightly and attendances averaged between fifteen and twenty members per meeting. Officers were limited to a Master, Senior and Junior Wardens, Treasurer, Secretary and a Tyler to guard the door of the lodge. All officers were elected and served for six months, elections and installations usually taking place on the festivals of St. John the Baptist (24 June) and St. John the Evangelist (27 December). Although elected every six months it was common for the Master to be elected for more than one period, but there is nothing to indicate that the installation of the Master included any sort of esoteric ceremony.

From the 1730s more lodge minute books survive and, together with other evidence, they enable us to build up a picture of how lodges came into existence. The first step was to petition the Grand Master to be allowed to form a lodge. If the petition was granted the Grand Master, or his Deputy, would summon the petitioners to meet him and they would be formally constituted into a lodge. If the new lodge was to meet outside London the Grand Master would send a written *deputation* to some local worthy brother authorising him to summon the petitioners and to constitute them on behalf of the Grand Master. A summary of the Constitution Ceremony as practised by the Duke of Wharton as Grand Master is given as an appendix to Anderson's 1723 *Constitutions*. The proposed Master of the new lodge was presented to the Grand Master—or his representative—and the Grand Master then asked the petitioners if the proposed Master was their unanimous choice. This being answered in the affirmative the Grand Master declared the lodge duly constituted and appointed the first Master. The Deputy Grand Master then gave the *Master's Charge* to which the Master had to submit, whereupon, he was installed and presented with the Constitutions, lodge book, and his jewel of office. The new Master then chose his Wardens, who had to be approved by both the Grand Master and the petitioners, who were given the *Warden's Charge* by one of the Grand Wardens and then installed by the Master. Once this was done the Constituting Officer signed a certificate of constitution which was returned to the Grand Secretary so that the new lodge could be registered and entered on the engraved *List of Lodges*. Once formally constituted the lodge could begin its work of making Freemasons.[2]

Until 1757 lodges under the premier Grand Lodge had no formal document authorising them to work as lodges.[3] Their authority to meet was the formal act of constitution by the Grand Master and their being registered with the Grand Lodge. In 1757 the premier Lodge adopted the Irish and Antients' practice of issuing warrants. Issued by authority of the Grand Master the warrant was the instrument permitting the lodge to meet and function as a lodge of Freemasons. The warrant designated the first Master and Wardens and empowered the lodge to elect their successors. It did not, however, bring the lodge into existence; it still had to be formally constituted.

The Antients had a slightly different practice. When a petition for a new lodge was submitted a dispensation was issued to the petitioners allowing them to meet and make Masons. If they proved that they could successfully hold and govern a lodge a further dispensation was issued permitting the holding of an emergency Grand Lodge 'for the space of three hours and no more'. If in London, the actual Grand Officers would preside; if in the country, the dispensation would designate certain local brethren to act as Grand Officers for the occasion. The emergency Grand Lodge was opened and the dispensation for holding it together with the original petition and the warrant for the lodge were read. The petitioners were then asked if they agreed to submit to the terms of the warrant, after which the Grand Master, or his representative, would declare the lodge duly constituted and proceed with the installation of the first Master and Wardens. Probably as a result of the Irish influence introduced by Laurence Dermott, the Antients began to issue warrants to their lodges as soon as their first Grand Master was installed. The warrant was of immense importance. No lodge could be considered as regular without a warrant and the document had to be present at every meeting for the proceedings to be considered valid.

William Preston in the first edition of his *Illustrations of Masonry* (1772) included an Appendix incorporating 'the manner of Constituting of Lodge' which he expanded in the eighth edition of 1792, which formed the basis of the present Consecration ceremony. It was incorporated in the 1815 edition of the *Book of Constitutions* but did not gain wide acceptance until the mid-nineteenth century. This was possibly because Grand Lodge had no occasion to use it, for between the Union and 1850 only two new lodges were warranted in London and the constituting or consecrating of new lodges in the provinces was the duty of Provincial Grand Masters. When more new lodges began to appear in London the Consecration ceremony was quickly adopted and in 1864 the Grand Secretary sent a circular letter to all Provincial Grand Masters in which he stated that 'the earliest possible opportunity ought to be taken for consecrating the Lodge, after the Grand Master's signature has been affixed to the Warrant'. Since then the Consecration ceremony has been essential and the lodge does not come into existence until it has been consecrated.

Although the Consecration ceremony incorporates non-denominational prayers it is not a religious ceremony in any sense. Its purpose is to dedicate the lodge to the Great Architect and, in the words of T. O. Haunch, 'it is the Masonic rite. . . . by which a new lodge is blessed for, and dedicated to the purpose for which it is regularly constituted, i.e. the practice of Freemasonry'.[4]

Tracing the development of the ritual is as difficult as tracing the origins of the Craft itself. Because printed rituals did not appear until as late as 1838[5] and because the eighteenth century and earlier Freemasons had a marked reluctance to commit ritual to paper, our knowledge depends very much on manuscript *aides-memoires* and printed exposures, the reliability of which must be called into question as they were produced for profit and to entertain the non-Masonic public. Certain versions of the Old Charges contain evidence of the taking of an oath and the giving of signs and words. Four manuscripts of Irish and Scottish provenance dating from 1696 to 1714 give details of a brief ceremony but not all ritual historians are convinced that they are evidence of Masonic ritual, being probably operative in origin.[6]

In the 1720s in England we begin to get printed exposures appearing in newspapers or as broadsheets.[7] The earliest appeared in *The Flying Post*, a London newspaper, for 11–13 April 1723, and is known as the *Mason's Examination*, a piece of doggerel which implies the existence of the three degrees of Apprentice, Fellow and Master. The third degree is believed to have been a late development originating in the 1720s. The first minute of the working of the third degree comes not in a lodge minute book but in that of the rather grandly named *Philo Musicae et Architecturae Societas Apoloni*—the Apollonian Society for Lovers of Music and Architecture—the members of which were all Freemasons. Their minutes[8] reveal that on 12 May 1725 'Brother Charles Cotton Esq., Broth^{r} Papillion Ball were regularly passed Masters.' There is no doubt that this was a reference to the working of the third degree for Cotton is known to have been initiated and passed to the second degree in a regular lodge at the Queen's Head Tavern, Hollis Street in the Strand, of which the Duke of Richmond was Master—at the same time being Grand Master. The proceedings of the Philo Musicae were, of course, completely irregular and they were strongly reprimanded by the Grand Secretary.

From 1726 we begin to get references of lodges working all three degrees. On 27 November 1725 a rather ambiguous Grand Lodge regulation of 1723 concerning the making of 'Masters and Fellowcraft only here [i.e. in Grand Lodge], unless by dispensation' was rescinded, enabling all lodges to work all three degrees. The 'making' and second degree were often conferred on the same evening, but the third degree took some time to gain acceptance. In many of the issues of the engraved *List of Lodges* in the 1730s and 1740s there are lodges referred to as 'Master's Lodges' and it is believed that their function was purely the conferring of the Master Mason degree. Throughout the eighteenth century there was no real necessity for anyone to go through anything other than the initiation ceremony for that qualified then to make claims on the Charity Fund.

It is not until 1730 and the publication of Prichard's exposure *Masonry Dissect'd* that we have any detailed indication of what all three ceremonies contained. From 1730 we have no further information until the publication of two further exposures, *Three Distinct Knocks* in 1760 and *Jachin and Boaz* in 1762, which show a certain development having taken place. After that we begin to get more authoritative information in the syllabus books for William Preston's[9] lecture system, Browne's *Master Key*,[10] and the publications of William Finch[11] from 1801 onwards, from which we can deduce the ceremonies of the three degrees.

What these various sources tell us is that the ceremonies themselves were fairly short. In essence the candidate entered, took an oath of fidelity and secrecy, and was given the word and sign. The greater part of the meeting was taken up with going through the catechetical lectures in which the ceremonies, principles and tenets, and symbols and emblems of the Craft were expounded and moralised upon. If the evidence of Prichard and the 1760s exposures can be accepted they show the catechetical lectures to have been fairly short and simple, with a minimum of symbolism. The last four decades of the eighteenth century, however, saw a growing interest in the philosophy of Freemasonry resulting in the publication of works like Calcott's *Candid Disquisition* (1769), Hutchinson's *Spirit of Masonry* (1775), Smith's *Uses and Abuses of Freemasonry* (1783), and Preston's *Illustrations* (1772). The influence of these works and Preston's lecture system gradually led to the catechetical lectures being greatly extended with a greater emphasis on moralising and symbolism.

The early eighteenth century in England was a great age of clubs and coffee houses and in many ways organised Freemasonry was little different from many other clubs and societies which then existed. Lodge meetings were usually held in a private room in an inn or tavern and there was very little difference between the actual meeting and the social board. Apart from items necessary for the actual ceremonies no special equipment was needed for much of the meeting, which generally took place with the members seated around a long trestle table. The Master would sit at one end with the two Wardens at the other and the members taking their places in order of seniority. The normal administrative business of the lodge and the working of the catechetical lectures would be done at the table. As well as carrying the symbols of Freemasonry the table would hold food, wine, punch and ale, tobacco jars, and church warden pipes. Eating, drinking, and smoking would take place throughout the meeting, except when the ceremonies were worked. Once the business of the meeting was concluded the Masonic items were removed from the table and the landlord brought in supper, at the conclusion of which the lodge would be closed.

The years immediately before and after the Union of the two Grand Lodges in 1813 were to bring further developments and great changes in the ritual. As a prelude to negotiations for the Union the premier Grand Lodge in 1809 ordered its lodges to reverse the alterations made in the words in the late 1730s. It then warranted a special Lodge of Promulgation[12] whose brief was to examine the ceremonies and determine how they differed from those practised in Scotland and Ireland and, by implication, the rival Antients Grand Lodge. Conscious of the obligations they had taken, the members of the Lodge of Promulgation did not officially write down their deliberations but from an examination of the lodge's minutes and other official and unofficial manuscript records we know that the Installation of the Master with an esoteric ceremony was recognised as a 'true landmark of the Order'. Deacons became mandatory lodge officers, alterations were made in the ceremonies of opening the lodge in each degree, and the ceremonies were brought into line with those of the Antients. The work of the Lodge of Promulgation paved the way ritualistically for the Union of the two Grand Lodges.

Once the Union had taken place further ritualistic alterations had to be made, resulting in the warranting of a special Lodge of Reconciliation[13] whose brief was to complete the reconciliation of the two former systems and bring about a standard form of ritual. Again nothing was officially written down concerning the work done by the Lodge of Reconciliation but some recently rediscovered manuscripts[14] show that a new arrangement of the ceremonies was produced and demonstrated and then completely rearranged in 1816. Rather than completing the reconciliation of the two former systems the Lodge of Reconciliation greatly extended the simple eighteenth-century ceremonies by including material from the catechetical lectures, which gradually dropped out of use. This extension of the ceremonies had three principal effects. The production of longer, more impressive ceremonies required a special room for them to be worked in, resulting in the development of lodge rooms reserved specifically for lodge meetings. This development into more dignified ceremonies also led to a separation of the meeting itself from the refreshment, which became a separate formal dinner or supper held in another room than the lodge. More important was an essential change in the nature of the meeting itself. The ceremonies, and their teaching of the principles of Freemasonry, became the whole basis of the institution and not simply entrance requirements for a benefit society.

The aim of producing a standard form of ritual was never achieved. As the revisions of the Lodge of Reconciliation were not officially written down and not allowed to be published the new system was passed on by demonstration and word of mouth. This combination of the method of promulgating the new system with a failure to suppress local traditions resulted in a variety of 'workings' of the same basic rituals in English lodges which makes visiting all the more interesting.[15] Most other Grand Lodges have a rigidly controlled ritual which is practised by all their subordinate lodges and in which no alterations or differences are permitted without the sanction of the Grand Lodge itself. In England, having settled the basic ceremonies in 1816, the United Grand Lodge had chosen not to intefere in ritual matters unless basic principles are involved, believing that each lodge had the right to decide which working it will adopt and how it might vary it to suit itself. Provided that the basic landmarks and outline of the ceremonies are used Grand Lodge does not interfere in details of language and performance of the ritual. The one area of the ritual in which Grand Lodge has involved itself in recent years is the traditional physical penalties included in the obligations, which will be discussed in Chapter 10.

The Installation of a new Master is an annual festival in each lodge. Although the Installation Ceremony has an esoteric content it is not a separate degree. It is believed that initially the Installation was simply the formal placing of the Master in the chair of the lodge and his investiture with his jewel of office without any esoteric ceremony being involved and without any additional 'secrets' being conferred. The earliest evidence we have for an esoteric Installation comes in the 1760 exposure *Three Distinct Knocks*, reputed to show the practice of Antients' lodges. It is clear by the 1770s that some lodges under the premier Grand Lodge must have been practising an esoteric Installation for by that time having been Master of a lodge was the qualification for exaltation into the Royal Arch—the word of an installed Master being the password to the Chapter. Preston in his *Illustrations of Masonry* does not have any esoteric content to the Installation Ceremony until the edition published in 1801. By the 1810 decision of the Lodge of Promulgation the premier Grand Lodge accepted the necessity of an esoteric Installation ceremony for the Master and held special meetings so that the present and past Masters of lodges could be properly Installed. The format of the Installation was settled in 1827 but the problem of the so-called Extended Ceremony of Installation, which includes a formal opening and closing of a Board of Installed Masters and the conferring of additional signs and words, was to rumble on throughout the nineteenth-century and was not finally settled until 1927.[16]

The Master of a lodge has to be elected by a ballot of those members present at a specific meeting each year. The Mastership is the highest honour which any lodge can confer upon one of its members. Since 1811 all candidates for election as Master must have served the office of Warden, for at least year. Before the Union the Master was usually elected and installed every six months but it was not uncommon for one Master to continue being re-elected for a number of years. On occasions elections were hotly contested and it was not unknown for a losing candidate for the Mastership to resign from the lodge with his supporters and either join another lodge or petition to form a new one. After the Union the present regulation was introduced whereby no one can serve as Master for more than two consecutive years except by dispensation of the Grand Master, which is only given in exceptional circumstances. The Master rules the lodge and is responsible for arranging and conducting the work during his year. He has the sole right to appoint his officers, with the exception of the Treasurer and Tyler, and has a casting vote when voting on a proposition results in a draw. At the conclusion of his year, after installing his successor, he becomes by right the Immediate Past Master of the lodge and sits on the left of the Master to assist him during his year of office.

The principal officers of the lodge, the Master and Wardens, were derived from the guild system. The Senior and Junior Wardens assist the Master in the ceremonies and in ruling the lodge. The Junior Warden has the responsibility for visitors to the lodge, in particular checking visitors who are unknown to the lodge to ensure that they are regularly-made Masons. The Secretary of the lodge keeps the minutes of the meeting and is responsible for preparing and issuing the summons for each meeting. In most lodges the Secretary continues in office for a number of years to ensure continuity in the administration of the lodge. The Treasurer of the lodge has always had to be elected annually by ballot of those members present at the election meeting. He is responsible for the finances of the lodge but any expenditure or raising of fees and dues can only be done by notice of motion followed by a resolution appearing on the lodge summons and a vote in open lodge. In the eighteenth century when the Treasurer physically looked after the lodge's money a number of lodges appeared to have had little faith in their Treasurers, despite having elected them, and insisted that they signed a bond as surety for the sums entrusted to them.

The Tyler, or Outer Guard, is the last of the original lodge officers.[17] His duty is to stand guard outside the door of the lodge to keep out intruders and to prepare the candidates for each degree. In the eighteenth century he was provided with a rather fanciful Turkish costume complete with turban, which was later replaced by a caped coat and tricorne hat, abandoned in the mid-nineteenth century. In the days when lodges drew their membership from a particular, small locality it was the duty of the Tyler to attend on the Secretary and personally deliver a copy of the summons to the meeting to each of the members. Before the introduction of Tracing Boards and their immediate predecessors, painted floor cloths, it was the Tyler's duty to 'draw the lodge' with chalk on the floor when a ceremony was to be worked. The 'lodge' was an oblong enclosing a drawing of the emblems and symbols of each degree. The designs became standardised and painted cloths were introduced followed by painted boards—Tracing Boards—one for each degree. The Tyler did not, however, have to remove his drawing for, as the exposures of the 1760s reveal, the candidate 'be he ever so noble a gentleman' was provided with mop and pail to remove the drawing to prevent non-Masons from seeing it.[18] The Tyler is usually elected by show of hands and receives payment for his work of setting the lodge room for the particular work of the meeting, looking after the lodge equipment, preparing the candidate for the ceremony, and guarding the door. In many Masonic Halls there is often a resident Tyler who tyles all the meetings in the building and acts as its caretaker. If the Tyler is a member of the lodge which he tyles he is not permitted to receive payment for his duties.

The office of Chaplain is what is termed an additional office; that is, the Master may appoint one but it is not mandatory for him to do so. Nor is it necessary for the Chaplain to be a clergyman as he has no religious duties to perform, Freemasonry being neither a religion nor a substitute for religion. His only function is to give the non-denominational prayers at the opening and closing of the lodge and at the beginning of each of the ceremonies. If no Chaplain is appointed the prayers are usually given by the Master.

Deacons are first heard of in Ireland in the early 1730s and were introduced from there into Antients' lodges by Laurence Dermott and the Irish founders of the Antients.[19] It was long believed that Deacons were not appointed in lodges under the premier Grand Lodge but recent research has shown that while not common there are instances of Deacons being regularly appointed in a number of premier lodges. The Deacons today have two functions. The Senior Deacon acts as a messenger between the Master and Senior Warden and is guide and conductor of the candidate in the second and third degrees. The Junior Deacon acts as a messenger between the Senior and Junior Wardens and is guide and conductor of the candidates during the intitiation ceremony.

The Inner Guard, as his name suggests, guards the lodge door from the inside. His duties are to guard the door, to admit latecomers, and to admit candidates for each of the ceremonies having ascertained that they are properly prepared and qualified to enter. The title was introduced at the Union of the two Grand Lodges in 1813, prior to which the duties appear to have been carried out by the Junior Warden or a Steward. It is not certain what duties the Stewards performed prior to the Union. They may have attended on the Wardens when Deacons were not appointed, guarded the inside of the door, and looked after the refreshments. Certainly since the Union they have had no ceremonial function other than being ready to stand in for an absent junior lodge officer, their services being reserved for the Festive Board. Their duties at the after-proceedings vary from lodge to lodge according to how the meal is arranged. In some lodges they do nothing, in others they will serve the wine at dinner, and in the Provinces where a Masonic Hall has its own catering facilities they will often serve the meal.

The Director of Ceremonies, with usually an Assistant Director of Ceremonies, is the guardian of the ritual and ceremonial of the lodge, an important task as the ritual has to be learnt and officers may not use their ritual books. His duties are to ensure the smooth running of the ceremonies, prompt the officers if necessary, and deal with any cermonial matters such as processions and the reception of distinguished visitors or latecomers. In some lodges the office is still styled Master of Ceremonies, a hangover from pre-Union days. Whether the duties of the Master of Ceremonies differed from those of the present Director of Ceremonies cannot be established from the ritual evidence we have.

Considering that brotherly love and relief are two of the great principles of Freemasonry it is surprising that the offices of Almoner and Charity Steward are fairly recent. The Almoner first appears officially in the 1884 edition of the *Book of Constitutions*. His duty is to look after the welfare of the members of the Lodge if they fall sick or on hard times and also the welfare of dependants after the death of a member. A good Almoner will check on members who have missed a few meetings to ensure that they are well and reports to the lodge on any who are sick. The Charity Steward was introduced as recently as 1975 and looks after the collecting of donations for either the lodge Charity Funds or for the major Masonic Charities. Working with the Treasurer he looks after and suggests disposals from the lodge Charity Fund.

As we shall see in the next chapter, music has been a part of Masonic meetings since the early eighteenth century and today the Master may if he wishes appoint an Organist. His main purpose is to provide incidental music for the ceremonies, in which he has a great freedom of choice provided that he avoids overtly religious items which could give offence to anyone present not of a particular religion.[20]

The lodge officers form a hierarchy leading from Steward to Master. The normal procedure is to pass through the offices as follows: Steward, Inner Guard, Junior Deacon, Senior Deacon, Junior Warden, Senior Warden, and Master. In most lodges the offices of Treasurer, Secretary, and Director of Ceremonies are undertaken by Past Masters who stay in these offices for a number of years to provide continuity. In most lodges the additional officers—Chaplain, Almoner, Charity Steward, Assistant Secretary, Assistant Director of Ceremonies, and Organist—are not progressive and may be held either by Past Masters or by members who may not wish to proceed to the Chair but still wish to be of active service to the lodge.

Today whilst the 'working' of the ceremonies may vary from lodge to lodge the basic format of the meeting will be the same. Each lodge meets on specific meeting dates, which cannot be varied without dispensation, and a meeting must be held regardless of whether or not there is a ceremony to perform. The number of meetings held a year is at the discretion of the individual lodge when it is formed and may only be varied by agreement of the members and by alteration of the lodge by-laws. On average, London lodges meet four times a year and lodges in the Provinces eight times, although some meet every month or every month except July and August. The Secretary has to issue a summons for each meeting giving the agenda to be followed. The members, and their guests, meet at the stated time and the lodge is ceremonially opened. The first item of business is the reading, confirming, and signing of the previous meeting's minutes, after which the order of business may vary from lodge to lodge. The *Book of Constitutions* lays down that no more than two candidates may be passed through a degree at any one time. At least 28 days must elapse before a candidate may progress from one degree to the next. Apart from ritual the meeting is taken up with the business of administering the lodge. Candidates for initiation or joining membership have to be proposed at one meeting and balloted for at the next, after their details have appeared on the summons. The Proceedings of Grand Lodge and, in the Provinces, the Provincial Grand Lodge have to be reported and any correspondence from either read and dealt with. It is customary for the lodge Almoner to report on the well-being of absent or sick members and to make recommendations when cases of need are discovered. Whilst the Master and Treasurer may have authority to dispense small sums most financial business of the lodge has to be agreed to by the members on propositions by the Treasurer. Once a year the Master, Treasurer and Tyler have to be elected together with Auditors and members for the lodge committee. Most lodges have some form of committee which has no authority to make decisions of its own but is a forum for discussing lodge business—the programme for the year, the interviewing of candidates, donations to charity—on which it will make recommendations which then have to be voted upon by the lodge, usually after notice of motion has appeared on a summons.

Whilst the majority of lodges are solely concerned with ritual work there are some lodges in which the only ritual performed is the opening and closing and the annual installation of the Master. These lodges fall into two groups—research lodges and those whose membership is limited to Installed Masters or Provincial Grand Stewards. The purpose of research lodges is the bringing together of those interested in research into the history, traditions, and practices of Freemasonry and the main work of the meeting is the presentation of a paper on some aspect of Freemasonry, usually followed by a discussion. Installed Masters' lodges and Provincial Grand Stewards' lodges are a means of continuing on a formal basis the fellowship developed during their year of office by those who have been Masters of lodges or Provincial Grand Stewards. The 'work' at their meetings usually takes the form of a talk on some aspect of Freemasonry or a demonstration of one of the ceremonies as it was performed in the past or as it is worked under another Grand Lodge.

In the middle of the nineteenth century there arose a number of what became known as 'class lodges', that is, lodges whose membership was limited to a particular group; e.g. school, University, and regimental lodges, those whose members came from a particular profession and whose members had a particular vocational interest in common. Unfortunately such lodges have an in-built weakness, for the success of a lodge depends on a regular supply of candidates and if the membership is limited to a particular group that supply may dry up. Since the end of the First World War it has not been possible to limit the membership of a lodge and many lodges which started out as 'class lodges' have abandoned their original limitation on membership.

It is a well-known fact that Freemasons wear distinctive regalia and the development of that regalia has paralleled the development of the lodge. The earliest reference to regalia comes in the premier Grand Lodge minutes for 24 June 1727 when it was ruled that the only jewels were the square for the Master, the level for the Senior Warden, and the plumb rule for the Junior Warden, which were to be in gold or metal gilt for the Grand Master and Grand Wardens and silver or base metal for the lodge Master and Wardens. On 17 March 1731 it was ruled that aprons should be of white lambskin, lined and edged with garter blue silk for the Grand Officers and white silk for all others excepting the Grand Stewards who were permitted to line and edge their aprons with red silk. It was also ruled that jewels of office were to be worn around the neck appended to garter blue silk ribbons for the Grand Officer, white silk ribbons for lodge officers, and red silk for the Grand Stewards.

Human nature being what it is, from the 1750s individual members began to decorate their aprons. Initially simple hand-painted designs were added to the plain white lambskin—a square and compasses or the Grand Lodge Arms. From the 1770s the designs become more and more elaborate incorporating a multiplicity of Masonic symbols, often combining those of the Craft with those of other degrees as they became more widely practised. Many fine examples survive in the Grand Lodge Museum and other places of hand-painted, embroidered (in silks or beadwork), or printed aprons. By the 1790s standardised designs were being produced from engraved plates and sold 'penny plain or tuppence coloured'.

As with aprons, so with Masonic jewels, as Masonic medals are called. To the original three for the Master and Wardens were soon added jewels of office for the Secretary (crossed pens), Treasurer (a key), and Tyler (a sword). When Deacons became more usual they adopted the winged Mercury, or Hermes, bearing a caduceus, possibly to mark their position as messengers. After 1750 individual members began to adopt their own unofficial jewels, usually incorporating a great number of Masonic symbols, not necessarily confined to the Craft. Two basic styles evolved, now known as plate and pierced jewels. The former were flat circular or oval plates, often in silver, on which the Masonic symbols were engraved; the latter were similar plates with the designs fretted out. Special presentation jewels were manufactured to mark particular services to a lodge, many of them being in gold or silver decorated with enamels and set in borders of paste or brilliants.

The Union of the two Grand Lodges brought about the standardisation of Craft regalia and jewels. A Board of Works had been set up to manage the property and furnishings of Grand Lodge but the first task was to design patterns for standardised regalia to be adopted by all members. They worked quickly and presented their designs at the March 1814 meeting of Grand Lodge. The designs were accepted and have only been varied since by the addition of new emblems for additional officers as they have been introduced. The designs were entered into the 1815 *Book of Constitutions as follows:*

JEWELS

The Grand Master, The compasses, extended to 45°, with the segment of a circle at the points and a gold plate included, on which is to be engraven an irradiated eye within a triangle.

Past Grand Masters, A similar jewel, without the gold plate.

Deputy Grand Master, The compasses and square united, with a five-pointed star in the centre.

Past Deputy Grand Masters, the compasses and square only.

Senior Grand Warden, The level.

Junior Grand Warden, The plumb.

Grand Chaplain, A book, within the triangle.

Grand Treasurer, A chased key.

Grand Registrar, A scroll, with seal appended.

Grand Secretary, Cross pens, with a tie.

Grand Superintendent of Works, a semicircular protractor.

Grand Director of Ceremonies, Cross rods.

Grand Deacons, Dove and olive-branch.

Grand Sword Bearer, Cross swords.

Grand Organist, A lyre.

The jewels of the grand chaplain, treasurer, registrar, secretary, superintendent of works, director of ceremonies, deacons, sword bearer, and organist, are to be within a wreath composed of a sprig of acacia and an ear of corn.

Provincial Grand Master, The compasses and square, with a five-pointed star in the centre.

Prov. Dep. Grand Master, The square.

All other Provincial Grand Officers, Jewels of the same description as those worn by the officers of the grand lodge.

The jewels of the provincial grand master and other provincial grand officers are to be placed within a circle, on which the name of the province is to be engraven.

All past officers of the grand lodge, or a provincial grand lodge, the jewel of their respective offices on a blue enamelled oval medal.

All the above jewels to be gold or gilt; and the collars to be garter-blue, four inches broad.

Masters of Lodges, The square.
Past Masters, The square and the diagram of the 47th prop. 1st B. of Euclid, engraven on a silver plate, pendant within it.
Senior Warden, The level.
Junior Warden, The plumb.
Treasurer, The key.
Secretary, The cross pens.
Deacons, The dove.
Inner Guard, Cross swords.
Tyler, The sword.

The above to be in silver. The collars to be light-blue riband, four inches broad: if silver chain be used, it must be placed over the light-blue riband.

APRONS

Entered Apprentice, A plain white lamb skin, from 14 to 16 inches wide, 12 to 14 inches deep, square at bottom, and without ornament, white strings.

Fellow Craft, A plain white lamb skin, similar to the entered apprentice, with the addition only of two sky-blue rosettes at the bottom.

Master Mason, The same, with sky-blue lining and edging, $1\frac{1}{2}$ inch deep, and an additional rosette on the fall or flap. No other colour or ornament shall be allowed except to officers and past officers of lodges, who may have the emblems of their offices in silver or white in the centre of the apron.

Grand Stewards, present and past, Aprons of the same dimensions, lined with crimson, edging $3\frac{1}{2}$ inches, and silver tassels.—The collars of the grand stewards lodge to be crimson riband, 4 inches broad.

Officers of the United Grand Lodge, present and past, Aprons of the same dimensions, lined with garter-blue, edging $3\frac{1}{2}$ inches, ornamented with gold, and blue strings, and may have the emblems of their offices, in gold or blue, in the centre.

Officers of Provincial Grand Lodges, present and past, Aprons similar to the officers of the United Grand Lodge, except that the garter-blue edging must not exceed two inches in width.

The masters and past masters of lodges to wear, in lieu and in the places of the three rosettes on the master mason's apron, perpendicular lines upon horizontal lines, thereby forming three several sets of two right-angles; the length of the horizontal lines to be two inches and a half each, and of the perpendicular lines one inch; these emblems to be of riband, half an inch broad, and of the same colour as the lining and edging of the apron. If grand officers, similar emblems, of garter-blue or gold. As a result of the 1815 regulations the design and wearing of regalia has been strictly controlled by Grand Lodge. No jewels other than those of the Craft or the Royal Arch may be worn as part of the Craft regalia unless they have been approved by the Grand Master. From the mid-nineteenth century the practice grew up of the wearing of Founder's jewels for new lodges and of lodges issuing a specially designed Past Master's jewel to each Master on the completion of his year of office. These jewels usually incorporated the lodge crest, the design of which has to be approved by the Grand Master. Commemorative jewels have been sparingly issued by the Grand Lodge itself: to commemorate the bicentenary, two hundred and fiftieth and two hundred and seventyfifth anniversaries of Grand Lodge; the building of the first, second, and present Freemasons' Halls; the Golden and Diamond Jubilees of Queen Victoria; the Installation of the Duke of Connaught as Grand Master in 1901, and the Celebration of Peace in 1919.

5

THE SOCIAL SIDE

ORGANISED FREEMASONRY developed in a great age of sociability and conviviality and the customs of the day were incorporated into Masonic usages. As we have seen, the premier Grand Lodge itself was originally formed in 1717 as a means for the members of the four London lodges to come together socially for the enjoyment of a 'Grand Feast'. The convivial side was as important as the business of electing a Grand Master and Grand Wardens. The Grand Festival has perhaps become more decorous but it still remains the high point of the Masonic year. There are those who have criticised the social side of Freemasonry, but in an Institution which has Brotherly Love as one of its aims a great deal would be lost if Freemasonry was limited to the proceedings carried out within the lodge room.

The first Grand Festivals were held in taverns but with the election of the Duke of Montagu as Grand Master in 1721 the Annual Assembly and Feast began to be held in the hall of one of the great livery companies of the City of London and continued to be held there until the first Freemasons' Hall was completed in 1776. The event was a very public one. The brethren all met at the town house of the incoming noble Grand Master and a procession, preceded and followed by bands of musicians, was formed to march from there to the hall at which the Festival was to take place. The brethren would march two by two dressed in their aprons and jewels and carrying the emblems, symbols, and banners of the Craft, followed by the nobility in their carriages and chariots. Not surprisingly such processions attracted public attention and in the 1730s they were caricatured in the press and an Order of Scald Miserable Masons began to hold processions a few days before the Grand Lodge procession, resulting in the latter being abandoned in April 1747 and a regulation being made that in future no 'public procession of masons cloathed in the badges of the Order' could be held without a dispensation.

Once the procession arrived at the hall a Grand Lodge was opened and the election of the new Grand Master was confirmed, after which the Grand Lodge was adjourned to dinner and the 'publick healths' were drunk. After dinner the new Grand Master was installed and invested his Grand Officers, who would then pass around the Hall for the new Grand Master to be proclaimed. This was followed by the 'General' or 'regular Healths', which ended the formal proceedings. The evening would then end with 'Orations, Musick and Mason songs' until the Grand Master formally closed the Grand Lodge. Various brethren had offered themselves as Stewards as early as 1721 to assist the Grand Wardens in preparing for the Feast, but in 1728 a significant development took place. Dr. Desaguliers proposed that twelve Stewards should be appointed to have the management of the Feast—the birth of the Grand Stewards.

The twelve Stewards were allowed to nominate their successors and were so successful in carrying out their duties that in 1731 they were given the privilege of having their own jewel of office and of lining and edging their aprons with red silk. A further privilege was added in 1735 when they were allowed to form a lodge whose membership was, and still is, limited to those who have served as Grand Stewards. The Grand Stewards continued to nominate their successors until the Union of the two Grand Lodges in 1813, after which the appointments became more formalised. The Duke of Sussex selected eighteen London lodges, many of which had provided Grand Stewards before 1813, to annually nominate from amongst their members a Grand Steward for appointment by the Grand Master. Pilgrim Lodge No. 238 gave up its right in 1834 and was succeeded by Jerusalem Lodge No. 197. The Old King's Arms Lodge No. 28 lost its right, on a technicality, in 1852 and was replaced by Old Union Lodge No. 46, but was restored to its privilege in 1904 so that there are now nineteen lodges with the privilege of nominating a Grand Steward. To be a Grand Steward is a highly prized honour, but it is also an expensive one as the Grand Stewards originally bore the whole cost of the Festival. They were allowed to charge a nominal dining fee—made more realistic this century—but the Grand Stewards have to cover any shortfall between the sum raised by the dining ticket and the actual cost of the Festival.

After the Union the Assembly became formalised into the Annual Investiture, at which the Grand Master was installed and appointed his Officers, for which Grand Lodge was opened and closed, whilst the Festival was separated off as a formal dinner without any Masonic ceremonial. Up to the outbreak of war in 1914 ladies were invited to the Grand Festival. It is not clear if they attended the dinner but they certainly joined with the brethren at its conclusion to hear a concert of vocal and orchestral music and to join in the singing of part-songs and glees. Since 1914 the Grand Festival has been purely a Masonic affair at which the Grand Stewards entertain the Grand Master, the Grand Officers and personal guests.[1]

Less fortunate than the Grand Stewards was an eighteenth-century group known as the Country Stewards.[2] In these days of Greater London and urban sprawl it is difficult to remember that in the eighteenth century Islington, Hampstead, Vauxhall, Ranelagh, and Gunnersbury were little country villages separated from the cities of London and Westminster. In the early 1730s it was decided to hold a Summer or Country Feast to honour the Deputy Grand Master at a suitable tavern in one of the villages around London. As with the Grand Feast it was soon realised that Stewards were required to organise the event, resulting in the creation of Country Stewards. Like the Grand Stewards, each year's Board of Country Stewards was given the right to nominate its successor and they were granted a special jewel to be worn suspended around the neck from green ribbon. In 1789 they successfully petitioned to have their own lodge, restricted to current and past Country Stewards, and to match their status with that of the Grand Stewards the Country Stewards petitioned the premier Grand Lodge in 1792 for the right to line and edge their aprons with green silk. Whether it was jealousy on the part of the Grand Stewards, or the intemperate manner in which the petition was presented, uproar ensued in Grand Lodge when the matter was debated and the petition was rejected, leading to the Country Stewards present storming out and declaring that if they could not have the green apron they might as well lose their special jewel and lodge. Tempers were allowed time to cool before the next Grand Lodge, at which the jewel and lodge were restored though the green apron was still refused. The hierarchy of Grand Lodge continued to be disturbed by the Country Stewards pressing their claim, resulting in the Deputy Grand Master, Admiral Sir Peter Parker Bt., stating in 1794 that as he was to be abroad on naval duties the Country Feast should be suspended until he could attend in person. Incredibly obstinate the Country Stewards in 1795 sent to the Grand Secretary a list of Stewards for that year and tickets for the Feast to be distributed to the Grand Officers. Rather brusquely the Grand Secretary returned the list and tickets stating that there could be no Feast or Stewards as the Deputy Grand Master had suspended the occasion till he could preside in person. Nevertheless they went ahead, held the Feast, and forfeited any support they might have had. No further official Country Feast was held therefore no further Country Stewards could be appointed. The Country Stewards Lodge continued to attend the Grand Lodge until 1799 when they disapeared for ever, their lodge warrant being used in 1802 to form what is now the Royal Lodge of Faith and Friendship No. 270 at Berkley in Gloucestershire.

As a fellowship or brotherhood the social side of Freemasonry is almost as important as the principles and tenets which are taught in the formalised setting of the meeting. Indeed it would be true to say that in its earliest days Freemasonry was very little different from the many other tavern and coffee house societies which were so popular in England in the early eighteenth entury. Since the great changes in ritual brought about by the Union of the two Grand Lodges there has been such a total separation of lodge meeting and Festive Board that it is often forgotten that originally there was no distinction between them.

Eighteenth-century lodges met in private rooms in taverns or coffee houses, with most of the evening being spent seated around a trestle table at which the administrative business of the lodge would be carried out and the catechetical lectures worked. Average attendance at a lodge meeting would be between twenty and thirty. In addition to the emblems of Masonry the tale would carry clay pipes and tobacco jars; bowls of fruit and nuts; bottles of wine, port, and brandy; bowls of punch and mead and jugs of ale. The alcohol was not simply there for refreshment, however, for the catechetical lectures were divided into sections, between each of which a formal toast would be drunk, often accompanied by a song. At a convenient point the Masonic 'work' would cease and the landlord, often himself a Mason, would bring in supper. Any unfinished business would then be dealt with, the lodge formally closed, and the evening rounded off with the singing of part songs and glees. With this consumption of refreshment and singing of songs it is not surprising that lodge minutes of the period often ended with a statement to the effect that 'the lodge was closed with feelings of true harmony and brotherhood'.

Eighteenth-century lodge Treasurers, being mindful of the charity and refreshment funds, were not slow to introduce fines for any misdemeanours. Fines of anything from two pence to a shilling—not inconsiderable sums when the average wage of a tradesman was about one pound—were levied for non-attendance at lodge; for arriving late; for falling asleep 'whilst the lodge was engaged in solemn business'—a not unusual occurrence when meeting and refreshment were combined; for being 'disguised in drink', as they termed over-indulgence; for 'escapes in modesty in language', as they termed swearing; for being improperly dressed; for refusing to take office in the lodge; and for smoking in lodge.[3]

After the ritual changes agreed by Grand Lodge in 1816 the conduct of lodge meetings was radically altered. The meeting became more formal and required a lodge room,[4] from which food, alcohol, and tobacco were banned. The social side of fellowship also became formalised into what is now called the Festive Board. Originally this was a simple supper during which loyal and Masonic toasts were honoured but it developed into what seem to us to have been gargantuan festivities. Surviving menus from the late Victorian and Edwardian periods list enormous banquets of eight to twelve courses, each offering as many as half-a-dozen choices and accompanied by its own wines, the whole being finished off with coffee, decanters of port and brandy, liqueurs, and fine Havana cigars. Dinner was often accompanied by music from a small military or string band and the formal toasting would be interspersed with vocal, instrumental, or comical entertainments. The oft-repeated comment by the late Arthur Askey and many of his contemporaries that they owed their early experience and popularity to working at 'weddings, barmitzvahs and masonics' has a great deal of truth to it. The First World War and its resultant social changes had their effect on the Festive Board, which gradually returned to what it was over a hundred and fifty years ago: a formal dinner of three or four courses, during which the members of the lodge and their guests can enjoy each other's company, followed by formal toasting.

Music played an important part in masonic proceedings. A wealth of Masonic songs have survived from the eighteenth century. Almost every Masonic publication of that time included a selection of Masonic songs, usually giving only the words to them. The earliest songs appeared in

Anderson's 1723 *Constitutions.*[5] From the mid-eighteenth century lodge minutes begin to record the purchasing or hiring of organs to assist in the music making, but many of the song books only include the melody with accompaniment for flute or recorder. Some lodges even initiated musicians as serving brethren[6]—i.e. they were made Masons but not members of the lodge—to provide music at their meetings. The Somerset House Lodge, now the Royal Somerset House and Inverness Lodge No. 4, had a strong musical tradition in the late eighteenth century and their music collection included concertos for harpsichord and string-players, Masonic songs, and collections of popular songs of the day.[7]

The premier Grand Lodge had purchased an organ shortly after its Hall was completed, but it was not until after the Union that a Grand Organist was appointed to provide music at Grand Lodge meetings. The first Grand Organist was Samuel Wesley and amongst his successors were many noted organists and composers of the day, including Sir Michael Costa, Sir Arthur Sullivan, Lionel Monckton, Sir Landon Ronald, Sidney Scott, and Henry Goss Custard. Whilst the Masonic press reports that they delighted the assembled brethren with their performance on the organ none of the Grand Organists appears to have composed any special music for Masonic occasions, unlike their more renowned brethren Mozart and Sibelius. Today the organist at Masonic meetings, at whatever level, simply provides accompaniment for the Opening and Closing Odes and suitable background music at appropriate points during the ceremonies.

In 1916 the Board of General Purposes had considered the questions of the use of instrumental and vocal music in lodges as a result of complaints that items were being used which could give offence because they were easily identifiable with a particular religion. As a result Grand Lodge agreed a ruling barring the use of such instrumental or vocal music. The matter came under consideration again in 1963 when Grand Lodge was considering the whole question of the relationship between Freemasonry and Religion. On 13 March 1963 the following policy statement was adopted as a Grand Lodge regulation to be obeyed by every lodge: 'instrumental or vocal music is not per se objectionable during Masonic meetings . . . but care must be taken that vocal music is such that it is not identified exclusively with a particular form of divine worship and that it does not offend the susceptibilities of a particular creed since Masonry is open to the adherents of every faith which requires belief in a Supreme Being, and that all other [musical] items should be scrutinised with the same care as any spoken additions. . . .'

The 'ladies' have had their part to play in the social side of Freemasonry. They were invited to take part in the dedication of the New Freemasons' Hall in 1776, being present at the beginning of the meeting for the formal handing over of the building by the Architects and Hall Committee; they also took tea and cakes and listened to a boys' choir whilst the Masonic ceremonial took place, returning to hear the speeches and a concert. Throughout the eighteenth century an Anniversary Ball was held to commemorate the dedication and concerts, poetry readings, theatrical performances, and soirees were regularly held in the Hall.[8] As we have already seen, throughout the nineteenth century ladies attended the Grand Festival and they were, and still are, guests at the Anniversary Festivals of the three great Masonic Charities.

At lodge level we find evidence from various parts of the country in the 1790s of ladies being invited to dine with the lodge once a year. In the Provinces in the nineteenth century a lodge or group of lodges in a particular area would join together to hold an annual ball at which, by dispensation, regalia would be worn. By the 1870s Masonic balls had become very popular and music still exists for 'Masonic' waltzes, gallops and the Lancers. By the end of the nineteenth century ladies' dinners and Masonic balls had begun to merge into what are now known as Ladies' Festivals. Many lodges now hold an annual dinner dance for their ladies, their families, and non-Masonic friends. In many small provincial Masonic Halls the ladies are involved in the life of the lodge by planning and carrying out the catering for lodge meetings, something which might not perhaps please the feminists but is done voluntarily by those concerned, who enjoy joining in with the fellowship of their menfolk.

Throughout the eighteenth and nineteenth centuries there was a long tradition of Grand Lodge and individual lodges giving theatrical performances, both in London and the Provinces. The brethren would arrange to fill the theatre for a particular performance and would attend in their regalia.[9] The performance would usually begin and end with specially written prologues and epilogues which were often afterwards printed for sale, the proceeds being added to the theatre receipts to swell the charity funds.[10] The performance would either be for the general charity fund or a benefit for a specific person or cause. Many playbills survive for Masonic 'bespeaks', usually decorated with Masonic symbols, and show a wide variety of performances from Grand Opera to potted Shakespeare, melodrama and farces, excerpts from well-known plays of the day, and what we would call variety programmes and circus acts.

Although the public procession held as part of the Grand Feast had been stopped in 1747, such processions were still permitted though they could only be held by special dispensation. Often they were for purely Masonic purposes. Provincial newspapers in the eighteenth and nineteenth centuries regularly carried reports of public processions by local lodges, often going from the lodge room to attend divine service. More impressive were the public processions, again usually to church, held during a Provincial Grand Lodge meeting. In addition to the Provincial Grand Officers and representatives of the lodges in the Province, all in their regalia and with their banners, the procession would include the town band and that of the local militia, the town council in their civic robes, and the local clergy in their vestments. As well as their own processions lodges would also take part, in regalia, in processions as part of local or national celebrations.

One public custom, often including a public procession, which has now ceased is the laying of the foundation stone of civic or religious buildings, bridges and monuments. This was regularly done with Masonic ceremonial up to the 1930s, since when it has died out of use except in the case of new Masonic buildings. The inhabitants of Holborn and Covent Garden turned out in force in 1808 to see the then prince of Wales (later King George IV) lead a Masonic procession from Freemasons' Hall to Bow Street, where in the presence of over a thousand spectators he laid the foundation stone of the Covent Garden Theatre (a predecessor of the present Royal Opera House). His brother, the Duke of Sussex, probably set some sort of record for laying foundation stones, usually in his capacity as Grand Master, of hospitals, public buildings and bridges as far north as Newcastle-upon-Tyne and as far west as Bristol. His record must have been almost matched by that of his great-nephew the Prince of Wales (later King Edward VII), who laid foundation stones with Masonic ceremonial not only at home but on his travels abroad, including Truro Cathedral and many churches.

What is believed to have been the largest ever Masonic gathering for a purely social reason was held on 8 August 1925 at Olympia in London. It was a Festival as part of the fund raising to provide money for the building of the present Freemasons' Hall. Over seven thousand brethren, presided over by the Grand Master, The Duke of Connaught, accompanied by the Prince of Wales (later King Edward VIII and Duke of Windsor), the Duke of York (later King George VI) and Prince Arthur of Connaught, sat down to a lunch at five miles of tables served by thirteen hundred waitresses. Over lunch they consumed six hundred pairs of best end of lamb, three thousand pounds of salmon, fifteen hundred chickens, and two hundred and fifty gallons of ice-cream. During the course of the lunch it was announced that £826,014. 11s. 6d. had been promised to the fund.

1 The Senior Grand Warden, c.1730. The portrait is alleged to be that of Sir James Thornhill (1675–1734), Senior Grand Warden 1728, by his son-in-law William Hogarth (1697–1764), Grand Steward 1735. Both ascriptions are doubtful. (Grand Lodge collection)

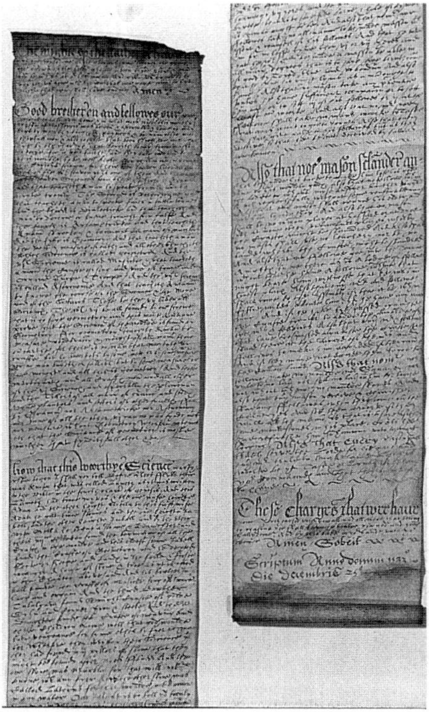

2

3

2 *Grand Lodge MS No. 1 of the Old Charges, 25 December 1583: a parchment roll 5 inches wide and 9 feet long. (Grand Lodge collection)*

3 *Engraved* List of Lodges *(1723), the first issue showing the inn signs and dates of meetings of London lodges.*

4 *Frontispiece to Anderson's* Constitutions *of 1723 showing John, 2nd Duke of Montagu passing the Constitutions to his successor Philip, Duke of Wharton.*

5

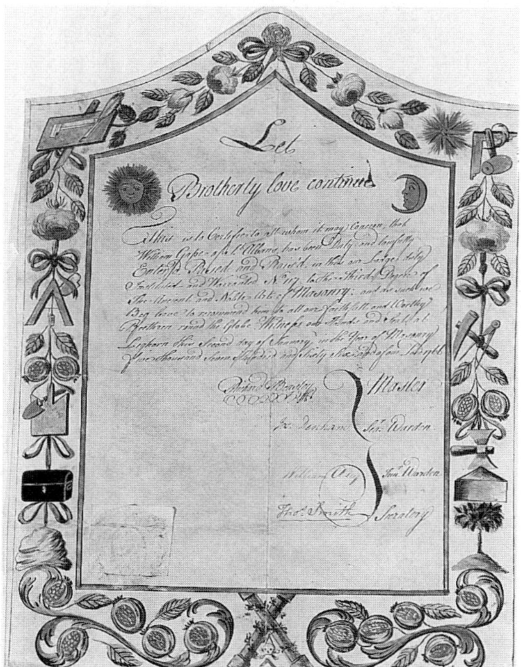

6

5 *Dermott's* Ahiman Rezon *(1764), the* Constitutions *of the Antients Grand Lodge. The frontispiece shows the Arms of the Antients Grand Lodge and those of the London Company of Masons.*

6 *Private Lodge certificate issued to William Gape by an English Lodge at Leghorn, Italy, in 1766. (Grand Lodge collection)*

7

8

7 London delftware bowl, c.1700. The transfer print was much used on eighteenth-century English pottery and engraved lodge summonses and certificates. (Grand Lodge collection)

8 Blank engraved summons for a Royal Arch Chapter, eighteenth century. Note the headdresses of the Principals. (Grand Lodge collection)

9 A selection of early Royal Arch jewels. Centre top is the earliest known, given to Dr James Rouby in 1766. (Grand Lodge collection)

10

11

10 HRH Henry Frederick, Duke of Cumberland, Grand Master 1782–90, in his robes as Grand Patron of the Royal Arch. Portrait by J. Hoppner (1758–1810) (Grand Lodge collection)

11 HRH Augustus Frederick, Duke of Sussex, Grand Master 1813–43. Statue by E. H. Baily, 1846. (Grand Lodge collection)

12 HRH Albert Edward, Prince of Wales (later King Edward VII), Grand Master 1874–1901. Portrait by L. Desanges. (Grand Lodge collection)

13

14

13 *The Freemasons' Hall and Tavern, engraving of 1784. The tavern frontage was extensively altered in 1788–90. (Grand Lodge collection)*

14 *The second Freemasons' Hall, 1869, and the adjoining Tavern. The architect was Frederick Pepys Cockerell (1833–78).*

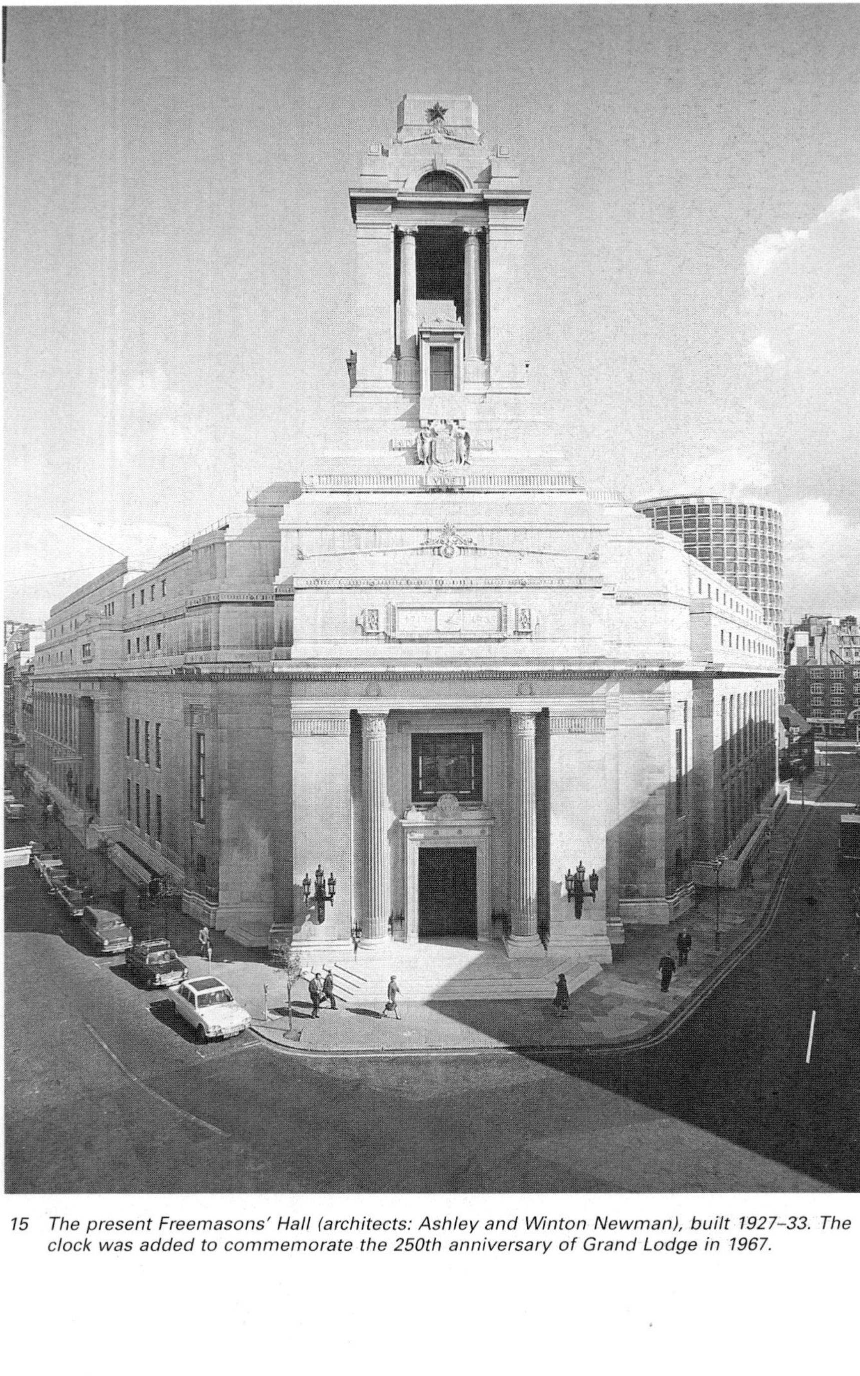

15 The present Freemasons' Hall (architects: Ashley and Winton Newman), built 1927–33. The clock was added to commemorate the 250th anniversary of Grand Lodge in 1967.

16 HM King George V and HM Queen Mary with HRH the Duke of Connaught (Grand Master 1901–38) leaving Freemasons' Hall after an official visit on 13 May 1934.

17 *Illustration, showing 'some prominent members of the Craft', from the* Pictorial World, *8 May 1875.*

18 *Engraving published with* Hiram, *one of the 1760s exposures of Freemasonry. Note the details of the jewels worn by the officers.*

19 *HRH Arthur, Duke of Connaught and Strathearn, Grand Master 1901–38, wearing full dress regalia as Grand Master and medals commemorating Peace (left) and the establishment of the fund to build the present Freemasons' Hall (right)*

20 *HM Queen Elizabeth The Queen Mother with Lord Scarbrough, Grand Master 1952–67, leaving Freemasons' Hall after a private visit, 1954.*

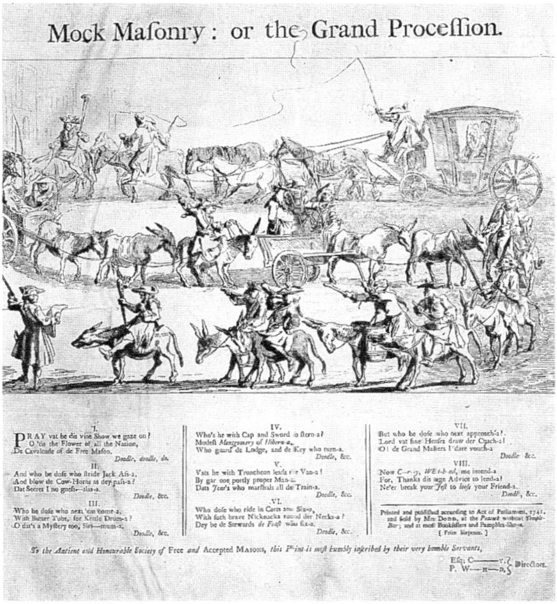

21

22

21 *One of the many broadsides and newspaper burlesques which led to the cessation of the annual Grand Feast procession in 1747.*

22 *The Rt. Hon. Lord Ampthill, Pro Grand Master 1908–35, and other Grand Officers processing to lay the foundation stone of the Shakespeare Memorial Theatre, Stratford-upon-Avon, 2 July 1929.*

23 *The Girls' School at Wandsworth Common; the Boys' School at Wood Green; and the Asylum for Aged and Decayed Freemasons at Croydon. Newspaper engraving, 1875. (Grand Lodge collection)*

6

ENGLISH FREEMASONRY ABROAD
Europe and North America

WITHIN a short time of its formation in 1717 the Grand Lodge began to export the Craft abroad. It is rumoured that lodges were constituted in Spain, France, Holland, and Belgium in the early 1720s but there is no supporting evidence. The first two foreign lodges for which there is evidence were constituted in Gibraltar and Fort William, Calcutta, in 1728/9. The Craft was spread abroad in three ways: by the issue of 'deputations to constitute lodges' as a result of the receipt of petitions from local Masons; by the appointment of Provincial Grand Masters for territories abroad with authority to constitute new lodges, which were then to be registered with the Grand Lodge; and by the constituting of travelling lodges in regiments of the Army, permitting them to meet wherever the regiment was stationed. The Antients Grand Lodge and the Grand Lodge of Ireland issued many such travelling warrants and although technically membership of the lodges was restricted to members of the regiment, many of these travelling lodges initiated civilian candidates when stationed abroad. When the regiment moved on to a new posting the civilians left behind would in turn petition one of the home Grand Lodges to be constituted as a stationary lodge.[1]

The development of English, and Irish and Scottish, Freemasonry abroad closely follows the development of Britain as an imperial power. When new areas of the world were discovered or opened up after 1730 the arrival of settlers, merchants, and the military usually brought with it the arrival of the Craft. In the same way, imperial decline was usually followed by lodges in the former colonies seeking Masonic independence from the home Grand Lodges and the setting up of their own sovereign and independent Grand Lodges.

In Europe English Craft Masonry was introduced into Belgium, Denmark, France, Germany, Gibraltar, Holland, Italy, Malta, Minorca, Russia, Switzerland and Turkey. Many of the lodges were short lived or assumed independence and many of the provincial Grand Masters appointed had no success in starting lodges. There were flourishing Provincial Grand Lodges in Hamburg 1737–1811; Frankfurt 1767–1823; Hanover 1746–1828; Holland 1756–70, when the premier Grand Lodge signed a treaty recognising the Grand East of the Netherlands and its territorial sovereignty over the Netherlands; Russia, where the first Provincial Grand Master was appointed in 1731, though the Provincial Grand Lodge did not come into existence until 1772 and lasted only until 1794, when Freemasonry was officially banned; and Minorca from 1772–94, when the Balearics were ceded to Spain. There are still flourishing District Grand Lodges in Gibraltar and Cyprus, but the former District Grand Lodge of Malta, started in 1813, has recently been reduced to the status of a Grand Inspectorate, most of its lodges having been transferred to England or having gone out of existence since the British withdrawal from the island.

English Freemasonry was introduced into North America by the appointment of Daniel Cox as Provincial Grand Master for New York, New Jersey and Pennsylvania in 1730, followed by the appointment of Henry Price as Provincial Grand Master for New England in 1733. In all, the premier Grand Lodge appointed 23 Provincial Grand Masters for various parts of what is now the United States of America between 1730 and the American War of Independence. The Antients Grand Lodge was no less active in warranting Provincial Grand Lodges for various parts of the Eastern seaboard. They were given the right to elect their own Provincial Grand Masters and because of the difficulties of communications and travel acted almost as independent Grand Lodges. The Antients Provincial Grand Lodge for Pennsylvania constituted over 50 lodges in North America and the Caribbean, most of which were not registered with the Grand Lodge. With the growing movement towards independence ties with the English Grand Lodges became even looser, and on the achievement of independence most of the Provincial Grand Lodges assumed their own independence and set the American pattern of each State of the Union having its own Grand Lodge.

INDIA AND ASIA

The issue of the deputation to constitute a lodge in Calcutta in 1728/9 was quickly followed by the appointment of Capt. Ralph Farr Winter as Provincial Grand Master for the East Indies in 1729. These two events began the great development of English Freemasonry in the Indian sub-continent. As more of the sub-continent came under British control so English Freemasonry expanded, but its course was not easy. Outside the main centres of government, military and trading stations tended to be temporary in character and lodges would be constituted, flourish for a few years then suddenly disappear when the English personnel were removed to a new station. Leadership also tended to be temporary, new Provincial Grand Masters being removed to other parts before they had an opportunity of establishing themselves. Provincial Grand Lodges were established in Bengal in 1729, Bombay in 1764, Madras in 1767, the Punjab in 1868, Northern India in 1951 and Ceylon (Sri Lanka) in 1810.

It was in India that the truly universal nature of the Craft was to be shown. The first native initiated, of which records have survived, was Omdat-ul-Omrah, Nabob of the Carnatic, in 1775. When the news reached the premier Grand Lodge in England they immediately resolved to honour him with 'a Masonic apron elegantly decorated, and a *Book of Constitutions* bound in a most superb manner' at a cost of £37.17s.6d. The initiations of Indians did not, however, meet with universal support and the lodges in India were to be bedevilled with problems over the subject for many years, some resolving—in a most un-Masonic manner—not to receive Indians as members. The matter was put to the Duke of Sussex, as Grand Master, in 1840 by the Provincial Grand Master for Bengal, James Grant. He received a very forthright reply from the Duke:

> The initiation of Hindus . . . is a question which has occupied H.R.H.'s attention for many years, and it has formed a part of his Masonic creed that provided a man believes in the existence of the Great Architect of the Universe and in futurity, and extends that belief likewise to a state of rewards and punishments hereafter, such a person is fully competent to be received as a Brother. Previously, however, to swearing any man to secrecy it is necessary to ascertain what religion

he professes in order to obligate him in the most formal and solemn manner possible; when once admitted into the Fraternity all questions of religion cease.

The issue continued to rumble on for two reasons. There were no problems over the initiations of Muslims, Parsees, or Sikhs as all those religions are monotheistic. Hindus were another matter. It appeared to the nineteenth-century English Masons in India that the Hindus had a multiplicity of gods and could not therefore satisfy the basic qualification for initiation: belief in a Supreme Being. As one writer has commented, 'if brethren had thought to inquire instead of ignorantly condemning, they would have found that to the Hindu his many gods are personifications of different aspects of the One God . . .' As K. M. Sem wrote: 'The Namless and Formless is called by different names, and different forms are attributed to him, but it is not forgotten that He is One God.' The second problem was caused by the Indians themselves and revolved around the caste system and the tensions between the various Indian religions. Resolution of these issues came in the second half of the nineteenth century and many Indians, regardless of caste or religion, flocked to join the Craft. They were fully integrated within the lodges, the books which they regarded as holy being placed alongside the Bible on the Master's pedestal.

With the arrival of independence in 1947 a movement was begun for the erection of a Grand Lodge of India, surprisingly, this did not meet with universal support and it was not until 1961 that the Grand Lodge was formed and even then not all the lodges under the home Grand Lodge elected to join it. There are still English District Grand Lodges in Bengal, Bombay, Madras, Northern India, and the island of Sri Lanka. A number of lodges in Pakistan—formerly the Punjab—also elected to stay under the Grand Lodge of England after the partition of the sub-continent and formed a flourishing District Grand Lodge until Freemasonry was banned by the State in 1973.

Surprisingly, the first lodge formed in China was the Amity Lodge, constituted at Canton in 1767. It was short lived, however, and English Freemasonry did not become properly established until 1844 and the appointment of a Provincial Grand Master, Samuel Rawson, in 1847. English Freemasonry in the trading stations on the China Coast flourished to such an extent that the district Grand Lodge was divided in 1875 into two Districts, Northern China, and Hong Kong and South China. The

English and Scottish Grand Lodges had considerable success in establishing the Craft in Hong Kong but encountered the same problems as Indian lodges over the question of a transitory population. All Masonic activity in Hong Kong was brought to a halt by the Japanese invasion during the Second World War, although the brethren who were interned in the civilian prison camp managed to continue their meetings, at great personal risk, and even to plan for the revival of the District when it became obvious that hositilities would soon end. Once normality was restored they were soon faced with the problems of the mainland lodges, which having survived the war did not survive the Communist takeover. Many went out of existence but a number transferred to Hong Kong, where they still meet, except the Northern Lodge of China No. 570 which continued to meet in Shanghai without government interference until it was erased by Grand Lodge in 1960 because of a lack of candidates. A similar situation had occurred in Japan, where a District Grand Lodge had been established in 1873 but became extinct when the Japanese entered the Second World War. Attempts to revive it after 1945 were unsuccessful and only one lodge, at Kobe, survives and now comes under the present Grand Lodge for Hong Kong and the Far East.

In the Eastern Archipelago a Provincial Grand Master for Sumatra was appointed in 1796 and had two lodges under his charge. With the exploration of Malaysia and the colonisation of Singapore sufficient lodges came into existence for a District Grand Lodge of the Eastern Archipelago to be formed by the appointment of a District Grand Master in 1858. The success of the District was brought to a halt by the events of the Pacific War but Freemasonry survived and quickly re-established itself and now has a flourishing, if widely spread, District of almost thirty lodges. A similar circumstance occurred in Burma, where a District Grand Master was first appointed in 1868. Having re-established itself after the Second World War the District faced possible extinction when a strict Muslim government came to power; but when the nature of Freemasonry was explained to the government the district was allowed to continue—and still continues—without interference. The lodges in Iraq and the Arabian Gulf were not so fortunate. English Freemasonry had been taken there during the First World War, but when the British mandate ceased and the various states became independent the strict Muslim governments placed a total ban on Freemasonry.

AUSTRALIA AND NEW ZEALAND

The earliest record of a Masonic meeting in Australia was an irregular one in Sydney in 1803. Regular Freemasonry was introduced into New South Wales by two Irish military lodges working between 1813 and 1820. The first English lodge came in 1828, followed by the appointment of a Provincial Grand Master in 1839. By the time of the formation of the United Grand Lodge of New South Wales in 1888 some ninety-two English lodges had been warranted in New South Wales. English Freemasonry came to South Australia in 1838 by a rather strange route. The South Australian Lodge of Friendship had been constituted in London in 1834 by Freemasons in London who were planning to go to South Australia and wished to continue their Freemasonry when they arrived. The lodge finally arrived in 1838. A Provincial Grand Master was appointed in 1847 and by the time of the formation of the Grand Lodge of South Australia in 1884 twenty-two English lodges had been created in the Province. The first English lodge in Victoria was warranted in 1841 and was followed by the appointment of a Provincial Grand Master in 1853. Victoria proved fertile soil for English Freemasonry, 114 English lodges being warranted to meet there by the time the Grand Lodge of Victoria was formed in 1889. One lodge, Combermere No. 752, chose not to join the new Grand Lodge and still works under the United Grand Lodge of England. Although the first English lodge in Western Australia was warranted in 1842, progress was slow and it was not until 1887 that a District Grand Master was appointed. When the Grand Lodge of Western Australia was formed in 1900 there were only thirteen English lodges in the state and one of them, Plantagenet No. 1454, chose to remain under the United Grand Lodge of England. It was the Irish, again, who introduced Freemasonry into Tasmania in 1827, but one of the resulting lodges changed its allegiance to England in 1844, leading to the formation of three further English lodges and the appointment of a Provisional Grand Master in 1856. A further twelve lodges were warranted by England before the formation of the Grand Lodge of Tasmania in 1890. Queensland became a separate state in 1859, the same year as the first English lodge was warranted to meet in Brisbane. A District Grand Master was appointed in 1862 and the District was to continue in existence until 1959. An attempt was made to form a Grand Lodge of Queensland in 1904, but failing to receive the support of the majority of the English, Irish, and Scottish lodges in the

State it was not officially recognised. The situation was remedied in 1921 when a further vote was held and the majority of the lodges agreed to join with the Grand Lodge to form the United Grand Lodge of Queensland. Six English lodges chose to remain English, hence the continuance of the English District Grand Lodge for so long a period after the formation of the Grand Lodge. Two of those lodges, Port Curtis No. 2255 and Geraldtown No. 3544, still remain on the English Register.

In New Zealand it is believed that the first Masonic meeting held in the South Island was organised by the crews of some whalers in 1837. English Freemasonry came to the South Island with the warranting of a lodge at Dunedin in 1860. In the North Island the first Masonic activity was the attendance of a number of brethren in their regalia at the laying of the foundation stone of St. Paul's Church, Auckland in 1841. This was followed by the warranting of an English and an Irish lodge in 1842. English Provincial (later District) Grand Lodges were established in Auckland in 1877; Canterbury in 1858; Otago and Southland in 1864; Wellington in 1875; Westland and Nelson in 1870. A Grand Lodge of New Zealand was formed in 1890 but had the support of only 40 per cent of the English, Irish, and Scottish lodges. Harmony was restored in 1897 when the Grand Lodge was recognised by England, followed by Ireland in 1898 and Scotland in 1899. The Grand Lodge of New Zealand flourished but the lodge which had chosen not to join it in 1890 continued under the home Grand Lodges. The five English Districts were amalgamated into two, one each for the North and South Islands, in 1973, and maintain a happy coexistence with the Grand Lodge of New Zealand.

SOUTH AMERICA, THE CARIBBEAN AND AFRICA

In 1730 Randolph Took was appointed Provincial Grand Master for South America but there is no evidence that he ever acted upon his patent. It was not until 1813 that an English lodge was established in British Guiana (now Guyana). A District Grand Lodge was set up in 1899 and now has twelve lodges. There were four English lodges in Haiti between 1809 and 1824 and a Provincial Grand Master was appointed in 1817. He was followed by the appointment of a Provincial Grand Master for Colombia in 1824, although there were no English lodges in that country, the only English lodge to meet there existing only from 1848 to 1857. English Freemasonry was introduced into Argentina in 1853 and a District Grand

Lodge of Argentina was set up in 1861. Its name was changed to South America Southern Division and it now has sixteen lodges in Argentina and one each in Uruguay and Chile. Between 1890 and 1912 a number of English-speaking lodges were set up in Brazil by its Grand Orient. To give them a collective identity they were placed under their own Grand Council, subordinate to the Grand Orient, in 1912. In 1935 they separated themselves, amicably, from the Grand Orient, were taken on to the English Register, and were formed into the District Grand Lodge of South America Northern Division, which still exists with eleven lodges in Brazil.

English Freemasonry was introduced into the West Indies and Caribbean by the appointment of a Provincial Grand Master for Antigua in 1738 and Barbados in 1740 and the setting up of a lodge in Antigua in 1738 and Jamaica in 1739. Numerous appointments of Provincial Grand Masters were made for various islands in the Leeward group, but they did little to promote the Craft, which had its greatest success in Jamaica. There are now District Grand Lodges for Bahamas and Turks (eight lodges); Barbados and the Eastern Caribbean (twelve lodges in Barbados, St. Vincent, St. Lucia, Montserrat, Grenada, and Antigua); Jamaica (twenty lodges); Trinidad (seven lodges); a Grand Inspectorate for Bermuda (four lodges); two lodges in the Virgin Islands, and one in Dominica.

Although the interior of the continent was largely unexplored three Provincial Grand Masters were appointed for Gambia, the Cape Coast, and 'the Coast of Africa and the British Islands in America' in 1736–7. None of those areas had any lodges, nor were any to appear on the African continent before 1800. A Provincial Grand Master for South Africa was appointed in 1801 and by 1876 the District—as it had then become—was so widespread that it was divided into Central, Eastern and Southern Divisions. There had been a flourishing Province under the Grand East of the Netherlands, the members of which in 1961 formed the Grand Lodge of Southern Africa. The English, Irish, and Scottish lodges in the area have been given the opportunity of joining with it to form a United Grand Lodge but have always declined, preferring to remain under the home Grand Lodges.

A short-lived Provincial Grand Lodge for Mauritius was formed in 1811 but had ceased to function by 1830 (its brass desk seal is now in the Museum of the United Grand Lodge of England). St. Helena received Provincial Grand Masters in 1801 and 1803 but the single lodge on the island did not survive the second appointment. The present St. Helena

Lodge No. 488 was warranted in 1843. Seven English lodges were formed in Egypt between 1862–7 and a District Grand Lodge of Egypt and the Sudan was formed in 1867 but did not survive the Suez affair and its aftermath in the 1950s. The Sudanese part survived into the 1960s, when Freemasonry was banned.

The development of English Freemasonry in Africa parallels the exploration and settlement of the continent. Today in addition to the three Districts in South Africa there are others for: East Africa, formed in 1926, with 32 lodges in Kenya, Tanzania, and the Seychelles; Ghana, formed in 1930, with 45 lodges, the first having been formed on the Gold Coast in 1810; Natal, formed in 1882, with 46 lodges; Nigeria, formed in 1913, with 27 lodges, one dating back to 1867; the Orange Free State formed in 1932, with 13 lodges, one dating back to 1864; Sierra Leone and The Gambia, formed in 1949, with 10 lodges, the oldest warranted in 1882; South West Africa (1958) with six lodges, the oldest warranted in 1925; the Transvaal (1895) with 120 lodges, the oldest warranted in 1878; Zambia, formed in 1967, but formerly under Rhodesia, with 14 lodges; and Zimbabwe (formerly Rhodesia), formed in 1929, with 31 lodges, the oldest warranted in 1893.

CANADA

The history of English Freemasonry in Canada is complex, involving intense rivalry between lodges and Provinces under the premier and Antients Grand Lodges and problems of communications both within Canada and between the Provinces and the Grand Lodges in London. The first Provincial Grand Master was appointed for Cape Breton and Louisburg in 1746. Nova Scotia received both a Provincial Grand Master under the premier Grand lodge and a warranted Provincial Grand Lodge under the Antients in 1757. Much of the early spread of the Craft was achieved by military lodges and civilian lodges being constituted by the Canadian Provincial Grand Masters and those in America before independence. The Canadian Provincial Grand Lodges had periods of great activity and others when they almost disappeared. With a certain amount of right on their side they complained bitterly of their neglect by the English Grand Lodges. In Ontario matters came to a head in 1855 when, angered by their problems with England, they declared themselves an independent Grand Lodge. The repercussions in England included a full investigation by the Grand Lodge, resulting in the formation of a Colonial Board to look after the overseas lodges and the forced retirement of the octogenarian Grand Secretary. The action of the Ontario lodges was soon followed by the other Provinces, resulting in the formation of Grand Lodges in New Brunswick in 1867; Nova Scotia in 1869; Quebec in 1869; British Columbia in 1871, and Prince Edward Island in 1875. The flourishing District Grand Lodge of Newfoundland refused to follow suit and remains under the United Grand Lodge of England to this day, with 27 lodges. Similarly the Royal Standard Lodge No. 398, Halifax, and the St. Pauls Lodge No. 374 and St. George's Lodge No. 440 in Montreal chose to remain English.

The events surrounding the secession of the Ontario Lodges led the United Grand Lodge of England to consider the best method of dealing with moves towards independence. The system was gradually evolved whereby the home Grand Lodges would poll their lodges in any area expressing a wish for independence. If a majority voted in favour the inevitable was faced and the new Grand Lodge was quickly accorded recognition as a regular Grand Lodge. The home Grand Lodges would recognise the new Grand Lodge's territorial rights by refusing to warrant any new lodges within its boundaries. In return the new Grand Lodge agreed to allow any of the English, Irish or Scottish lodges which did not wish to join with them to continue meeting under the home Grand Lodges without any interference. If only a minority voted for independence the home Grand Lodges would recommend dropping the plan until it had majority support. If the minority then seceded and formed a Grand Lodge, the home Grand Lodges would not accord it recognition or allow its members in the area to have Masonic intercourse with the seceders. This situation arose in both New South Wales and Queensland, where a minority seceded and formed unrecognised Grand Lodges which existed alone until the majority in the two States voted for independence and formed United Grand Lodges.

With the appearance of new Grand Lodges throughout the world a new problem arose: that of a regular and irregular Freemasonry. The Grand Lodge of England had simply accepted the appearance of the Irish and Scottish Grand Lodges without question and a happy and cooperative relationship has always existed between the three. England's first problem arose in 1756, when the lodges in the Netherlands declared themselves an independent Grand Lodge. Relations were strained between the two until 1770, when a Treaty was signed in which England acknowledged the sovereignty of the Grand East of the Netherlands and its territorial rights within its national boundaries. A similar situation arose in 1771 with the Grand Lodge in Berlin. European Freemasonry had developed along different lines from that in Great Britain, particularly in its adoption of additional degrees, and certain elements within European Freemasonry were using it for political and anti-clerical ends. These problems were to become worse in the nineteenth century and were complicated in the 1870s by the Grand Orient of France, which had been recognised for over a hundred years, dropping all reference to a Supreme Being in its rituals and removing the Volume of the Sacred Law from its lodges. They were immediately informed by England that unless these changes were reversed recognition would be withdrawn and English Masons would be banned from attending meetings of lodges under the Grand Orient or of lodges at which members of that obedience were present. The Grand Orient chose to go its own way and has ever since been regarded as irregular by all regular Grand Lodges.

England had a three-tier system in the nineteenth century in its relations with other Grand Lodges. Full recognition with an exchange of official representatives; fraternal correspondence where there was some doubt as to the origins or regularity of a Grand Lodge, meaning essentially that the respective Grand Secretaries exchanged correspondence without full recognition being given; and non-recognition, which meant that no English Freemason could have a Masonic contact with members of an unrecognised Grand Lodge. This made life complicated for an English Mason who travelled abroad and wished to attend meetings. After the end of the First World War matters had become so complex, with new Grand Lodges springing up all over the world, that the three British Grand Lodges held a conference and agreed basic principles upon which they would recognise new Grand Lodges. These were adopted by the United Grand Lodge in 1929 and have continued to be the guidelines for deciding questions of recognition ever since.

They read as follows:

BASIC PRINCIPLES FOR GRAND LODGE RECOGNITION

Accepted by Grand Lodge, September 4th, 1929. The M. W. The Grand Master having expressed a desire that that Board would draw up a statement of the Basic Principles on which this Grand Lodge would be invited to recognise any Grand Lodge applying for recognition by the English Jurisdiction, the Board of General

Purposes has gladly complied. The result, as follows, has been approved by the Grand Master, and it will form the basis of a questionnaire to be forwarded in future to each Jurisdiction requesting English recognition. The Board desires that not only such bodies bvt the Brethren generally throughout the Grand Master's Juridiction shall be fully informed as to those Basic Principles of Freemasonry for which the Grand Lodge of England has stood throughout its history.

1. Regularity of origin; i.e., each Grand Lodge shall have been established lawfully by a duly recognised Grand Lodge or by three or more regularly constituted Lodges.

2. That a belief in the G.A.O.T.U. and His revealed will shall be an essential qualification for membership.

3. That all Initiates shall take their Obligation on or in full view of the open Volume of the Sacred Law, by which is meant the revelation from above which is binding on the conscience of the particular individual who is being initiated.

4. That the membership of the Grand Lodge and individual Lodges shall be composed exclusively of men; and that each Grand Lodge shall have no Masonic intercourse of any kind with mixed Lodges or bodies which admit women to membership.

5. That the Grand Lodge shall have sovereign jurisdiction over the Lodge under its control; i.e., that it shall be a responsible, independent, self-governing organisation, with sole and undisputed authority over the Craft or Symbolic Degrees (Entered Apprentice, Fellow Craft, and Master Mason) within its Jurisdiction; and shall not in any way be subject to or divide such authority with a Supreme Council or other Power claiming any control or supervision over those degrees.

6. That the three Great Lights of Freemasonry (namely, the Volume of the Sacred Law, the Square and the Compasses) shall always be exhibited when the Grand Lodge or its subordinate Lodges are at work, the chief of these being the Volume of the Sacred Law.

7. That the discussion of religion and politics within the Lodge shall be strictly prohibited.

8. That the principles of the Antient Landmarks, customs, and usages of the Craft shall be strictly observed.

7

THE ENGLISH ROYAL ARCH

MEETINGS of the Royal Arch are called Chapters and the ultimate authority is a Grand Chapter. The members address each other not as Brother but as Companion. In English Royal Arch Masonry, and in those other Grand Chapters which have adopted the English Ritual, the Chapter is presided over by three Principals who rule co-equally. They represent Zerubabel, Prince of Jerusalem, Haggai the Prophet, and Joshua the High Priest. They are assisted by two Scribes, Ezra (who acts as Secretary of the Chapter) and Nehemiah; a Principal and two Assistant Sojourners; a Treasurer; and a Janitor who stands guard outside the door of the Chapter. The drama of the ritual is set in Jerusalem immediately after the return from the Babylonian Captivity when Zerubabel is preparing to rebuild the City and Temple. The Chapter represents the Grand Sanhedrim, whose deliberations are interrupted by the arrival of three Sojourners from Babylon who ask to be permitted to assist in the rebuilding work They are set to clear the ground of Solomon's former Temple to receive the foundations of the new Temple. In doing so they discover a hidden vault which they break open and enter. Inside the Principal Sojourner discovers a scroll—the lost Volume of the Sacred Law—and a pedestal on which are engraven the initials of the three Grand Masters who built the original Temple. They report their discoveries to the Sanhedrim and are rewarded by being constituted members of the Chapter. As in the Craft, the Royal Arch ritual is an allegory. The three Principals and two Scribes are biblical characters but historically could not have been in Jerusalem at the same time. In Ireland and many of the Grand Chapters in the United States of America the legend is not that used in England and Scotland but is based upon the repair of Solomon's Temple under Josiah. The intent of the ritual is the same however: to lead the Companion, without transgressing the bounds of religion, to a contemplation of the nature of and his relationship with his God, whatever his religion may be.

The Royal Arch in England is defined by Article 2 of the Articles of Union of 1813 as being part of 'pure ancient Masonry'. In the exaltation ceremony the candidate is informed that he must not regard himself as having taken a fourth degree, the Royal Arch being described as the Master Mason's degree completed. As a result the Craft and Royal Arch in England are closely linked constitutionally, administratively and thematically. This very close relationship is peculiar to England for complex historical reasons. In all other constitutions the Craft and Royal Arch are totally separate, the Royal Arch being governed by autonomous and sovereign Grand Chapters. To understand how this close relationship came about we need to examine the origins and development of the Royal Arch in the eighteenth century.

The origins of the Royal Arch are as uncertain as those of the Craft. It is now generally accepted that the Royal Arch originated in the 1730s, but whether in England, Ireland or, possibly, France is still highly arguable. There have been various theories published as to the origins of the Royal Arch.[1] It has been suggested that it evolved either from material discarded when the third degree was settled in the 1720s or that this degree was deliberately mutilated to provide for a new degree. As we have little evidence concerning the development of the third degree, and none at all for its mutilation or splitting into two, those theories have been discounted. Vibert[2] suggested that the Royal Arch originally formed part of the ceremony of the Installation of the Master of a Craft Lodge, but there is no evidence for this ceremony, at the time at which the Royal Arch was developing, being anything other than a ceremonial placing of the Master in the chair without any esoteric content, and Vibert's theory has generally been dismissed. Others have suggested that the Royal Arch was a natural extension of the third degree: a loss having been made in that degree, it was necessary to invent a further degree in which the loss could be repaired. Others would argue that at the time in which the Royal Arch was evolving, the 1730s, the loss was repaired in the third degree by the introduction of the substituted secrets.[3] Some, less charitably, have suggested that the Royal Arch was an inevitable result of human vanity. They argue that initially the third degree had been strictly controlled but was becoming more widely practised in the 1730s, resulting in the development of the Royal Arch as a 'special' and limited degree to replace the formerly exclusive Master Masons' degree.

The search for origins has not been helped by the marked lack of early evidence. The earliest undisputed printed reference is in Fifield Dassigny's *A serious and impartial enquiry into the cause of the present decay of Free-Masonry in the Kingdom of Ireland*, published in Dublin in 1744, in which the author relates a curious incident which had happened a number of years previously when

> a certain propagator of a false system some few years ago in this city [Dublin] who imposed upon several very worthy men under a pretence of being Master of the Royal Arch, which he asserted he had brought with him from the city of York; and that the beauties of the Craft did principally consist in the knowledge of this valuable piece of Masonry. However he carried on this scheme for several months and many of the learned and wise were his followers, till at length his fallacious art was discovered by a brother of probity and wisdom, who had some small space before attained that excellent part of Masonry in London and plainly proved that his doctrine was false.

Thus it would appear that the Royal Arch was known in at least London, York and Dublin by 1744.

Laurence Dermott stated that he had been exalted in his Dublin lodge in 1746, but it is not until 1753 that we have the first extant minutes of the conferring of the Royal Arch, occurring not in the British Isles but within a craft lodge in Fredericksburg, Virginia. The lodge minutes record that on 22 December 1753 three members of the lodge were 'Raised to the Degree of Royall [sic] Arch'. For many years it was believed that the earliest extant English record of an exaltation was that of a now defunct lodge at Bristol,[4] under the premier Grand Lodge, in which on 13 August 1758 two members of the lodge were 'raised to the Royal Arch degree'. A recently rediscovered letter in the Grand Lodge archives, however, now proves Thomas Dunckerley's claim that he was exalted within his mother lodge, the now defunct Lodge of Antiquity at Portsmouth, on 15 August 1754. The letter was written to the Grand Secretary on 14 March 1824 by Edward Sibley, then lodge Secretary, requesting permission for the lodge to revive its former practice of working the Royal Arch within the

Lodge. Sibley states that the original minute book of the lodge often includes the Proceedings of a Chapter, including one held on 16 August 1754 at which Dunckerley together with a John Shakespeare and a Caleb Whitehorn were exalted.

From the 1760s onwards there is ample evidence of the Royal Arch being worked in England within Craft lodges. The growing popularity of the degree did not please members of the premier Grand Lodge. Despite the fact that it was being worked within their lodges they refused to acknowledge it as part of their system. The Grand Secretary in 1759—Samuel Spencer—in writing to an Irish brother who was attempting to claim charity on the strength of his being both an Antient mason and a member of the Royal Arch stated quite bluntly 'We are neither Arch, Royal Arch not Antient so that you have no right to partake in our Charity.' Spencer, again, writing officially to a brother in Frankfurt in 1767, stated the premier Grand Lodge's attitude to be that 'the Royal Arch is a Society which we do not acknowledge and which we hold to be an invention to introduce innovation to seduce the brethren'. Quite how Spencer squared these official pronouncements with his own conscience is hard to imagine as he himself had become a Royal Arch Mason. As late as 1792 the premier Grand Lodge stated its attitude to be 'That this Grand Lodge do agree with its Committee that the Grand Lodge has nothing to do with the Proceedings of the Society of Royal Arch Masons.' As a result of these, and similar, pronouncements it has often been claimed that the premier Grand Lodge was antagonistic to the Royal Arch, but this is something of a misunderstanding. They were not willing to accept the Royal Arch as an integral part of Freemasonry or to permit it to be worked within their lodges, but they made no objection to their members joining it as a separately organised society.

Indeed, it was members of the premier Grand Lodge, led by their Grand Master Lord Blayney, who set up the first Excellent Grand and Royal Chapter of the Royal Arch of Jerusalem by virtue of a Charter of Compact dated 22 July 1766. Evidently the involvement of their Grand Master in the formation of a Masonic body which they did not officially recognise upset the premier Grand Lodge, for the Charter of Compact shows evidence of having been tampered with. The date was altered to 1767 and a 'P.' was inserted between 'Blayney' and 'Grand Master' implying that the event took place after Blayney had finished his term as Grand

Master.[5] As well as being the instrument by which the first Grand Chapter came into existence the Charter of Compact incorporated the first regulations for its govenrment and that of its subordinate chapters.

The new Grand Chapter was a completely autonomous body, having its own regulations and Grand Officers.[6] It issued charters to form subordinate chapters in England, Wales, Scotland, Europe and other parts of the world. In all some 185 chapters were chartered between the formation of the Grand Chapter and 1817. The only connection between the Grand Chapter and its chapters and the premier Grand Lodge and its lodges was one of common membership. In no way were either the Grand Chapter or its chapters attached to or subordinate to the premier Grand Lodge and its lodges. It must be admitted that the Grand Chapter's work as a regulatory body was not an unqualified success. After an initial burst of energy it had become almost moribund by the 1790s and had lost contact with many of its chapters. Fortunately there was a revival of interest in the late 1790s and by 1800 the Grand Chapter had reasserted its authority and re-established contact with many of its chapters. It began to attract many senior members of the premier Grand Lodge and in June 1803 the Earl of Moira, Acting Grand Master of the premier Grand Lodge under the Prince of Wales, was exalted in the Grand Chapter and became First Grand Principal the following year. He it was who in 1810 proposed that the Duke of Sussex be exalted in the Grand Chapter, and upon that being accomplished immediately resigned as First Grand Principal in favour of the Duke.

The exaltations of Moira and the Duke of Sussex within Grand Chapter were not unusual circumstances. Those who formed the Grand Chapter in 1766 are believed to have been meeting as an independent Chapter for at least a year before the signing of the Charter of Compact by which they assumed the status of a Grand Chapter. After that event the Grand Chapter acted as both a regulatory body and a private chapter, exalting new members and accepting other Companions as joining members. At first the two functions were kept separate and distinct, with the Grand Chapter business being carried out at specially convened meetings. The distinction soon became blurred and by the 1780s the private Chapter functions were being carried out within the Grand Chapter, which appears to have functioned as such as and when business arose requiring its attention. Indeed the Grand Principals were elected and installed in the same manner as those of subordinate chapters, on an annual basis, until the election of Lord Rancliffe as First Grand Principal in 1794.

As had happened in the Craft, in the late 1770s the Grand Chapter began to introduce a Provincial system with the appointment of Grand Superintendents responsible for existing chapters and the formation of new ones in a particular area of the country. The ubiquitous Thomas Dunckerley did much to popularise the Royal Arch for the Grand Chapter in his capacity as Grand Superintendent in and over Hampshire, the Isle of Wight, Essex, Dorset, Wiltshire, Devon, Somerset, Kent, Suffolk, Durham, Sussex, Cornwall, Gloucestershire, Herefordshire, Nottinghamshire and Surrey. Whether he visited the more northerly of his charges is not known, but he certainly did much work in the West Country and the Home Counties.

The rival Antients Grand Lodge had completely the opposite response to the Royal Arch to that of the premier Grand Lodge, largely as a result of the great support given to it by Laurence Dermott.[7] On his first appearance as Grand Secretary in 1752 there is reference to the Royal Arch in his report on an imposter who 'initiated many persons for the mean consideration of a leg of Mutton for dinner or supper . . . whom they pretend to have made Royal-Archmen. . .' Again in the Grand Lodge held on 2 September 1752 'every piece of real free-masonry was traced and explained; except the Royal Arch. . .' by Dermott. So much had he influenced the Antients that when their constitutions—Ahiman Rezon—were published the Royal Arch was styled the 'fourth degree' and characterised as 'the root, heart and marrow of masonry'.

The Antients had no objection to the Royal Arch being worked as a fourth degree within their lodges. Indeed they considered their lodge warrants to be sufficient authority to work any of the known Masonic degrees whether or not those degrees were mentioned in the warrant. Their practice, if they wished to work other than the three Craft degrees, was simply to call those entitled to attend a special meeting, often on a Sunday, open a lodge in the third degree, then open it further into the particular degree to be conferred. They certainly did not have separate units for these degrees; the members simply formed inner circles within the lodge and the minutes of their meetings were recorded in the lodge minute book. By the 1790s those Antients lodges which worked the Royal Arch had evolved a sequence of intermediate steps between the Craft and

Arch. A typical example is the Kent Lodge (now) No. 15, which worked the three Craft degrees followed by the Past Master, the Mark (in two sections), the Excellent and High Excellent, then the Royal Arch itself, which could be followed by the Knights Templar. That each of these intermediate steps was a separate degree is shown by entries in the lodge accounts recording the payments for regalia and certificates by those who had taken them.

The question of whether or not the Antients had a Grand Chapter is one on which many historians agree to differ.[8] Until 1771 all matters pertaining to the Royal Arch were settled in the Antients Grand Lodge. In that year some Arch matters having arisen, those present in Grand Lodge resolved 'that as several members of Grand Lodge were not Royal Arch masons, the Chapter were the properest persons to adjust and determine the matter'. In December 1773 the Grand Lodge resolved that 'a General Grand Chapter of the Royal Arch shall meet on the first Wednesday in the months of April and October in every year to regulate all matters of that branch of Masonry, and that at such meetings a faithful copy of the Transactions with a list of all the Royal Arch masons of the respective lodges shall be returned to the Grand Secretary to be Inrolled.' Whether the General Grand Chapter ever met is not known and no records or minutes of any meetings have survived. Certainly the General Grand Chapter had no separate existence and its transactions had to be ratified by the Antients Grand Lodge, so that if it did exist it was no more than a committee of suitably qualified members of the Grand Lodge. Nor is there any extant record of the Antients appointing Grand Officers for the Royal Arch. When they began to issue Royal Arch certificates the spaces for the signatures of the three Grand Principles, or Grand Masters, Z, H, and J as they were often referred to by the Antients, were signed by suitably qualified senior Grand Officers of the Antients Grand Lodge.

The question of the placing of the Royal Arch arose in the negotiations leading to the Union of the two Grand Lodges. With two such opposing views—complete acceptance by the Antients and non-recognition by the premier Grand Lodge— a careful compromise was necessary. The Antients were satisfied by the acceptance of the Royal Arch as a part of 'pure ancient Masonry', whilst the premier Grand Lodge was satisfied by the actual working of the Royal Arch being removed from the lodges into Chapters which, to satisfy the Antients, were separate from but linked to

Craft lodges. The Duke of Sussex was so preoccupied with the settling of the Craft Union that it was not until 1817 that any specific arrangements for the Royal Arch were made. In the interim the two former sides continued working the Royal Arch as they had before the Union, with Edwards Harper, joint Grand Secretary, being given special responsibility for dealing with any Royal Arch enquiries that arose.

Questions did come up, resulting in 1817 in the rather hurried so-called Union of the two Grand Chapters. The original Grand Chapter had not met since 1813 and the Antients' Grand Chapter, as a committee of that Grand Lodge rather than an autonomous body, had presumably ceased to exist once the Union of the two Grand Lodges had taken place. However, to placate the former Antients a meeting was held in 1817, at which the members of the Grand Chapter and former Antients Royal Arch members met in separate rooms at Freemasons' Hall and then proceeded to the Grand Hall, where the Duke of Sussex awaited them and formed them into the United Grand Chapter, a title which was soon dropped in favour of Supreme Grand Chapter. New Grand Officers were appointed and a new code of Regulations was adopted by which the Royal Arch became firmly linked to but worked separately from the Craft.[9]

Administratively the Craft and Arch were linked by certain designated Officers of the United Grand Lodge, if properly qualified, automatically holding similar office in the Grand Chapter. Additionally, any matter not specifically covered by the Royal Arch Regulations was to be considered as being covered by the Book of Constitutions of the United Grand Lodge. Separation of the working was evolved by the regulation that in future the Royal Arch must be worked in a properly chartered Chapter and not in the lodge. The Chapter, however, could not have a separate existence but had to be attached to—and carry the number of—a Craft lodge. To achieve this all those Chapters that were working under charters issued by the original Grand Chapter had to return their original charters and apply for one attaching them to a Craft Lodge. All those former Antients lodges that had worked the Royal Arch had to cease doing so, form themselves into a chapter, and apply for a charter attaching themselves to a Craft lodge of their choice. If for any reason the lodge should go out of existence the chapter could not exist independently but must attach itself to another lodge.

The Royal Arch has a Provincial system similar to that of the Craft.

As we have seen, the original Grand Chapter had begun to appoint Grand Superintendents to oversee and stimulate Royal Arch activity in the Provinces. This system was continued and expanded after the formation of Supreme Grand Chapter in 1817. Provinces are based roughly on the old county boundaries and the Grand Superintendent is appointed by and represents the First Grand Principal, the equivalent of the Grand Master in the Royal Arch. He is the supreme local authority in his Province and has responsibility for managing Royal Arch affairs within it and must hold a meeting of his Provincial Grand Chapter at least once a year. He is empowered to appoint Provincial Grand Chapter Officers and to appoint, or promote, those who have given service to the Province to Past Provincial Grand Chapter rank. As the Royal Arch spread abroad chapters were grouped into Districts, ruled over by a Grand Superintendent with the same powers as those appointed for Provinces at home.

Tracing the development of the Royal Arch ritual is made exceptionally difficult by the almost total absence of evidence for it during the first forty years of its existence.[10] The Royal Arch did not attract the same interest as the Craft, as a result of which there are no early printed exposures of the Royal Arch ritual. From the original Grand Chapter's minutes, and those of private chapters, we can deduce that the ritual was based on the story of Zerubabel and the preparations for the building of the second Temple of Jerusalem and that the working of the ceremonies included the giving of catechetical lectures. What the ceremonies actually consisted of is a mystery. The earliest manuscript rituals date from as late as the early 1780s[11] and from that date to the major revision of the Royal Arch ritual in 1834 we have some 50 ritual manuscripts—of varying states of completeness—and half-a-dozen printed texts from which to draw conclusions.[12]

The exaltation ceremony was in two parts. The actual ceremony, in which the candidate ceremonially entered the Chapter, advanced to the pedestal, took his obligation, and was given the signs and words, was fairly brief and at its conclusion the candidate became a spectator for the remainder of the ceremony. The main part of the ceremony was an enacted catechetical lecture in three sections—between the Principals and the Principal Sojourners—in which the discovery of the vault and its contents, the symbolism, signs, word and the 'history' of the Royal Arch were explained to the candidate. Additionally, there was another catechetical lecture in which the ceremony was explained and moralised upon together with the material in the enacted lecture, sections of which were often given when no candidate was available for exaltation.

It is difficult, from the limited information available, to draw general conclusions about the working of the Royal Arch, or decide what differences—if any—there were between the working in Chapters under the original Grand Chapter and those used by Antients in their lodges. As we have seen, the Antients practised a series of intermediate degrees between the Craft and the Royal Arch but, from existing evidence, this would not seem to have been the case in chapters under the Grand Chapter. It may perhaps be inferred from the fact that no Chapter of Reconciliation was set up in 1817 that the two former workings were compatible and that there was no necessity to bring them into line with each other, as there had been in the Craft as a result of the move towards a Union of the two Grand Lodges. What is apparent is that by the 1830s there was some confusion in the Grand Chapter itself as to what ceremonies constituted the Royal Arch, resulting in the First Grand Principal setting up a Special Committee whose brief was to determine what the ceremonies were and to demonstrate them to the Grand Chapter for approval and promulgation—after amendment if necessary— as the official ritual to be adopted by all chapters.

As had happened in the Craft with the Lodge of Reconciliation, the Special Committee greatly exceeded its brief. The simple eighteenth-century ceremony was extended by including material from the enacted catechetical lecture, the candidate remaining a participant throughout the ceremony. The remainder of the enacted lecture was divided into two set-piece Lectures: the Historical—given by the Third Principal—explaining the legendary history of the three epochs in Freemasonry culminating in the Royal Arch; and the Symbolical—given by the Second Principal—in which the forms, symbols and decorations of the chapter are explained and moralised upon.

The Special Committee introduced a new set piece, the Mystical Lecture, to be given by the First Principal, in which the signs were explained and a complicated explanation of the words and symbols found on top of the pedestal in the vault was introduced. This explanation has caused some controversy, for those who formulated it were not Hebrew scholars and used, and gave meanings to, certain Hebrew words which were capable of giving offence to Jewish members. This matter was discussed in depth in 1982 and alternatives were produced.[13]

The Special Committee also completed the removal of all overtly Christian references in the Royal Arch, to make it as universal as the Craft and therefore open to men of all faiths. The two earliest ritual manuscripts we have—dating from *c.*1784—show the Royal Arch to have been overwhelmingly Christian in content. Prayers were given in the name of Jesus Christ, readings were from the Old and New Testament, candidates were raised as 'Knights Companions of the Holy Order of St. John of Jerusalem', and the symbolism of the Lectures contained many Trinitarian references. Although special prayers were available for non-Christian candidates it is hard to see how they could have accepted many other items in the Lectures, particularly in the Sheffield MS, which has a final section entitled the *Mystical Knowledge of the Temple* in which the architecture, furnishing and decorations of Solomon's Temple are given in intensely Christian symbolism, much of it plagiarised from Bunyan's *Solomon's Temple Spiritualised.*[14] The later manuscripts see a diminution of the overt Christian references, a move completed by the Special Committee—a deliberate move to make practicable the inclusion of the Royal Arch in the definition of 'pure ancient masonry' evolved at the Union of the two Grand Lodges.

The Special Committee made two further alterations to bring the Craft and Arch closer, both of which concerned the qualification for entry into the Royal Arch. The first was to remove the intermediate degrees which had been practised by the Antients—the Mark, Excellent and High Excellent Mason— all of which virtually dropped out of use, though they were later revived as separate and autonomous Orders. The second was a complete change of the password required for entry into the chapter by a candidate. Both the Antients and the Grand and Royal Chapter had required candidates for the Royal Arch to be either Masters or past masters of a Craft lodge and they were required to give the word and sign of an Installed Master on entry into the chapter room. Clearly, even in the eighteenth century, when the Master of the lodge could be changed every six months, this put a limitation on the number of possible candidates for exaltation. A subterfuge was soon developed, now known as the Passing the Chair ceremony. By this the candidate for the Royal Arch who had not served as Master of a lodge could temporarily occupy the chair and receive the necessary sign and word to use as a pass to enter the chapter. The Passing the Chair ceremony could take place either in a Craft lodge on the normal night of Installation or in what was termed a 'previous lodge' opened within the chapter. In neither case did the candidate who 'passed the chair' qualify as a Past master: he was regarded as a virtual rather than an actual Past Master. There had always been those who, rightly, regarded the Passing the Chair ceremony as an unconstitutional means of gaining the secrets of the Chair. Their view appears to have prevailed in 1834 when the necessity to be an Installed Master to be exalted was dropped and a new password was adopted. From 1835 onwards it was only necessary to be an Installed Master if you wished to occupy the Principal's chairs in the Royal Arch.

Although the Special Committee and the Chapter of Promulgation had revised and rearranged the Ceremony of Exaltation, their additional aim of promulgating an agreed ritual to be adopted by all chapters was never achieved. As in the Craft, there was a great reluctance to write down the Royal Arch ritual and its publication was regarded as a Masonic offence.[15] The new system was demonstrated in London by the Chapter of Promulgation and passed on by word of mouth. This, combined with an inability to suppress local traditions, had resulted in all manner of local differences in the working of the same basic ceremony.

The special committee had also laid up problems for the future. Their convoluted explanation of what had been found on the plate of gold on top of the pedestal was both to cause problems within the Royal Arch itself and lead to unfounded accusations of devil worship and even blasphemy from outside Freemasonry. The problems within the Royal Arch came to a head in the 1970s when a special committee was again set up to look at the Royal Arch ritual, resulting in Supreme Grand Chapter agreeing further revisions of the ritual in 1989, particularly to the Mystical Lecture, which simplified the ritual and removed those items which had given offence to Jewish Companions in particular.

The Royal Arch has always had its own distinctive regalia. The 1766 Charter of Compact, as well as being the authority by which the Grand and Royal Chapter worked, also contained its first regulations and was illustrated with drawings of the jewel to be worn by the Companions. The Charter and the 1766 *Regulations* of the Grand Chapter ordered that:

(a) the Principals should wear proper robes and caps;
(b) all others should wear white aprons with indented borders of scarlet and scarlet ties and that the apron bib should have a 'T over an H' [for Templum Hierosolymae—the Temple at Jerusalem] in gold embroidery or sequins;
(c) every Companion should wear a jewel of the prescribed pattern—two interlaced triangles within a circle with the centre of the interlaced triangles having a different device according to rank.

The Charter of Compact gave no indications as to what the robes or caps of the Principals were to be. In 1777 the Chevalier Ruspini, founder of the Girls' School, laid designs for robes before the Grand Chapter which were adopted and agreed and appear in the 1782 Regulations as scarlet faced with ermine for the First Principal (Zerubabel); mazarine blue (a light sky blue) faced with sable for the Second Principal (Hagai); grey faced with sable for the Third Principal (Joshua), and plain red for Past First Principals. The colours were slightly altered after the formation of Supreme Grand Chapter in 1817. The First Principal still wears a scarlet robe, as an emblem of regal dignity. The second Principal wears a purple robe, as an emblem of Union—purple being a mixture of blue (the Craft) and scarlet (the Royal Arch). The Third Principal wears a blue robe, as an emblem of universal friendship and benevolence. The Scribes and Sojourners, since 1778, have worn white linen surplices, but the reason for the adoption of this mode of dress is not now known.

In all but a very few old chapters the wearing of headdresses by the Principals and Sojourners had dropped out of use. It was not until the 1796 Regulations that descriptions of the Principal's headdress were given. The First Principal was to wear 'a turban or crown', and the Third a 'purple Hiera cap having a silver plate at the front with the words Holiness to the Lord in Hebrew characters'. These descriptions did not appear after the 1807 Regulations but enterprising regalia manufacturers continued to advertise them up to the First World War. From engraved certificates and early decorated aprons it would appear that the Sojourners in the eighteenth century wore academic mortarboards, but they are now to be found only in one chapter at Hull.

The jewel which decorated the Charter of Compact continues to be worn by all members of the Royal Arch, the colour of the ribbon from which it hangs denoting their status. As in the Craft, unofficial and presentation jewels were introduced. One popular example was of the pierced type and features the arch, pedestal, and other Royal Arch symbols. As many of the hallmarked examples carry the maker's mark of Thomas Harper, Deputy Grand Master of the Antients, they have been assumed to have been made for those who entered the Royal Arch under the Antients. Again as in the Craft, in the mid-nineteenth century individualised jewels began to appear for Past Principals and for founders of new chapters, usually carrying on the ribbon the crest or badges of the particular chapter.

With the formation of Supreme Grand Chapter in 1817 regulations were introduced to standardise regalia and to provide emblems of office for Grand Officers. The current regulation patterns are as follows.

The jewels of the officers of a Chapter comprise an equilateral triangle bearing the emblem of office, all in gilt:

First Principal	a celestial crown on an irradiated circular plate
Second Principal	an all-seeing eye on an irradiated circular plate
Third Principal	an open book on an irradiated circular plate
Scribes	crossed quill pens
Treasurer	a key
Director of Ceremonies	crossed wands interlaced by a laurel wreath
Principal Sojourner	the square on an irradiated circular plate
Assistant Sojourners	the square
Organist	a lyre
Steward	a cornucopia or horn of plenty
Janitor	a sword

Provincial and District Grand Chapter Officers from the Scribes downwards have the same emblems on an equilateral triangle surmounting a double circle enclosing the name of the Province or District. Grand Officers have their emblem of office surmounting an equilateral triangle which in turn surmounts a double circle enclosing two laurel branches; Past Grand Officers have the laurel branches replaced by the words Supreme Grand

Chapter. Additional emblems for Grand, Provincial and District Officers are:

Registrar	a charter surmounting a quill pen
Sword Bearer	two swords in saltire
Standard Bearer	a standard suspended from a pole by a cord.

The President of the Committee of General Purposes of Supreme Grand Chapter has the Arms of the United Grand Lodge of England as his emblem of office to mark the relationship between the Craft and Royal Arch in England. The jewel of a Grand Superintendent of a Province or District comprises an equilateral triangle bearing a double circle enclosing two interlaced triangles with an irradiated triangle in their centre. The jewels of the three Grand Principals consist of a pair of compasses, extended to forty-five degrees, enclosing an irradiated plate, bearing the emblem of office, from which is appended three interlaced equilateral triangles. The emblem for the First and Pro First Grand Principals is a celestial crown, for the Second an all-seeing eye, and for the Third an open book. The jewels for the Provincial or District Second and Third Grand Principals are those of the Second and Third Grand Principals surmounting an equilateral triangle laid over a double circle enclosing the name of the Province or District.

In addition to their jewels of rank or office all Companions wear the jewel of the Order appended to a ribbon on the left breast. The ribbon for a Companion is white, that for a Principal or Past Principal crimson, and that for those above the rank of Past Principal a tri-coloured ribbon of dark blue, crimson, and light blue.

Principals and Officers of a chapter wear their jewels of office appended to collars of crimson ribbon four inches wide. Provincial and District Grand Officers and holders of London and overseas Grand Rank wear their jewels suspended from a tri-coloured ribbon (dark blue, crimson, and light blue). Grand Officers have collars of tri-coloured ribbon four inches wide. In Grand Chapter and when acting officially the Grand Officers and Second and Third Provincial and District Grand Principals wear their jewels suspended from gold or metal gilt chains.

All Companions wear the sash of the Order over the left shoulder. Of crimson ribbon with indented blue edges, it has fringed ends secured by a gilt triangle enclosing a triple tau. Companions have a silk fringe and Principals and all above that rank have gold fringing. Companions have the triple tau on a white background, Principals and Past Principals on a crimson background, and all above that a dark blue background. It is worn over the left shoulder to show that it is a mark of honour and not formerly intended to hold a sword.

The apron of the Royal Arch is of white lambskin, from fourteen to sixteen inches wide and twelve to fourteen inches deep, with a triangular overlap. The apron and overlap have an edging of indented crimson and dark blue not more than two inches wide, except for Grand Officers who have a double indented border not more than four inches wide. In the centre of the overlap is a gold-edged silk triangle having a gold triple tau at its centre, white silk for Companions, red silk for Principals and Past Principals, and dark blue for all above that rank. Two gold-fringed ribbons are suspended beneath the overlap, the colour of the ribbons and the lining of the apron corresponding to that of the silk triangle on the overlap and denoting the rank of the wearer. Provincial and District Grand Chapter Officers have their emblem of office within a double circle enclosing the name of the Province or District in gold embroidery on the centre of the apron. Grand Officers have their emblem of office embroidered in gold between branches of laurel.

8

THE ADDITIONAL DEGREES AND ORDERS

BEYOND the Craft and Royal Arch there are, in England, fourteen additional Masonic Orders which a Freemason may join, together with an Order which although not Masonic per se requires its candidates to be Master Masons. All of these additional degrees and Orders require their candidates to be Craft masons, some also require them to be members of other Orders.[1] Some of them are universalist, simply requiring a belief in the Supreme Being, but others require their candidates to profess the Christian faith. Though often referred to as higher degrees, this description is a misnomer. Although some of them include in their titles numbers higher than the three degrees of the Craft, all are dependent upon the Craft for their membership and all of their members as Craft Masons are subordinate to the Grand Master and the regulations and Constitutions of the United Grand Lodge. Any suggestion that a particular Order, because its constituent degrees are given a higher numerical status than those of the Craft, therefore constitutes a secret elite controlling the Craft is ludicrous. The governing bodies of the various additional degrees and Orders are independent of the Craft and of each other and only have authority over their own particular degrees. They certainly have no authority over the Craft or Royal Arch, nor do the Craft or Royal Arch have any control over the government, organisation or administration of the additional degrees or Orders.

The additional degrees and Orders worked in England today are:

The Mark Degree
The Royal Ark Mariner Degree

The Knights Templar*
The Knights of Malta*
The Ancient and Accepted Rite*
The Royal and Select Masters, also called the Cryptic Rite
The Order of the Allied Masonic Degrees
The Order of the Secret Monitor
The Order of the Red Cross of Constantine*
The Knight Templar Priests*
The Royal Order of Scotland
The Operatives
The Order of Light
The Order of Eri*

Those marked * require candidates to profess the Christian faith. The Order which is not Masonic per se but which requires candidates to be Master Masons is the Societas Rosicruciana in Anglia, known colloquially as the Soc. Ros. or Rosicrucians.[2] The largest of the additional degree is the Mark, whose membership is approximately 10 per cent of that of the Craft.

These degrees and Orders are additional to the Craft and Royal Arch in the sense that in the terms of the definition of 'pure ancient Masonry' given in the Articles of Union of 1813 a Freemason is regarded as complete when he had taken the Craft degrees and the Royal Arch. Indeed the terms of that declaration preclude any sort of formal recognition of the additional degrees and Orders by the United Grand Lodge or Supreme Grand Chapter of England. That lack of official recognition, however, in no way precludes a member of the Craft and Royal Arch from participating fully in meetings of the additional degrees. Many senior members of the Craft and Royal Arch hold high office in the additional degrees and Orders.[3] They do not form a progressive system with the Craft and Royal Arch as a basis. Nor do they form a cohesive system amongst themselves. With the exception of four Orders which require their candidates to be members of the Craft, Royal Arch and one additional degree, these degrees can be taken in any order.

Despite the comments of many non-Masonic commentators and a minority of Masonic writers, the various degrees and Orders do not form a cohesive and progressive philosophical, spiritual or religious system gradually leading a Freemason to greater secret knowledge or salvation. What the additional degrees and Orders do is to continue and further emphasise particular aspects of the principles and moral teachings presented in the Craft and Royal Arch. Whilst the additional degrees have a religious basis in that they require a belief in a Supreme Being, or specifically require candidates to be Christian; and despite the fact that many of them base their ritual dramas on stories from the Bible and include prayers in their ceremonies, like the Craft and Royal Arch none of them are in themselves religions or substitutes for religion. Nor, despite the claims of Walton Hannah in his *Christian by Degrees*, do any of the Christian Orders contain any sacramental elements or any practices which approximate to or in any way attempt to replace elements of the Christian liturgy.[4]

As with the Craft and Royal Arch, the origins have yet to be discovered of those additional degrees and Orders which arose in the eighteenth century. French Freemasons in that century had very fertile Masonic imaginations and invented literally hundreds of additional rites, degrees and Orders, many of which had only a handful of members or had simply been created on paper but were never actually worked. Most of them passed into oblivion when their creators died. Many of them had introduced into them mystical, alchemical, and occult features, or a combination of all three, leading to their developing further and further away from the basic principles and customs of Freemasonry and in most cases losing any tenuous connections with Freemasonry that they might originally have possessed.[5] Many of those additional degrees in France incorporated the word Scottish (Eccosais or Eccosaise) in their title from a mistaken belief that they were based upon Orders brought from Scotland by Jacobite Freemasons after the abortive Jacobite risings in 1715 and 1745. Many of them also included a reference to Heredom or Heredon, from an erroneous belief that there existed a mysterious and sacred Mount Heredom near Kilwinning from which all masonic orders originated. Fortunately, few of these French inventions were introduced into England.

There was a similar burst of activity in England in the 1860s and 1870s when a group centred around Rober Wentworth Little, Kenneth Mackenzie, Francis Irwin, John Yarker and W. Wynn Westcott 'revived' or 'arranged' a number of what Ellic Howe has termed fringe Masonic Rites.[6] A combination of wide reading and fertile imaginations led them to revise or construct a series of increasingly complex and overcomplicated

Rites, such as the Order of Ishmael, the Swedenborgian Rite of Primitive Phremasonry, The Fratres Lucis, Royal Oriental Order of the Sat B'hai and the Antient and Primitive Rite of Memphis and Misraim.[7] All of these Rites had been carefully worked out on paper with elaborate designs for regalia and furnishings. Not all were Masonic per se but all required candidates to be Master Masons. With the exception of the Swedenborgian Rite and the Antient and Primitive Rite—both of which had miniscule memberships—it is doubtful if any of them were ever worked by other than a handful of their members conferring grades and titles upon each other by post.

The additional degrees began to appear in England in the 1750s, but it was not until the 1790s that they became widespread and organised. At the time of the Union of the two Grand Lodges, 1813, the Duke of Sussex was head of a number of them and they were quietly pushed into the background whilst he concentrated upon making the Union of the Grand Lodges secure. After his death in 1843 they began to appear again and gradually established their own governing bodies. It must be admitted that under the Grand Mastership of the Earl of Zetland (1843–70) there was a certain unease on the part of the Craft at what appeared to be a proliferation of new degrees; but provided that none of them made any attempt to infringe upon the prerogatives of the Craft or Royal Arch there was no attempt to prevent their emergence or to bar members of the Craft from joining them. The election of the Prince of Wales as Grand Master of the Craft in 1874 did much to remove any remaining unease, for he was already Grand Master of the Knights Templar, became Grand Master of the Mark, and Grand Patron of the Ancient and Accepted Rite. As a result of his enthusiasm, continued by his brother the Duke of Connaught, who occupied the same offices, the present situation was arrived at whereby the additional degrees and Orders are accepted as graceful additions to 'pure ancient Masonry'.

The principal additional degrees and Orders are as follows:

THE MARK DEGREE

The largest of the additional degrees, the Mark Master Mason, can be traced back in England to the mid-1750s.[8] Originally worked in lodges and as part of the Royal Arch, an attempt was made to have it incorporated as part of the Craft, placing it between the Fellow Craft and Master Mason degrees. The attempt, in 1856, was at first successful, but when the Grand Lodge minutes were put for confirmation the Grand Registrar moved for non-confirmation of the portion adopting the Mark Degree, arguing that as it was not included in the 1813 definition of 'pure ancient Masonry' Grand Lodge could not agree to its incorporation in the Craft. As a result, an independent Grand Lodge of Mark Master Masons was set up within a few days of the rejection by the Craft.[9] The Mark ritual deals with an incident during the building of Solomon's Temple and the degree takes its name from the candidate choosing his 'mark' in the early part of the ceremony—a tenuous connection with operative masonry and the practice of the operative mason choosing a distinctive mark with which to sign his work. In the words of one writer, the Mark Degree 'teaches the lesson that education is the reward of labour and contains a dramatic message, that fraud can never succeed.'[10]

The Mark is organised on the same style as the Craft, with a Grand Lodge as government, a General Board as policy maker, Provincial and District Grand Masters, and individual lodges. The regalia for the Mark is similar to that of the Craft and includes aprons, collars, and jewels. Like the Royal Arch there is a distinctive breast jewel worn by all Mark Masters regardless of rank—a keystone appended to a ribbon bearing a mallet and chisel. The keystone, mallet and chisel are the principal symbols of the Mark degree. The Mark Benevolent Fund was instituted in 1868 and has an annual festival presided over by the Provincial Grand Masters in turn. Although principally it assists Mark Master Masons and their dependents, the Mark Benevolent Fund also makes non-Masonic and general grants, including £500,000 towards the purchase of the land and the building of Lord Harris Court at Sindlesham, Berkshire for the Royal Masonic Benevolent Institution, Lord Harris having been Grand Master of the Mark 1954–1972. Since 1982 the Grand Master of the Mark has been HRH Prince Michael of Kent.

THE ROYAL ARK MARINER

Now attached to the Mark Degree, the origins of this degree are unknown.[11] Claims that a Grand Lodge of Ark Mariners was warranted in 1772 and later given a confirmatory Charter by the Duke of Clarence (later King William IV) do not stand up to examination. The earliest record of the degree being worked comes in Bath in 1790, and Thomas Dunckerley appears to have worked it in connection with his Knight Templar Conclaves. The degree had almost disappeared when in 1871 the 'revival' of the Grand Lodge of Royal Ark Mariners was announced, headed by one Morton Edwards.[12] A conflict immediately arose as certain Mark Lodges had also begun working the degree. Mark Grand Lodge began to negotiate with Edwards but he proved so tricky that Mark Lodge simply annexed the Royal Ark Mariner degree, eventually buying out Edwards' interest in it for £25. As a result the Grand Master of the Mark Degree is ex officio Grand Master of the Royal Ark Mariners. Mariner lodges are attached to and carry the same number as Mark lodges and the degree is governed by a Grand Master's Royal Ark Council whose members are suitably qualified members of the Mark General Board. Until 1990 matters pertaining to the Royal Ark Mariner degree were considered within Mark Grand Lodge meetings. In December 1990 the Annual Assembly of Royal Ark Mariners was re-introduced.

The Royal Ark Mariner ritual is based upon the story of Noah and his ark. The presiding officer of a Royal Ark Mariner lodge, the Commander, represents Noah and the Senior and Junior Wardens his sons Shem and Japeth. The ritual further emphasises and moralises upon the cardinal virtues, using the triangle and the working tools with which Noah built the ark—the axe, the saw, and the auger—to point the moral lesson. The principal emblems of the degree are the triangle, rainbow, and a dove with an olive branch in its beak. The collars and apron edging are of rainbow-coloured ribbon from which hangs a segmented silver arc, representing a rainbow, from the centre of which hangs a dove carrying an olive branch in its beak.

THE ROYAL AND SELECT MASTERS

Commonly known as the Cryptic Degrees, this Order consists of four separate degrees: Most Excellent Master, Royal Master, Select Master and Super Excellent Master. The first three fill in details of the building of Solomon's Temple and the fourth is concerned with the Temple up to its destruction by Nebuchadnezzar. To many members they form a continuing link between the events of the Craft and Royal Arch rituals. Candidates for the degrees must be members of the Craft, Mark, and Royal Arch. The origins of the four degrees may have been in the Excellent and Super Excellent degrees worked by the Antients, but there is no evidence for them having been worked in their present form until 1871 when the Grand Council of New York warranted four Councils to meet in London. These formed the Grand Council for England in 1873.[13]

The regalia consists of a triangular white apron edged in crimson ribbon trimmed with gold braid. Masters, Past Masters, Divisional and Grand Officers have their emblem of office embroidered in gold on the apron. All members wear the breast jewel of the Order, which is an imperial crown from which is suspended a white enamel, skeletal equilateral triangle with the point downwards, the whole suspended from a crimson ribbon. All of the rank of Master and above wear crimson collars to which are appended their jewel of office.

THE ALLIED MASONIC DEGREES

Formed in 1879 the Grand Council of the Order of the Allied Masonic Degrees arose out of a desire to have a governing body for a number of degrees which owed allegiance to no central authority.[14] It now controls five degrees: St. Lawrence the Martyr, Knight of Constantinople, Grand Tilers of Solomon, Red Cross of Babylon, and Grand High Priest. There is no link between any of the five degrees, each of which has its own separate legend and set of officers, but are collectively grouped as a Council. Candidates must be Craft, Mark and Royal Arch Masons. The Council is opened as a lodge of St. Lawrence, both for the working of that degree and for the administrative business of the Council. The ritual is based on the story of St. Lawrence the Martyr and impresses on the candidate the virtues of fidelity and fortitude. The Knight of Constantinople degree is based on an incident in the life of Constantine and illustrates the virtues of humility, equality and justice. The Grand Tilers of Solomon takes the candidate back to Solomon and his Temple and exemplifies the quality of mercy. The Red Cross of Babylon has links with the Royal Arch—the ritual tracing the journey of Zerubabel from Persia to Jerusalem—and teaches the importance of truth. The Grand High Priest ritual is based on an incident in the life of Abraham and exhorts the candidate to dedicate his life to his God.

The regalia of the Allied Degrees is very simple. Originally each member simply wore a bar from which was suspended five miniature jewels representing the five degrees. Recently a single jewel was introduced in the shape of a pentagonal plate, each segment of which carries an emblem of one of the degrees. Grand officers wear a thistle green collar, edged with gold lace and embroidered with gold oak leaves and acorns, from which hangs a jewel in the form of the seal of the Order.

THE ORDER OF THE SECRET MONITOR

The Order of the Secret Monitor is believed to be descended from an early eighteenth-century Dutch Order of David and Jonathan.[15] It was brought to England in 1875 by a Dr. Zacharie, who formed a Grand Council in 1887. The Order originally consisted of one degree and a bitter argument arose between the Grand Council and that for the Allied Masonic Degrees, both claiming the sole right to work the degree. The argument was not finally settled until 1931, when the allied Masonic Degrees relinquished its claim. The Secret Monitor now has three degrees: Secret Monitor, Prince, and Supreme Ruler. Membership of the Craft is the only qualification necessary for admission. Individual units are called Conclaves and have four unique Officers: the Visiting Deacons, whose duties include keeping in touch with members between meetings. The rituals are based on incidents in the lives of David and Jonathan and teach the beauties of friendship and fidelity.

The regalia consists of a jewel in the form of interlaced equilateral triangles and three arrows with the letters D and J, members of the two degrees being distinguished by the colouring of the jewel ribbon. Supreme Rulers wear a collarette of orange-purple-orange stripes from which the jewel of the Order is suspended. Provincial and Grand Officers wear sashes and collarettes indicating their ranks.

THE KNIGHTS TEMPLAR AND KNIGHTS OF MALTA

The full title of the Order is the United Religious, Military and Masonic Orders of the Temple and of St. John of Jerusalem, Palestine, Rhodes and Malta, in England, Wales and Provinces Overseas. The Order has two degrees, Knight Templar and Knight of Malta, joined by a 'passing' degree, Knight of St. Paul or Mediterranean Pass. The governing body is the Great Priory and the members meet in Preceptories (Knights Templar) and Priories (Knights of Malta). Candidates for installation as Knights Templar must profess the Christian Faith and be members of the Craft and Royal Arch. The Malta degree is only conferred upon those who have taken the Templar degree.[16]

The Knights Templar probably originated in France, where there was a revival of interest in Chivalric Orders in the 1740s.[17] Evidence of its being worked in England dates back to 1777 and by 1791 there were sufficient Conclaves for Thomas Dunckerley to form a Grand Conclave with himself as Grand Master. Dunckerley was succeeded in 1796 by Lord Rancliffe, but on his death the Grand Conclave went into abeyance until it was revived with the Duke of Kent as Grand Master in 1804. On the Duke becoming Grand Patron in 1807 he was succeeded by Waller Rodwell Wright[18] who in turn relinquished the Grand Mastership to the Duke of Sussex in 1813. The Duke was so preoccupied with the formation of the United Grand Lodge that he allowed the Grand Conclave to decline and no meeting was held until after his death. The Grand Conclave was revived in 1845, later changing its name to the United Order.

The Knight Templar ritual places the candidate in the position of a pilgrim travelling symbolically through hardship and dangers until he is received as a Knight. It teaches the virtue of humility and urges the candidate to live his life as a Christian knight. The Knights wear a costume similar to that of the medieval Templars—a white tunic bearing a red cross, a hooded cloak, and a sword. Rank is denoted by the type of cross used and by the addition of embroidered emblems of office to the cloak.

The Knights of Malta ritual deals with the history of the Knights Hospitallers and their journey from Palestine to Malta It emphasises the Christian virtues. The Knights wear a red tunic with a white Maltese cross on the breat and a black, hooded mantle with a white Maltese cross on the left breast, a sword and a black velvet cap. The jewel is a white Maltese cross with silver lions between its arms.

THE ANCIENT AND ACCEPTED RITE

This Rite of thirty-three degrees had its origins in France in the 1750s as a twenty-five degree Rite of Perfection.[19] It was taken to the West Indies in 1761 by one Stephen Morin, and from there to Charleston in South Carolina where it was extended to thirty-three degrees and reintroduced to Europe as such. In the late eighteenth century its Rose Croix and Ne plus ultra degrees were introduced into England and were worked in Knights Templar Conclaves. The Duke of Sussex received a Charter from France in 1818 to form a Supreme Council but did not act upon it. On his death in 1843 a number of English brethren received a patent from

America admitting them to the thirty-three degrees, thus enabling them, in 1845 to form the present Supreme Council.

In England the first three degrees of the Rite are not worked, being equivalent to the Craft degrees; the fourth to seventeenth degrees are conferred by name and the eighteenth degree—Sovereign Prince Rose Croix—is worked in full. All business takes place within a Rose Croix chapter. The ritual teaches that salvation is only possible by following the principles of the Christian faith. The nineteenth to twenty-ninth degrees are again conferred by name only and the thirtieth is worked in full at a Higher Degrees meeting convened by the Supreme Council. Promotion to the thirtieth degree is an honour conferred only on those who have presided over a Rose Croix chapter. Promotion above the thirtieth degree, in England, is a great honour and the degrees can only be conferred upon a strictly limited number of members. The thirty-third degree is reserved solely to the actual members of the Supreme Council, Inspectors-General of Districts, and as an honour to certain distinguished brethren who have given great service to Freemasonry in general.

The regalia is different for each degree. For the eighteenth it is a rose pink collar beautifully embroidered with symbols referred to in the ritual, from which hangs the jewel of the degree which incorporates the compasses, a rose, a celestial crown, an eagle and a pelican. Members of the thirtieth degree wear a heavily embroidered black sash fringed in silver and a collarette of silver edged black watered silk from which hangs a crown from which is suspended a black double-spreading eagle with a sword in its talons. The thirty-first degree regalia is an embroidered collar of white watered silk trimmed with gold lace. From a white collarette a black eagle with gilt wing-tips and tail is suspended. The collar for the thirty-second degree is of black watered silk edged with silver lace and embroidered with the emblems of the degree. With it is worn a gold-edged red silk collarette from which hangs a black eagle with gilt wings, legs and claws. Members of the thirty-third degree wear sashes of white watered silk edged with gold lace with a golden rose and scarlet bow at the base, from which is suspended a jewel with a number thirty-three at its centre. The silver eagle is worn suspended from a black oxidized chain by members of the degree, from a silver chain by Inspectors-General who are members of the degree, and from a gold chain by members of the Supreme Council.

9

MASONIC CHARITY

One of the basic principles of Freemasonry is Charity, in its sense of relieving the wants of others, and it has been one of the motivating forces in Freemasonry from its earliest days. Indeed, as we have seen, there are those today who believe that Freemasonry originated in the late sixteenth and seventeenth centuries as part of a self-help movement, being originally groups of local stonemasons who banded together to support each other in times of need. By beginning to accept non-operatives they gradually turned into social rather than trade-orientated groups. Whether or not that is the case certainly by the time purely non-operative lodges emerged regular attendance at lodges and paying dues into the box guaranteed members assistance in times of hardship or illness, with added assistance to dependants if a member should die. Once Freemasonry became organised after the formation of Grand Lodge in 1717 this system of casual relief was to continue as a feature of lodge life. It still continues today, with many lodges having their own Benevolent Funds from which immediate relief can be given to members or their dependants.

With the beginnings of a formalised Grand Lodge administration in 1723 attention was turned to the formation of a centralised Charity Fund. At the Quarterly Communication held on 21 November 1724 the Earl of Dalkeith, the previous year's Grand Master, proposed that each lodge should take up a collection to be sent to Grand Lodge to form a Joint Stock for charitable purposes and that a Treasurer should be appointed to administer it. The Grand Master, the Duke of Richmond, requested those present to consider it in their lodges before it was debated in Grand Lodge and appointed a Committee to make recommendations. A year later, on 25 November 1725, the Committee made its report, which was adopted and ordered to be entered on the minutes. Action on the report, however, was slow and it was not until 24 June 1727 that the then Grand Master, the Earl of Inchiquin, appointed Nathaniel Blackerby as Treasurer and set up a Committee of seven to administer the fund. It was not until two years after that, at the Quarterly Communication of 25 November 1729, that representatives of the lodges present were called over to pay their lodge's contributions to the Charity Fund. The fund was augmented a month later by a new regulation instituting a fee of two guineas payable to the charity by every new lodge for its constitution.

The years 1730–3 were to see discussion of and agreement to new regulations for the Charity at almost every Quarterly Communication. The Committee was twice expanded, by the addition of the Masters of twelve lodges to the original seven Grand Officers (28 August 1730) and then by being completely reconstituted (13 December 1733) to consist of all the Grand Officers and the Masters of all the lodges which had contributed to the fund during the previous twelve months. The Committee of Charity, however, was not in any way independent. Whilst it could, on proper examination of each case, give immediate relief up to a grant of five guineas it had to keep minutes of each meeting which had to be presented to and approved by the next Quarterly Communication. Any grant over five guineas could not be dispensed without the approval of the Grand Lodge.

A significant widening of the brief of the Committee of Charity took place on 13 December 1733, when it was resolved that, the pressure of business at Quarterly Communications having become so great, all matters pertaining to the administration of the Craft should first be discussed by the Committee of Charity, who would then report on them and make recommendations to Grand Lodge. Thus the Committee of Charity not only dispensed charity but also acted as a general committee and policy-making body. It continued in this dual capacity, with its policy-making function becoming increasingly more important, until the Union of the two Grand Lodges in 1813.

The same situation occurred with the Antients Grand Lodge. One of the reasons for its formation had been its founder's dissatisfaction with the methods of the premier Grand Lodge. Not being recognised as regularly made Masons they were unable to claim casual relief from lodges in England or from the central Charity Fund. Once established the Antients

Grand Lodge instituted registration fees and quarterly due from members, a portion of which was automatically transferred to a charitable fund. A Stewards' Lodge was set up to consider applications and, like the opposition's Committee of Charity, it soon found itself with the power to act as a reporting Committee, board of enquiry, and policy-making body.

In the Provinces local charities were developed, particularly to assist those who fell ill at a time when there was no Welfare State or free medical services. In 1799 a national Masonic Benefit Society was set up with the agreement of the premier Grand Lodge. Members paid an annual fee of one guinea, in return for which they were guaranteed medical fees and a subsistence allowance in times of sickness. The scheme proved very popular, so much so that by 1830 the possible claims against the Benefit Society's fund so outweighed its actual assets and income that it had to be wound up.

The late eighteenth-century saw the beginnings of two of what are now regarded as the four major Masonic Charitable Institutions: the Royal Masonic Institution for Girls and the Royal Masonic Institution for Boys.

The Institution for Girls was the brainchild of the Chevalier Bartholomew Ruspini. An Italian surgeon-dentist, Ruspini arrived in England in 1759 and began to practise in Bath and London. Attracted to Freemasonry he became an ardent member of a number of lodges and a Grand Officer in the premier Grand Lodge. He began to discuss the idea of a Masonic Charity to support the daughters of indigent or deceased brethren with some of his friends in 1787 and on 28 March 1788 his Committee first met to plan for a school. They worked quickly and within nine months had purchased a property in Somers Place East (between the present Euston and St. Pancras Stations), converted it into a school, and installed fifteen girls between the ages of five and ten years under a Matron and domestic staff. Ruspini's profession had brought him into contact with many members of the Royal Family, and the Grand Master, the Duke of Cumberland, and his wife were persuaded to become patrons of the new charity, which was named in their honour the Royal Cumberland Free Masons' School. The girls were well looked after, but the regime was somewhat spartan. Education was limited to reading, writing, arithmetic, and domestic economy including needlework, the results of which were sold to help finance the School. By 1795 the School had outgrown Somers Place and a new site was purchased in St. George's Fields (now Westminster Bridge Road) where a custom built school was erected at a cost of £3,000 to cater for up to 60 girls.

Admission to the school was by petition from the lodge of the petitioner's father. Each petition had to be presented to the Court of Governors and a complicated system of voting was used—a sliding scale on which brethren or lodges had an increasing number of votes in proportion to their donation to the charity. By 1802 sixty girls were being looked after at the school and at a special festival in 1838 to celebrate the jubilee of the School it was announced that the school had educated five hundred girls in its first fifty years. Within a few years of the Jubilee celebrations it was realised that the Free Masons' Girls' School had outgrown the building at St. George's Fields and the search began for a larger site, resulting in the transfer in 1852 to the borders of Clapham and Wandsworth Common. By 1864 the number of girls had increased to a hundred and over the next twenty-four years more property was acquired, a separate Junior School was begun (in 1880), and accommodation was provided for two hundred and fifty girls between the ages of seven and sixteen.

The Centenary of the Girls' School was celebrated on 4 June 1888 with an enormous Festival at the Royal Albert Hall in the presence of the then Prince and Princess of Wales (later King Edward VII and Queen Alexandra), the former in his capacity as Grand Master of the United Grand Lodge of England and Grand Patron of the Girls' School. The Festival realised the then magnificent sum of £50,000, enabling a special Centenary Hall to be built and further repairs and expansions to be made to the existing buildings. The new century was to see a number of changes in the Institution. In 1904 the Junior School was moved into its own premises at Clapham, where it remained until it was moved out of London altogether in 1917 when a new Junior School was opened at Weybridge. In 1907 consideration was given to the support of girls other than placing them as boarders at the School, resulting in the system of grants for education at schools near their homes, which still continue today. The resultant increase in the work of the Institution led to the setting up of an office opposite Freemasons' Hall in Great Queen Street.

By 1920 the school had again outgrown its facilities and there was no further room for expansion at Clapham, which it was felt by then had become a less desirable area for a girls' school. The decision was made to move out of London altogether and the search for a suitable site resulted in 1926 in the purchase of Rickmansworth Park, Hertfordshire, from Viscountess Bonnington for £61,500. An architects' competition was held to provide the best design for housing and schooling four hundred girls and the teaching and domestic staff necessary for such an enterprise. The competition was won by Denman and Sons of Brighton but work could not begin until 1929 as a condition of the sale was that Lady Bonnington remained in residence until 1928. Work began immediately on the School Houses, on 16 July 1930 the foundation stone of the main school block was laid with Masonic ceremonial by the then Grand Master, HRH the Duke of Connaught and Strathearn. The move from Clapham was completed by April 1934—the old school which had served since 1852 having been sold to the Peabody Trust, which levelled the site to construct blocks of workers' flats. The enterprise was crowned on 27 June 1934 when the School was formally opened by HM Queen Mary.

The post-war years, the development of the Welfare State, and changing social attitudes had their effect on the Girls' School. The provision of out-education grants, and the better provision of state education, gradually led to a preference for girls being educated locally rather than boarding at the School. In 1965, with places being available at the School, agreement was given to the introduction of fee-paying girls—often the daughters of Freemasons in the services or government officers whose careers took them abroad for long periods—and in 1972 the first day girls were accepted. As a result of the Bagnall Report and the closure of the Boys' School a greater change has been brought about with preparations being made for the School to become a co-educational establishment and the appointment of a Headmaster.

Although the original aim of the Institution was simply to clothe and educate the girls until they reached the age of sixteen and were able to take charge of their own lives the system was expanded to one of taking a paternalistic interest in the welfare of the girls for the remainder of their lives. Nowadays girls who go on to further education continue to be assisted until their formal education ceases. Girls who do not wish to go on to further education are given assistance in finding vocational training or suitable jobs and guidance and any necessary assistance continues until they are settled. Once formal assistance ceases the Institution does not lose interest in the girls, who know that the Institution is there to help or advise them if problems arise.

The Royal Masonic Institution for Boys had a double foundation due to the existence of the two Grand Lodges in England before 1813. The first Boys' Charity was formed in July 1798 by William Burwood—Junior Grand Warden of the Antients Grand Lodge in 1789—and members of the United Mariners Lodge (now) No. 30. Unlike Ruspini and the founders of the Girls' School the founders of the Boys' Charity had no intention of starting a school but simply wished to provide clothing and tuition fees for the sons of indigent or deceased Freemasons. The plan quickly gained support of the Antients Grand Lodge with the Grand Master—the Duke of Atholl—becoming the Charity's Patron in 1801 and the Grand Lodge making annual grants to the Charity from 1803. From an initial six boys in 1798 the Charity had become responsible for fifty-five boys by 1813.

A curious situation arose in 1808. Sir Francis Columbine Daniel, who had been a member under both Grand Lodges and a founder of the Antients' boys charity, had been expelled by the Antients, resulting in him devoting all his energies to the Royal Naval Lodge (now) No. 59. With the support of his lodge Daniel instituted a boys' charity for the premier Grand Lodge. Like the Antients' charity there was no intention of forming a school, money raised being used to clothe and out-educate boys.

Although the two Grand Lodges were united in 1813 it was not until 1816 that the two Boys' Charities became one under the patronage of the Grand Master, HRH the Duke of Sussex. The Institution continued to clothe and out-educate the boys and when, in 1830, the idea of building a school was raised it was peremptorily dismissed by the Grand Master, who gave it as his opinion that the money donated by the brethren was for the support of the boys and not to be wastefully expended on supporting bricks and mortar. The desire for a school did not disappear, however, and in 1852 a building fund was instituted leading, in 1856, to the purchase of a property in Lordship Lane, Wood Green. Forty-five of the boys cared for by the Institution were moved to Wood Green in 1857 and in 1863 the foundation stone of new school buildings was laid. Further building took place in 1865, enabling the School to house one hundred boys.

As with Girls, the remainder of the nineteenth-century was taken up with expanding the existing property. In 1884 a preparatory school for fifty boys was opened in property adjacent to the original school and the entrance age was dropped to seven years. By 1890 the School was looking after 260 boys. It had become clear that the Wood Green property had outlived its usefulness and that no space was available for expansion, necessary to provide suitable accommodation to teach the boys scientific and technical subjects. In 1896 agreement was reached to purchase for £13,000 the Bushey Grove Estate near Watford. Another architectural competition was held to provide suitable school and boarding accommodation, resulting in Messrs. Gorden, Lowther and Gunston of London, being granted the contract at an estimated cost of £99,000.

Before work on the new school could begin the Centenary of the Institution took place. As with the Girls ten years earlier, the Royal Albert Hall was called into service on 10 June 1898. Three thousand eight hundred and twenty stewards dined under the Presidency of the Prince of Wales, with as many spectators in the galleries. Spontaneous cheers and applause broke out when it was announced that the Festival had resulted in the raising of £141,203 for the Institution, the largest sum ever raised up to that date. In addition it was announced that Grand Lodge had donated £2,000 to the scholarship fund as a memorial to Queen Victoria's Diamond Jubilee of the previous year, and that the Old Masonians' Lodge No. 2700 had been formed for ex-pupils, teaching staff, and those connected with the administration of the Institution.

Work began on the new School at Bushey in 1900. The foundation stone was laid on behalf of the Grand Master by his brother HRH The Duke of Connaught on 12 May 1900 in the presence of over fifteen hundred visitors. The new buildings were completed by October 1902 and the School moved from Wood Green to Bushey for the start of the new term in January 1903, the old school being sold in June 1903. A large increase in the number of boys receiving assistance as a result of the First World War led to consideration being given to building a separate junior school. Suitable premises were found in the Manor Estate at Bushey, which was purchased in 1919. Sufficient funds had been raised to enable work to start in 1926 and on 8 June HRH the Duke of Connaught laid the foundation stone. Work was completed by 1929 when four hundred boys were admitted.

The expansion of the 1920s was not maintained The Junior School was never fully used after the Second World War and in 1969 the decision was taken to transfer the remaining Juniors to the Senior School and from September 1970 the two were merged into one School. This proved only a temporary measure. Continually rising costs and a preference for out-education forced the Council in 1975 to recommend that the School be closed. The recommendation, after much spirited and often very public debate, was accepted and the School finally closed in 1977.

The work of the Institution, however, did not cease but returned to its original form of supplying grants to clothe and educate the boys. From 1975 all boys accepted by the Institution were placed in Schools approved by the Board of Management. As with the Girls, interest in the Boys did not cease once they had finished their schooling. In 1922 the Masonic Boys' Welfare Fund was established to provide benefits for the boys once they had left either Bushey or the School in which the Institution had placed them. In the words of one of the Institution's own publications, the Fund does 'a great deal of quiet and unostentatious work in assisting ex-pupils to establish themselves in their chosen careers at a time when their earned income is usually very small'.

The formation of the Royal Masonic Benevolent Institution was fraught with difficulties. As early as 1830 it had been suggested that some form of Institution, with residential facilities, should be formed to take care of aged brethren but it was not until Dr. Robert Crucefix took up the idea in his periodical *The Freemasons' Quarterly Review* that any action was taken. Crucefix advocated the funding of an Asylum for Aged and Decayed Freemasons and met with a group of like-minded friends on 22 June 1835 to organise a Committee to manage the setting up of such a fund. Unfortunately they began to arrange matters, including a Festival, before gaining the support of Grand Lodge and, more importantly, the Grand Master. When the Committee petitioned the Grand Master for his support he replied that as he had no official cognizance of the Committee and as it had not been constituted by any Masonic authority he could not give it his support. The Committee tried to get themselves put on a proper footing but, unfortunately, misrepresented a public statement of the Grand Master and for a period of four years the two sides gradually grew farther and farther apart, the situation reaching a climax with Crucefix being suspended from his Masonic privileges for six months and the Grand Master stating publicly that he did not believe the aged would be best served by the provision of an Asylum—the upkeep and staffing of which would be a perpetual drain on the Institution's finances—but that a system of annuities would be a more proper way of disbursing the money subscribed.

Despite the official objections the Asylum project met with general approval and Festivals and other entertainments were held to swell the subscriptions donated by the brethren. To show that the Committee had serious intentions a building fund was instituted and limited annuities were given to show that the Institution was keen to get about its business. The Grand Master counteracted this by persuading Grand Lodge in 1842 to set up the Royal Masonic Benevolent Annuity Fund financed by quarterly donations of £100 from the Fund of Benevolence. This only caused the Asylum Committee to cease granting any new annuities and concentrate its efforts on increasing the building fund. By 1847 they had sufficient funds to choose a site at Croydon and ask architects to produce schemes for housing fifty occupants, providing each with two rooms, the necessary offices, and accommodation for staff. Unfortunately, after such a long battle, Crucefix did not live to see the opening of the Asylum in 1850.

By 1849 many of those who had been involved in the early disagreements, including the Grand Master, had died or ceased Masonic activity. Common sense prevailed and discussions took place to promote an amalgamation of the Asylum scheme and the Grand Lodge Annuity Scheme. In May 1850 the two united to form the Royal Masonic Benevolent Institution for Aged Freemasons and their Widows. The new Institution continued the work of its two forerunners, taking over the management of the Asylum at Croydon—and gradually enlarging it—and continuing to grant annuities to those who did not wish to or could not be accommodated in the Asylum.

It is in the last twenty years that the Benevolent Institution has really come into its own with the development of residential accommodation in various parts of England and Wales. In 1947 Harewood Court at Hove in Sussex came into existence, providing self-contained flats and communal areas, a pattern which was to be repeated with every development. The Benevolent Institution now has eleven homes, in addition to Harewood Court, which are fully operational.

Devonshire Court, Oadby, Leicester (1966)
Scarbrough Court, Cramlington, Northumberland (1967)
Prince George, Duke of Kent Court, Chislehurst, Kent (1968)
Connaught Court, Fulford Park, York (1971)
Lord Harris Court, Sindlesham, Berkshire (1972)

Albert Edward Prince of Wales Court, Porthcawl (1973)
Queen Elizabeth Court, Llandudno (1979)
James Terry Court, Croydon, Surrey (1980)
Cornwallis Court, Bury St. Edmunds (1981)
Zetland Court, Bournemouth (1982)
Cadogan Court, Exeter (1985)

In addition the RMBI has now taken administrative and financial responsibility for three residential developments originally founded by the Hannay Residential Trust of the Province of West Lancashire. They are Tithebarn, Great Crosby, Liverpool (1956), Fairlawn, Lytham St. Annes (1961) and Ecclesholme, Eccles near Manchester (1977).

The last of the Masonic Charities to be formed was the Royal Masonic Hospital. This had its origins in the First World War when the Hospital for Women in Fulham Road was bought and opened as the Freemasons' Hospital and Nursing Home to care for the war wounded. When peace returned it was clear that the Hospital could meet a real need within the Craft and the decision was made to retain it. Although Fulham Road was a purpose-built Hospital it was old and in need of renovation and re-equipment. Rather than raise money to modernise, the decision was taken to find a site and start afresh with a purpose-built hospital and nursing home. A site was found at Ravenscourt Park, in West London, and fund raising began in earnest. Sufficient was raised by 1932 for the foundation stone to be laid by the Grand Master, HRH the Duke of Connaught, with the assistance of five royal 'brothers'—the Prince of Wales (later Duke of Windsor), the Duke of York (later King George VI), Prince George (later Duke of Kent) and Prince Arthur of Connaught. The building was completed by 1933 and officially opened on 12 July by King George V, accompanied by Queen Mary, who announced that it was to be known as the Royal Masonic Hospital.

The Hospital reverted to its original status as a war hospital in 1939 and over eight thousand servicemen were given treatment. When the National Health Service came into being in 1948 the Hospital was not taken over by the state and has continued ever since as a private Hospital. In August 1949 a School of Nursing was opened at the Hospital, which now has a high reputation for the training it gives. Although extensions had been built in the 1950s it was clear by 1968 that the operating theatres and equipment of the Hospital needed replacing. A 'Redevelopment and Modernisation Fund' was set up in 1970 and a special appeal to the Craft was launched. Unfortunately the 1970s was a decade of economic difficulties in Britain and as well as raising funds for redevelopment the Hospital, for the first time, suffered an operational loss in 1972 and had to issue further appeals for general funds. The redevelopment and modernisation was successfully carried out, but at much greater cost than estimated, resulting in the Hospital being the best equipped of all the private Hospitals. Economic problems have continued, however, and in 1984 serious consideration began to be given to the question of disposing of the Hospital and creating a new Charity to give assistance to the sick in their own localities rather than bringing them to Ravenscourt Park.

A meeting of Governors of the Hospital turned down the proposal to sell and the 'discussions' continued and, sadly, became more acrimonious. At the time that this book was going to press the Charity Commissioners had stepped in and appointed a Receiver and Manager to try and sort out the Hospital's finances and to decide whether or not it had a viable future. General care of the sick was taken out of the hands of the Hospital in 1990 when the New Masonic Samaritan Fund was established to provide assistance with medical care not only at the Royal Masonic Hospital but at any Hospital which provided the best care at the most reasonable cost and most conveniently to the patient.

The three great Masonic Charitable Institutions were conceived of and funded independently of Grand Lodge. They relied totally on the generosity of individual brethren and lodges for their financial stability. The Girls, being the oldest, set the pattern for fund raising which was to be followed by the two junior Institutions. In 1789 to mark the first anniversary of the Girls' School a church service—led by the Bishop of Winchester—followed by a Festival Dinner was held. Collections were taken at both, benefiting the School Fund by £82.10s.6d. The Anniversary Festival became an annual event for all three Institutions. Initially money was raised by collections at the church service and dinner, but it soon became formalised into a system whereby a prominent Freemason was invited to be Festival Chairman and brethren throughout the country were invited to be Stewards by payment of a minimum donation and a Steward's fee. The three Annual Festivals became even more formalised in the mid-nineteenth century when the present system was adopted of inviting a Provincial Grand Master to be Festival Chairman with enough notice for his Province to work for five or seven years towards raising increasingly enormous sums of money for 'their' Festival. Those who qualified as Stewards for the Festival were entitled to wear a special jewel—usually incorporating some emblem representing the Province or the Provincial Grand Master—during the year of the Festival, ladies being entitled to qualify as Stewards and also wear the jewel. The Festival collection would not be limited to donations from the sponsoring Province but would include donations from other Provinces, London lodges, and lodges abroad under the United Grand Lodge of England.

Apart from the Festival collections the only income the Institutions receive is derived from fixed grants from Grand Lodge, individual donations and legacies, and investment income. The system is far from satisfactory. The principal source of income is the Annual Festival and as this depends largely on the size of the sponsoring Province annual income can fluctuate wildly and financial planning is made difficult by the lack of knowledge of what the next year's income will be.

The Royal Masonic Hospital has never had an annual Festival and depends on patients' fees and donations and legacies from individuals and Masonic groups. Treatment at the Hospital is not free. Patients pay according to their means, any shortfall being made up from the Samaritan Fund. As a result it has been necessary for the Hospital to issue special appeals from time to time, with the Grand Master's permission, to enable expansion, modernisation and re-equipment to be carried out.

Despite the existence of the independent Charities, Grand Lodge did not neglect its duties. As we have seen, the two Grand Lodges which existed before 1813 each had their own central Charity Funds controlled by the Grand Lodge. After the Union of the two Grand Lodges a Board of Benevolence was set up to deal with petitions for Charity. It was funded by an agreed percentage of the annual dues, which each member paid for every lodge to which he belonged, being set aside in a separate Fund of Benevolence. The Board was composed, initially, of members chosen by the Grand Master from amongst the present and past Grand Officers and the actual Masters of Lodges. Meeting monthly, its purpose was to aid petitioners, their widows and children from any recognised Constitutions. As we shall see, it also had authority to recommend grants for non-Masonic purposes and give annual fixed sums to the three Institutions.

The Masonic Charities evolved to fill specific needs and served their various purposes admirably. With the growing development of the Welfare State, the introduction of the National Health Service, and the great improvement in state education a number of brethren began to question whether the Charities were serving a useful purpose or were simply duplicating state facilities. Foremost among those who believed that the time had come for a major investigation into the Charities and a reappraisal of their functions was the present Grand Master, HRH the Duke of Kent. In June 1971 the Pro Grand Master, Lord Cadogan, announced the Grand Master's intention of setting up a wide-ranging Committee of Enquiry into the Masonic Charities and their funding. At the Quarterly Communication of 8 September 1971 it was announced that the Committee of Enquiry had been set up under the Chairmanship of the Hon. Mr. Justice Bagnall and that its terms of reference were:

1. To consider in the light of present economic and other circumstances whether the Charities, that is the three Masonic Institutions and the Royal Masonic Hospital, are serving the interest of the Craft and achieving their several charitable purposes in the best possible manner.
2. To consider the several methods at present adopted for raising funds for the purpose of each of the Charities and whether any additional or alternative method or methods could with advantage be adopted.
3. To consider whether competition between the Charities in seeking funds or otherwise is in the best interest of the Craft and of the Charities.
4. To consider whether competition between the Provinces in the provision of funds for the Charities is in the best interests of the Craft and of the Charities.
5. To consider the general principles of administration of the funds, assets and property of each of the Charities.
6. To consider any other matters that appear to the Committee to be closely related to any of the foregoing matters.
7. To make recommendations on all or any of the foregoing matters.

The Committee took submissions from and enquired into the Charities themselves but also took a great deal of oral and written evidence from lodges and individual brethren of all ranks within the Craft. They also examined how comparable non-Masonic Charities were organised and funded. Their work took a considerable amount of time and their report was not presented to the Grand Master until 1974. His reaction to the report was given to the Craft in his address to the Annual Investiture on 29 April 1974 and is worthy of quotation in full. The Grand Master said:

Now, Brethren, I would like to turn to a subject of the utmost importance to Freemasonry. As you will all know, the Committee of Inquiry which I appointed in 1971 to look into the whole question of our Masonic Charities has completed its deliberations and submitted to me its report. I have studied the report in the greatest detail and discussed it at length with my immediate advisers. Inquiries made by my Committee were most thorough and searching and indeed no comparable appraisal of our charities had been made previously—at least not within living memory. I have already thanked each member personally and they have featured among those receiving honours today, but I would like to say a special word to them now. I appreciate immensely all that they have done, the great amount of trouble that each one had taken and the time that they have freely given in their busy lives in the preparation of this excellent report. As in any Committee, the main responsibility fell upon the Chairman, R. W. Bro. the Hon. Sir Arthur Bagnall and to ensure that his outstanding contribution be remembered I would like the report to be known in future at the Bagnall Report. The whole Craft owes to him and his Committee a very great deal.

Brethren, I now turn to the all-important question of what is to be done and I would like the Craft to know that in the main I have accepted the recommendations made in the report. These will entail considerable alteration in the structure of our charities as we know them today, not with a view to reducing our charitable activities, as charity is the very essence of Freemasonry, but rather to bringing them up to date so that our financial resources can be concentrated where they are most needed, now and in the future. There are four major items of re-organisation about which I want to tell you today as they are the essential features of our proposed new charitable structure. The first of these is to do with education. I would like to see the Royal Masonic Institution for Girls and the Royal Masonic Institution for Boys brought together to form a new body known as the Educational Trust and furthermore I envisage that the two schools themselves will in due time amalgamate to form a single co-educational establishment at Rickmansworth. The object of the Trust is to establish a charity operating over the whole field of education which, as well as maintaining a Masonic School, will give help wherever State provision is deficient. Thus the Craft will be able to help dependants of Freemasons from earliest childhood right through to adult education.

The second change concerns our work for the aged and the sick. I propose that the Royal Masonic Benevolent Institution and the Royal Masonic Hospital should be brought together to form a single Trust which, for the moment I have in mind to call the Foundation. I know how concerned the Craft is that our old people should be properly looked after. One of the limiting factors, apart from money, is that we have nowhere to accommodate those who are too frail to live on their own or in one of our existing homes. The new Foundation should have both the flexibility and the experience to close this gap in the best possible way. I would like to say a word here about our great Hospital with its needs for essential modernisation coming at a time of spiralling inflation. The part that it will play in the Foundation will be further considered following a thorough examination of the financial implications of the various alternatives which are open to us. I have called for this report to be made at the earliest possible moment and hope to be able to tell the Craft of my decision before the end of the year. An additional task of the Foundation will be to discharge the functions at present carried out by the Board of Benevolence.

The third major change is the introduction of the new Central Charity, for which I much prefer the title of Grand Charity. The purpose of establishing this fund is twofold: firstly to allow additional monies to be directed to one or other of the Trusts when it is most needed, and secondly, which I consider most important, to enable the Craft to support non-Masonic charities and thus carry out charitable activities into fields beyond the bounds of Freemasonry.

And now I come to the last of the four major changes. This has to do with the management of the three Charities, that is the Educational Trust, the Foundation and the Grand Charity. Each of these will be a separate entity under the ultimate control not of those whose contributions to it have been recorded, but of the Craft as a whole acting through the membership of Grand Lodge. The principal officer of each charity will be known as its President and will be appointed by me annually in the same way as the President of the Board of General Purposes with whom they will each rank equally.

In order to co-ordinate and implement the changes which will necessarily take place and to bring them into phase with each other, I have asked the Assistant Grand Master [the Hon. Fiennes Cornwallis, now Lord Cornwallis, Past Pro Grand Master] to preside over a Steering Committee which will be fully representative both of the charities and of the Craft generally. I am glad to say that he has agreed to do so and I expect this work to begin in the very near future. This Committee will have permanent accommodation in Freemasons' Hall.

The Craft will be reassured to hear that it is proposed to continue the Festival system and to give further consideration as to how best to fit it into the framework of the changes which I have outlined already.

You have now heard the main features of the report and I am arranging for copies of what I have just said, together with a copy of my Committee's recommendations, to be sent to all Lodges immediately. I hope that many people will provide themselves with full copies of the report and study it in details as I am sure they will find it of great interest. I hope too that all those concerned in the administration of the charities as they now exist will see virtue in the changes proposed and give the Steering Committee their full support and co-operation.

The Steering Committee, known as the Grand Master's Committee, began its work immediately but its task was not an easy one. As the Institutions and Hospital were autonomous bodies with Royal Charters and Charitable status there were many legal difficulties to be sorted out and some changes in the Bagnall Report's suggestions had to be made to satisfy the Charity Commissioners. Additionally it must be admitted there was a certain reluctance in some quarters to agree to change. The Craft has always had an emotional reaction to changes in the Charities and whilst it was acknowledged that changes needed to be made there were those who would rather have some alterations in the existing Charities than the major reorganisation which resulted from the Bagnall Report.
Many of the problems were solved, however, and the new Charities have come into existence as follows:

(i) *The Foundation for the Aged and Sick's* trust deed was signed on 28 November 1979 but for complicated legal reasons—largely a result of the Hospital remaining a general hospital rather than specialising in geriatric cases—the Benevolent Institution and the Hospital remain separate and will do so until the future of the Hospital is decided.

(ii) The Grand Charity's trust deed was signed on 16 April 1980 and it began its work on 1 January 1981 when the duties and assets of the former Board of Benevolence were transferred to it. Independent of Grand Lodge its controlling body is the General Meeting, the membership of which is composed of those qualified to attend Grand Lodge. The work of dealing with petitions, considering grants to Masonic Charities, and the dispensing of non-Masonic Charity is carried out by a Council and its Petitions Committee.

(iii) *The Masonic Trust for Girls and Boys'* trust deed was signed on 8 September 1982. The complete amalgamation of the Boys' and

Girls' Institutions was delayed because of peculiar legal and practical complications. A special Court of the Boys' Institution met on 21 February 1985 and resolved to surrender its Royal Charter and to pass the Institution's assets to the new Trust. The complete merger of the Boys and Girls into the Trust took place on 1 January 1986. The Trust will significantly widen the scope of assistance given to the children of distressed or deceased Freemasons and, for the first time, will allow assistance to be given, funds permitting, to any child regardless of whether or not its father was a Freemason, and grants to be made to any charity established for the benefit of distressed children.

The Grand Master is Grand President of all three Charities, each of which is presided over by a President, appointed by the Grand Master, which office is an active office in Grand Lodge. The Charities each have their own Councils composed of members appointed by the Grand Master and elected by London and the Provinces. Each has its own annual Festival sponsored by the Provinces in rotation, the first of which took place in 1986.

Contrary to public opinion, Masonic Charity is not solely directed at Freemasons and their dependants. The records show a long tradition of non-Masonic charity dating back to 1733, when the Deputy Grand Master recommended that the Masters and Wardens of all lodges should make a collection amongst themselves to assist the Trustees for the Settlement of the American Colony of Georgia 'to send distressed persons to Georgia where they may be comfortably provided for'. From that time onwards grants were regularly made to help those suffering the effects of natural disasters both at home and abroad, to assist national Charities, and to ameliorate the effects of war. Freemasonry has had a long connection with the Royal National Lifeboat Institution, providing assistance in setting up Lifeboat Stations and paying for ten lifeboats, the last of which was presented in 1980 and named in honour of HRH the Duchess of Kent, the Duke of Kent himself being in the curious situation of presenting the lifeboat to himself in his two capacities as Grand Master and President of the RNLI.

Until recently the major non-Masonic charitable effort was made as part of the celebrations of the 250th anniversary of the formation of Grand Lodge in 1967. The then Grand Master, the Earl of Scarbrough, suggested providing a major fund for medical research. As a result over £600,000 was raised and formed into a Trust Fund, the income of which is administered by the Royal College of Surgeons. Over the years the income has been used to provide laboratories and specialised equipment and to pay the salaries of specialist researchers principally into heart disease and cancer. The income from the Trust is still being administered by the Royal College and an annual report of progress and new research is made to Grand Lodge and printed in its Proceedings.

The new Grand Charity is now the principal dispenser of grants to non-Masonic Charities and organisations. At the end of each year some £300,000 is dispensed in sums from £500 to £5,000 to national charities concerned with welfare and medical research covering all types of mental and physical disabilities. To mark the link, direct or indirect, between Freemasonry and operative stonemasons donations of £5,000 have been given to the restoration funds of the great Anglican cathedrals of England and Wales. Each year the Grand Charity selects two or three major projects to receive major awards over periods of three to five years. Recipients of major grants since 1981 have been:

1981 £50,000 Duke of Edinburgh's Award Scheme
£250,000 Royal Association for Disability and Rehabilitation.
1982 £25,000 South Atlantic Fund
£175,000 Dept. of Health and Care of the Elderly Nottingham University Medical School
£100,000 Research Team for the Care of the Elderly Welsh National School of Medicine
1983 £40,000 Royal College of Nursing
£100,000 Liverpool School of Tropical Medicine
£100,000 Royal Marsden Hospital
1984 £20,000 British Red Cross African Famine Relief Fund
£250,000 to Hospices throughout England and Wales
1985 £250,000 to establish a Chair in Gerontology at the University of Cambridge.
£45,000 University of Oxford for research into brain disease in the elderly

1986 £250,000 Mental Health Foundation to combat drug abuse
1987 £250,000 Crisis at Christmas
£250,000 Great Ormond Street Children's Hospital
1988 £500,000 to be divided amongst Hospices in England and Wales over the period 1989–91
1989 £90,000 Monoclonal Antibody Laboratory, University of Keele
£78,000 Royal Post Graduate School of Medicine
£50,000 Marie Curie Memorial Foundation
1990 With the assistance of the Charities Aid Foundation two endowment funds, of £250,000 each, were established to benefit for ten to fifteen years charities in the field of caring. The Carer's National Association and Contact a Family are the first two Charities to benefit.
1991 £250,000 Age Concern
£250,000 Help the Aged
£525,000 to be divided between Hospices in England and Wales in the period 1992–1995
1992 In celebration of the 275th Anniversary of Grand Lodge and the 25th Anniversary of the Installation as Grand Master of HRH The Duke of Kent, KG,:
£1,250,000 (plus £500,000 from the Masonic Trust for Girls and Boys) to Cottage and Rural Enterprises to establish a community for the handicapped at Rowde, Wiltshire
£500,000 Home Farm Trust
£250,000 Camphill Village Trust
£50,000 Elizabeth Fitzroy Homes
1993 £500,000 Cancer Relief Macmillan Nurses Pediatric Nursing Services to train new Nurses.

In addition to the centralised charities many Provincial Grand Lodges and individual lodges have their own Benevolent Funds, and just as the Grand Charity supports Masonic and non-Masonic cases so Provincial and Lodge Benevolent Funds will support both.

In addition to the Grand Charity contribution, which forms part of his Grand Lodge dues, the individual Freemason, provided it does not overstrain his personal or family commitments, can contribute to the Central Charities by covenant. In many lodges it is the custom to take a Charity collection either at the end of the meeting or at the Festive Board and it is usually up to the Master how each collection is disposed of. In many lodges it is the custom for one collection a year, often at a meeting near Christmas, to be given to the local hospice, hospital or childrens' home.

Charity is not solely concerned with money but also involves the giving of time and practical assistance. Many lodges and individual Masons give freely of their time to local charities, visiting those who are sick or disabled, arranging events for children's homes, and entertaining the elderly and housebound. Often both the financial and the practical help is given without any attendant publicity—in the true spirit of charity—but the uninformed criticisms of Freemasonry's detractors have forced the bushel to be at least lifted up from the light, if not totally removed.

10

ATTACKS ON THE CRAFT

FROM time to time, since its earliest organised days, the Craft has been criticised, attacked or satirised in the media and books. The attacks in the 1980s were by no means a new thing but what was new was their vehemence and the great amount of interest that they stirred up. Why the attacks should have surfaced at this time is something of a mystery. The catalyst was probably the publication of Stephen Knight's *The Brotherhood*,[1] a supposedly long researched, serious and impartial study of Freemasonry but containing many factual errors, a great deal of third-hand rumour and speculation and gross exaggerations. Why the public and the media took such a great interest in such a mediocre book was probably the result of the intense privacy in which the Craft had conducted its affairs over the previous forty years. For reasons now not known the Craft at the end of the 1930s began to become very introspective, to the extent that, over the years, the general public lost contact with it and it began to appear in their eyes as a vast, secretive organisation. Prior to the outbreak of the Second World War the situation was very different. Reports of Masonic meetings and information on Masonic personalities appeared regularly in the national and local press. There were two weekly Masonic newspapers, *The Freemason* and *The Freemasons' Chronicle*, and a monthly magazine, *The Masonic Record*,[2] which were available from newsagents and station bookstalls, all three reporting meetings and other Masonic events in great detail as well as carrying articles on all manner of Masonic subjects.

Until 1984 the official response to anti-Masonic comment was one of 'no comment', which may in itself have contributed to the distancing of the Craft from public life. That attitude of 'no comment' came under review by the Grand Master himself, who signalled a limited change of that attitude in his Address to Grand Lodge at the Annual Investiture held on 25 April 1984 in which he said:[3] "Brethren, you will be aware that the Craft has recently been the subject of another 'exposure', this time by an author who seems to make it a speciality to attack Freemasonry. Many of his arguments are on the basis that because some Freemasons may have misused the Craft, the Craft itself is corrupt, and that because we are staunchly private, our privacy is sinister. At the same time, fresh impetus seems to have been given to renewed expositions attempting to show why Freemasonry is incompatible with Christianity and it is even reported that local authorities are debating whether membership of the Craft is compatible with local Government.

Our response was, in the traditional manner, to be largely unresponsive. This may have temporarily dampened the delight which the media seem to take in Mason-bashing—and it is remarkable how resolute but courteous refusal to comment dampens debate—but I am beginning to wonder whether our stonewalling attitude is necessarily the best for the interests of the Craft. Giving little or no information may stifle immediate interest, but it does nothing to discourage malicious speculation or to dispel unnecessary suspicion. I believe that we—and I mean in particular the Board of General Purposes as the body which recommends Grand Lodge's policy—shall need to give the matter close attention before very long.

I am not advocating a reversal of our traditional attitude and still less an active Public Relations Campaign. I believe, however, that we should do more in preparing ourselves, as suggested here two years ago, to explain to people, who may genuinely want to know for respectable reasons, what the Craft stands for and to stress the positive aspects of what it does for the world in general and for us personally.

In this we should not simply fall back on traditional elliptic phrases, for instance explaining Freemasonry as a 'system of morality': nor do we convey very much by negative explanation such as saying simply that Freemasonry is not a religion, or that it prohibits political discussion in its Lodges.

How, then, do we start? Logically at the beginning, explaining that Freemasonry is a society of men which developed, perhaps historically, from the Guilds of mediaeval operative Stonemasons. Its members follow ancient principles, which I discussed in 1980 and can summarise under the well-known headings. We profess Brotherly Love by treating other men charitably and as equals. We practise Relief: we care for our own (though not as a benefit society), and we care increasingly for those who are not Masons. We strive for Truth: in calling for high moral standards, hoping that we can attain them in our own lives and perhaps influence others in the same way.

What does Freemasonry do for its members and the community? I do not need to dwell on its charitable works, which I believe are well enough known and understood by us all, particularly since the publication at the end of last year of the useful booklet 'Information on Masonic Charities'. I think we could well emphasise however that, in context of our ancient principles, contributions to non-Masonic Charity and pastoral or practical involvement in charitable works are very important.

We can then go further and say that Freemasonry extends the family. It should introduce us to more friends, or at least to friendly acquaintances. Its Charities may be on hand to support families if their circumstances change for the worse but—like families—they cannot always help.

As to the religious aspect, we should emphasise that Freemasonry is an ally of religion and is firmly rooted in religious belief. In all our rituals and at our meals, we are reminded of the deity to whom we owe our being. It is sad, in these days of ecumenism and, in some quarters, tolerance, that it should be considered a criticism of Freemasonry that it is not specifically Christian. It will certainly help if the phrase 'Freemasonry is my religion' is never uttered again: I cannot think of any words more likely to give a false impression of the Craft. We may pray, as our forebears did, more than others pray now, but the Craft does not and cannot provide any of the usual characteristics of a religion.

When we say that we profess Brotherly Love we mean that Freemasonry encourages Brethren to help each other in a charitable and generous way. We emphatically do not mean using Masonic connections for personal gain or preferment."

The Grand Master's comments and suggestions were immediately taken into consideration by the Board of General Purposes and resulted in a number of organisations who were contemplating holding enquiries into Freemasonry being agreeably surprised when they were invited to meet senior members of the Craft to discuss the subject. To help brethren explain Freemasonry the Board produced four leaflets—*What is Freemasonry*; *Freemasonry and Religion*; *Freemasonry and Society*; and *Freemasonry's External*

Relations—and a half-hour video *The Freemasons*. The Grand Secretary and Grand Lodge's Librarian and Curator appeared on radio and television as official spokesmen, and many journalists found themselves being invited to discuss Freemasonry. Further, critics in the media now found that factual errors in their comments no longer went uncorrected.

Criticism of Freemasonry falls into four main areas: that it is a secret society; that it is a religion, substitute for religion or that it is anti-Christian; that it exists solely to further the material or social interests of its members; and that it is a 'conspiracy' secretly manipulating government and the law at all levels.

Freemasonry is neither a secret society nor, as it has sometimes been characterised recently, a 'society with secrets'. The only 'secrets' in Freemasonry are the traditional words and signs of recognition used as proof of membership. As a careful reading of the obligation taken in each degree shows, these are the only secrets that a Freemason binds himself to keep. He does not, as has been claimed by some anti-Masonic writers, bind himself not to reveal his membership; not to discuss Freemasonry in any way with a non-Mason; or to protect a fellow Freemason regardless of the circumstances. On the contrary, a Freemason is at perfect liberty to declare his membership to anyone he chooses; has the freedom to discuss Freemasonry, excepting the traditional secrets, with anyone he cares to; and although he obligates himself to protect the honour, reputation and confidences of a fellow Freemason it is a promise strongly qualified by the following statement: 'murder, treason, felony and all other offences contrary to the laws of God and the ordinances of the realm being at all times most especially excepted'.

It is a strange secret society that publishes its *Constitutions* and *Regulations*,[4] which can readily be purchased over the counter at Freemasons' Hall. It is an equally strange secret society whose meeting places are easily identified, either by their exterior decoration or from having the words 'Masonic Hall' over their doors or on a brass plate on the doorway, and which are listed in telephone and street directories. So secret is it that members of the public can walk into its London headquarters, visit its Library and Museum, and be taken on a conducted tour of the Grand Temple and Ceremonial Suite. Can one really call an organisation which keeps minutes of its meetings at all levels, those of the Grand, Provincial and District Grand Lodges being printed by outside printers, and issues for circulation amongst members a *Grand Lodge Year Book* and Provincial *Year Books* listing lodges and chapters with their meeting dates and places and lists of members, again produced by outside printers, a secret society?

That Freemasonry as an institution and individual Freemasons value their privacy is another matter, but does not make the institution a secret society. Grand Lodge has always declined to publish a complete membership list, believing that as Freemasonry is a voluntary organisation the privacy of its members must be respected and that if anyone wishes to publish their membership that is a matter for the individual and not the business of Grand Lodge. In this it is in the same position, although larger numbers are involved, as any other institution, society or club whose members are there by choice and which similarly neither publish lists of members nor reveal details of membership without the consent of the members concerned. In this computer age with its necessary regulations concerning data protection there is a great deal of doubt as to whether or not Grand Lodge has authority to publish a list of members without the consent of each member being obtained.

Add to that the practical problems of producing such an enormous list (nearly 360,000 names) and the large expenditure in terms of time and money involved in producing a list which is by its nature out of date before it is completed, and you have the reasons why, in addition to respect for privacy, Grand Lodge does not publish a membership list. As the compiler of an article in *City Limits*[5] found to his cost when he identified a name in the list of Grand Officers in the Grand Lodge *Year Book* with the Chairman of one of the major clearing banks, who happened to have the same surname and initials, a list of names without a great deal of additional information, which is not available in the Grand Lodge Registers, is of little use.

Attacks on English Freemasonry on religious grounds have been made periodically over the last three hundred years, varying from sermons by individual clergymen to the total ban on membership by the Roman Catholic Church and the recent reports by the Methodist Conference in 1985, and the General Synod of the Church of England in 1987.

The first Papal *Bull*[6] against Freemasonry was issued in 1738 and did not attack the Craft purely on religious grounds but claimed that by having 'secrets' known only to Masons it offended against the relationship between a Roman Catholic and his priest, from whom he should have no secrets.

Later Papal *Bulls* attacked Freemasonry on grounds of anti-clericalism and political involvement, confusing a number of European political associations, which had adopted quasi-Masonic trappings, with regular Freemasonry. Having consistently opposed Freemasonry since 1738, the penalty under Canon Law for being a Freemason being excommunication, the Roman Catholic Church's attitude became somewhat blurred after Pope John XXIII's Second Vatican Council. To clarify the subject the then Pro Grand Master, Earl Cadogan, wrote to the Archbishop of Westminster and received a reply enclosing a statement issued in 1974 by the (Roman Catholic) Bishops of England and Wales on the subject. Its text is as follows:

'STATEMENT ON FREEMASONRY

Canon 2335 of the Code of Canon Law forbade Catholics to join the Freemasons or any similar organisation under pain of excommunication. The ban was imposed because in many countries Freemasonry was regarded as being a secret society plotting against Church and State. Times change. The Holy See has reviewed the Church's present relationship with Freemasonry. Widespread consultation failed to produce a uniform response from the World's Bishops. So the Sacred Congregation for the Doctrine of the Faith has recently told Bishops that universal legislation is to remain unchanged, at least until the revision of the whole Code of Canon Law. But the Congregation has ruled that Canon 2335 no longer automatically bars a Catholic from membership of masonic groups. In particular cases it is to be subject to the restrictive interpretation applied to penal legislation. And so a Catholic who joins the Freemasons is excommunicated only if the policy and actions of the Freemasons in his area are known to be hostile to the Church.

The Bishops of England and Wales have taken note of this guidance. They wish to clarify procedure in their countries until such time as the universal law of the Church is reformulated.

A Catholic should regard himself as first and foremost a member of the Catholic Church, finding his inspiration for Christian living in the Church and his fellowship within that community. But if he sincerely believes that membership of Freemasonry does not conflict with this deeper loyalty he should approach his Bishop through his parish priest to discuss the implications of such membership. Local conditions would of course

1 *Chronometer in pinchbeck, enamel and lacquer, by William Staples of London, c.1790. (GL collection).*

2 *Leeds creamware teapot, c.1770. (GL collection).*

3 *English masonic engraving by William Tringham, London, 1755. (GL collection).*

4 *Member's jewel of the Royal Alpha Lodge No. 16, which since 1818 has been the Grand Master's personal lodge.*

5 *Wedgwood cup and cover. Three examples were commissioned to celebrate the 275th Anniversary of Grand Lodge in 1992. They were presented to HM The Queen, HRH The Duke of Kent, KG, and the Grand Lodge collection.*

6 Arms of the United Grand Lodge of England granted by the College of Arms in 1919.

7 Glass enamelled with the Arms of the premier Grand Lodge, by William Beilby, c.1760. (GL collection).

8 Hand painted Royal Arch apron, c.1800, presented to Francis, 2nd Earl of Moira. (Moira Lodge No. 92).

9 English lambskin apron, handpainted with Masonic symbols, c.1780 (GL collection).

10 *The pupils of the Masonic Girls' School being presented to the Grand Master,* c. 1795. *Painting by J. Stothard. (Rickmansworth Masonic Girls' School).*

11
HRH The Duke of Sussex, KG *Grand Master 1813–43. Anonymous portrait in regalia of Grand Master. (*GL *collection).*

12 HRH Albert Edward, Prince of Wales (Edward VII), being welcomed as a Past Grand Master, 1870. Painting by S. Rosenthal. (GL collection).

13 Third Degree Tracing Board by Josiah Bowring (1757–1831), dated 1819. (Lodge of Honor and Generosity No. 165).

14 Wedgwood jug, 20 inches high, inscribed 1803 and decorated with transfers referring to all the then known Masonic degrees. (GL collection).

15 *John Hervey, Grand Secretary 1868–80. Portrait in oils by H. Tetterborn, 1870. (GL collection).*

16
James Asperne in his regalia as a Grand Steward, 1813. Portrait in oils by Samuel Drummond. (GL collection).

17 *HRH The Duke of Kent, KG, Grand Master, opening the public exhibition at Freemasons' Hall, 4 July 1986 with John Hamill, Librarian and Curator of the United Grand Lodge of England.*

18 Grand Lodge meeting at Earls Court, London on 10 June 1992 to celebrate the 275th Anniversary of the Grand Lodge and the 25th Anniversary of the Grand Mastership of HRH The Duke of Kent, KG.

19 Members of Quatuor Coronati Lodge No. 2076, the premier Lodge of Masonic Research, November 1993.

20 *HRH The Duke of Kent,* KG, *Grand Master since 1967. Portrait by Derek Hill commissioned by Grand Lodge in 1986.*

have to be kept in mind. A Catholic who has in the past left the Church to become a Freemason is urged to seek reconciliation.

Priests, religious and members of Secular Institutes are still forbidden by the universal law of the Church to accept membership of the masonic order or similar organisations.'[7]

Thus the attitude of the United Grand Lodge since 1974 has been that, provided a Roman Catholic is satisfied in his own conscience that his joining Freemasonry will not compromise his religious beliefs and will not produce conflict within his immediate family, there is no reason, because he satisfies the inalienable qualification of a belief in the Supreme Being, why he should not be accepted into the Craft.

Matters became somewhat muddied when Canon Law was revised in the late 1970s.[8] The new Canon made no reference at all to Freemasonry and Catholics believed that the old objections had been dropped. Cardinal Ratzinger, Prefect of the Sacred Congregation for the Doctrine of the Faith, quickly published an unsigned article in *L'Osservatore Romano* for 5 December 1985, stating that although Freemasonry was not explicitly mentioned in the new Canon it was implicitly there as an organisation which worked against the Church! He added that local ecclesiastical authorities had no power to vary the ban, but Roman Catholic Bishops in many parts of the world continue to follow the line adopted by the English Bishops in 1974.

The *Report* of the Faith and Works Committee of the Methodist Conference[9] and its adoption by that Conference in July 1985 came as a shock to the many Methodists who were also Freemasons. The Committee had been asked to enquire into the compatibility of Freemasonry and Methodism. Rather than doing this they concentrated on public misconceptions of Freemasonry, recommended that Methodists who were Freemasons and those who were thinking of becoming Masons should think very carefully about membership of the Order. They also recommended a ban on Masonic meetings in Methodist premises, a rather empty gesture as no Lodge meetings were held in Methodist premises.

The principal criticisms from Methodists themselves were that the *Report* dealt not with the nature of Freemasonry but popular misconceptions of it; that the Committee had been composed solely of non-Masons and had done its job in a hurry; that few Methodists who were Freemasons had been consulted or asked to give evidence; and that there were far more important matters that the Conference should have been debating instead of attacking an institution which had always supported religion. The post-Conference issues of *The Methodist Recorder*, which treated both sides with great fairness in their reporting of the debate, contained many letters from Masons and non-Masons criticising the *Report*. Not unnaturally the adoption of the *Report* caused great distress to Methodists who were Freemasons, and their families. They were not, however, content to let matters rest. An Association of Methodist Freemasons was formed which lobbied at all levels within the Church and presented a public exhibition in the town in which successive Conferences were held. Their work was rewarded at the 1993 Conference when a large number of Memorials were presented to Conference resulting in the 1985 *Report* being referred back for further examination.

In the wake of the Methodist *Report*, the General Synod of the Church of England, in 1985, set up a working group to enquire into the compatibility of Freemasonry and Christianity. Unlike the Methodists, the Synod included two Freemasons on its working party and took a great deal of evidence from Grand Lodge and other Masonic authorities.[10] Having done all it thought possible to explain Freemasonry to the Synod Working Party and having answered all the direct questions received, Grand Lodge was all the more dismayed when the Working Party's *Contribution to discussion*,[11] as it termed its report, was published and accused the Craft of four types of heresy and the Royal Arch of blasphemy. The *Contribution to discussion* stopped short of actually declaring Freemasonry incompatible with Christianity and, contrary to press reports, did not demand that Anglicans withdrew from Freemasonry. It did cause a great deal of distress to many Freemasons, and their families, who were devoted Anglicans and great supporters of their local churches.

The *Contribution to discussion* was debated for three hours at the General Synod in York in June 1987, and was adopted, and recommended for discussion within the church, by a large majority. The Craft took the Synod at its word and has continued to discuss Freemasonry at all levels within the Church, finding that it has rather more friends within the Church than the Synod.

The media had a field day with both the Methodist and the Synod *Reports*. The accuracy of their reporting left a great deal to be desired, claiming, completely without foundation, that both Churches had banned their members from being Freemasons. Sadly, when in 1986 the General Assembly of the United Reformed Church debated Freemasonry[12] and made no adverse criticisms of it the press were noticeably silent.

The question of the relationship between Freemasonry and Religion had been brought before the Board of General Purposes causing them to lay before Grand Lodge a policy statement on 12 December 1962, reconfirmed on 9 December 1981.[13] Knowing that some Churches were to investigate Freemasonry the statement was again looked at and a leaflet *Freemasonry and Religion* was produced which, since 1987, has read as follows:

FREEMASONRY AND RELIGION

Introduction

This leaflet is intended to deal with a topic mentioned in the leaflet 'What is Freemasonry'. It explains the United Grand Lodge of England's view of the relationship between Freemasonry and Religion.

Basic Statement

Freemasonry is not a religion, nor is it a substitute for religion. It demands of its members a belief in a Supreme Being but provides no system of faith of its own.

Freemasonry is open to men of all religious faiths. The discussion of religion at its meetings is forbidden.

The Supreme Being

The names used for the Supreme Being enable men of different faiths to join in prayer (to God as each sees Him) without the terms of the prayer causing dissension among them.

There is no separate Masonic God; a Freemasons' God remains the God of the religion he professes.

Freemasons meet in common respect for the Supreme Being as He remains Supreme in their individual religions, and it is no part of Freemasonry to attempt to join religions together. There is no composite Masonic God.

Volume of the Sacred Law

The Bible, referred to by Freemasons as the Volume of the Sacred Law, is always open at every Masonic meeting.

The Oaths of Freemasonry

The obligations taken by Freemasons are sworn on or involve the Volume of the Sacred Law. They are undertakings to help keep secret a Freemason's means of recognition and to follow the principles of Freemasonry.

The physical penalties which are purely symbolic do not form part of an Obligation. The commitment to follow the principles of Freemasonry is, however, deep.

Freemasonry Compared with Religion

Freemasonry lacks the basic elements of religion:

a. It has no theological doctrine and by forbidding religious discussion at its meetings will not allow a Masonic theological doctrine to develop.
b. It offers no sacraments.
c. It does not claim to lead to salvation, by works, secret knowledge or any other means. The secrets of Masonry are concerned with modes of recognition and not with salvation.

Freemasonry Supports Religion

Freemasonry is far from indifferent to religion. Without interfering in religious practice it expects each member to follow his own faith, and to place above all other duties his duty to God by whatever name He is known. Its moral teachings are acceptable to all religions.

Freemasonry is thus a supporter of religion.

The imputation that men join Freemasonry for material or social gain is of comparatively recent date in Masonic history and first arose in the late nineteenth century. To join Freemasonry for this reason is to go against all that it stands for. Indeed on a number of occasions from his initial interview until he receives his Grand Lodge certificate on the completion of his taking the three degrees a Mason is asked for a categorical declaration that such is not the reason for his joining. He is firmly told that any attempt to use his membership for material or social gain is contrary to the principles and tenets of the Craft. Before he is admitted to the lodge for initiation he signs a declaration which includes a statement that material gain is not his reason for seeking admission;[14] on his entry to the lodge he is asked to publicly make that declaration; and when he is presented with his Grand Lodge certificate he is told that he must never have it framed and displayed in his home or place of work as that could constitute advertising his membership in the hope of gain.

Freemasons are as human as any other group of people and it would be dishonest to try and claim that no Freemason has ever attempted to misuse his membership; but the very few who do join for material gain or later attempt to use their membership in that way soon discover that they will be shunned by their fellow members, and that if they persist in their attempts they will become subject to Masonic discipline, varying from temporary suspension of membership to total expulsion depending on the gravity of the offence. This code of internal discipline exists not simply as a deterrent but as a practical means of stopping Freemasonry being used for improper purposes and therefore being brought into disrepute.

This emphasis on not using Freemasonry for personal gain is one of the reasons why Freemasons have become so reticent about advertising their membership. It is an almost classic Catch 22 situation: being open about membership leads to accusations that that openness is simply for personal gain, and being reticent is taken as an admission that Freemasonry is a secret society with something to hide.

Many of the accusations of Freemasonry being simply used for personal gain are based upon the mistaken belief, fostered by Freemasonry's detractors and inaccurate newspaper reports, that a Freemason is bound by his obligation to support and prefer a fellow Freemason before anyone else. A careful reading of the ritual shows how erroneous this belief is. Every Freemason is taught that his duties are to his God, to the laws of the land, to his family and to his professional or business responsibilities, and in that order. Only when he has satisfied those duties does any responsibility he might feel he has to his brethren come into play. It is a rather sad comment on society today that it is prepared to believe that an employer will employ or promote someone simply because they are a Freemason, regardless of their experience, ability or qualifications.

It is all too easy to make accusations of Masonic connivance or corruption in matters of employment or business, but it is significant that on the occasions when complaints are made testable evidence is rarely ever produced; the 'evidence' usually consisting of innuendo and supposition. In recent years a number of attempts have been made to blame Freemasonry for various decisions not liked by others. The London Borough of Hackney spent around £500,000 to have an eminent Queens' Counsel investigate 'Masonic corruption' in the running of their Borough. They were not pleased when his report, in which he acknowledged unprecedented assistance from Grand Lodge, showed no evidence whatsoever of Masonic corruption but a great deal of simple mismanagement and maladministration. In 1992 and 1993 a round dozen of complaints of Masonic interference in local authority planning decisions were investigated by various local government Ombudsmen (none of whom were Freemasons), who again found that Freemasonry was a red-herring in their investigations.

What annoys Freemasons is the suggestion by critics that because a very few Freemasons have erred, sometimes in a spectacular and very public way, then the institution itself is corrupt and that the majority of its members if they are not misusing their membership are at least capable of doing so. Even the late Stephen Knight in both his book *The Brotherhood* and in his appearance on Radio 4's *Tuesday Call*[15] readily admitted that because one Freemason misused or attempted to misuse his membership that did not mean that the Craft itself was corrupt.

The popular belief that Freemasons go around giving odd signs and handshakes to identify each other is another distortion and legend. The traditional modes of recognition are simply used as a means of testing a stranger visiting a lodge where he is not known to any of the members. The present writer can honestly say that in twenty-four years of membership he has never come across anyone at a non-Masonic gathering who has attempted in this way to signify that he was a Freemason. There have been odd occasions when because of an odd turn of phrase occurring in a conversation I have suspected that someone might be a Freemason, but this is simply because Freemasonry—like the Armed Forces, the professions and many vocations—has its own terminology and phraseology which with usage becomes unconsciously part of a Freemason's normal language and is used in general conversation without any deliberate intention to use it as a signal to other Freemasons.

Freemasonry entered the realms of conspiracy theory largely as a result of claims by two contemporary writers, Robison and Barruel, that the French Revolution was hatched in French Masonic lodges.[16] As a result Freemasonry has subsequently been held responsible for the American War of Independence,[17] the Paris Commune of 1870, the South American Revolutionary movements of the nineteenth century,[18] the Russian Revolution,[19] and the First World War. These claims have been based upon the fact that some participants in the events were, or were claimed to be, Freemasons, totally ignoring the fact that in most cases there were Freemasons on both sides. The belief that Continental Freemasonry was a radical political movement arose from the autocratic and strictly stratified social structure of Europe in the eighteenth century, to the rulers of which the Masonic ideals of fraternity, equality and toleration were anathema, resulting in Freemasonry being banned at various times in Austria, Spain, Portugal, the Austrian Netherlands, Russia, and parts of Germany and Italy.

Because of different political and social structures Freemasonry never suffered from government intervention in England. The nearest it came was in 1799 when the Unlawful Societies Act[20] was passed banning societies which required their members to take oaths. In its original form it would have effectively prevented any Masonic lodges meeting. As a result of the leaders of both the Grand Lodges in England explaining to the Prime Minister the nature of Freemasonry and how it was both a supporter of law and the throne, and was in turn supported by members of the Royal House, Freemasonry was specifically exempted from the provisions of the Act. The exemption was conditional upon each lodge Secretary annually providing to his local Clerk of the Peace a return of the members of his lodge. This provision remained in force until it was removed by Parliament in 1967 as part of the Criminal Law Amendment Act of that year, one of those rag-bag Acts beloved of Parliamentary lawyers in which a host of obsolete Acts, or provisions resulting from Acts, are rescinded in one large sweep.

Although Freemasonry was thus recognised as a respecter and supporter of lawfully constituted authority this did not prevent the conspiracy theorists from weaving their fanciful tales of it being a vast and secretive network manipulating government and the law in all their forms and at all levels; there have even been claims that Freemasonry is an arm of the intelligence service and has been infiltrated by agents of foreign intelligence services.[21] The conspiracy theorists base their claims on three false premises: that because lodges meet in private they are therefore secret and provide scope for plotting and corruption; that Freemasons are bound to support each other regardless of the circumstances and to promulgate Masonic views; that the 'secret' registers of Freemasonry give the rulers of Freemasonry and individual Freemasons access to a vast network of the population, by which means they can manipulate and control society. The facts are somewhat more mundane.

As was stated at the beginning of this chapter, Freemasons do not meet in secret. Meetings are private, but as an anti-Masonic element in Britain demonstrated, it is a simple matter to set up a video camera outside a Masonic Hall and film the 'secret' Masons arriving for their meetings.[22] Although conspiracy theorists will not accept that no business other than Masonic business is transacted at lodge meetings, and even if admitted to see for themselves would more than likely claim that the meeting had been 'fixed' for their attendance, it is a simple fact that masonic meetings are taken up with working the ceremonies and the normal business required for the well running of any society or club: there is simply no time available to get up to any of the machinations claimed by the detractors of Freemasonry. The total ban on the discussion of politics, religion or any other non-Masonic subject is rigidly adhered to.

As has already been explained, Freemasons are not bound to support each other regardless of the circumstances. They are bound to put their religious, civil, civic and family duties before any obligations they might feel towards another Freemason. As the present Grand Secretary has publicly said on a number of occasions, Freemasonry is as interested as the police, local authorities or any other body in finding *provable* evidence that Freemasons have misused their membership so that the necessary Masonic disciplinary action can be taken. Too often, however, such allegations are so vague and third-hand, or are based on a fallacious equation that because X, Y and Z are Freemasons therefore collusion must have taken place, that they are impossible to investigate. There is also a complete misunderstanding of the authority conferred by rank in Freemasonry. The Master of a lodge only has authority within the lodge and the members only owe allegiance to him within the lodge. His authority does not extend outside the meetings of the lodge. Freemasons are so conversant with this situation that they have found it difficult to understand why, particularly in the areas of local government and the police, concern has been expressed that those who are in a superior position in their professional lives are occasionally in a subordinate position to their professional juniors in a Masonic situation. To those involved there is no conflict as the two facets of their lives are separate and distinct and do not impinge upon one another.

A policy statement on a Freemason's duties was issued as a leaflet entitled *Freemasonry and Society*, the latest printing of which, dated 1988, reads as follows:

Introduction

This leaflet is intended to expand a topic mentioned in the leaflet 'What is Freemasonry'. It explains the United Grand Lodge of England's view on Freemasonry and Society

Grand Lodge's Policy

It must be clearly understood by every member of the Craft that his membership does not in any way exempt him from his duty to meet his responsibilities to the society in which he lives. The Charge to the new Initiate calls on him to be exemplary in the discharge of his civil duties; this duty extends throughout his private, public, business or professional life.

Respect for the Law

Freemasonry demands from its members a respect for the law of any country in which a man may work and live.

Principles

The principles of Freemasonry do not in any way conflict with its members duties as citizens, whether at work or at home or in public life, but on the contrary should strengthen them in fulfilling their public and private responsibilities. Thus there is no conflict of interest between a Freemason's obligation and his public duty.

If an actual or potential conflict of duties or interests is known to exist or is forseen, a declaration to that effect should be made.

It may on occasions be prudent to disclose membership to avoid what others mistakenly imagine to be a potential conflict or bias, but this must be a matter for individual judgement.

Use of Membership

A Freemason must not use his membership to promote his own or anyone else's business, professional or personal interests. This is made clear directly or by interence several times during a Freemason's early career so that no Freemason can pretend to be ignorant of it. A Freemason who transgresses this rule may be suspended from Masonic activities or even expelled.

Duty as a Citizen

A Freemason's duty as a citizen must always prevail over any obligation to other Freemasons, and any attempt to shield a Freemason who has acted dishonourably or unlawfully or to confer an unfair advantage on another Freemason is contrary to this prime duty.

Personal or Business Difficulties

If it could be proved by evidence that any personal failure or business difficulty was attributable to 'Masonic influence', Masonic authority would take a serious view of the fact, as it would be contrary to the Principles of Freemasonry.

Secrecy

*Freemasonry is not a secret society.

*Like many other societies it regards some of its internal affairs as private matters for its members.

*There is no secret about the aims and principles. Copies of the constitutions and rules can be obtained from Freemasons' Hall by interested members of the public.

*The secrets of Freemasonry are concerned with its traditional modes of recognition. Its ceremonies are private.

*In ordinary conversation there is very little about Freemasonry which may not be discussed.

*On inquiry for acceptable reasons, Freemasons are free and will be proud to acknowledge their own membership.

The Registers of Grand Lodge contain very little personal information concerning members. For the majority of members it is simply their age, occupation and some indication of their address at the time of their initiation or of their subsequently joining additional lodges, together with the date of cessation of membership. It is only in the case of Grand Officers, Provincial and District Grand Secretaries, and Lodge Secretaries that up-to-date information is kept concerning addresses, for the simple reason that they have to be sent agendas for Grand Lodge meetings and other administrative papers from time to time. It is not possible to tell from the Registers family relationships between members or a member's religious, political or other views, since they are not relevant to their membership. As the Registers are kept by hand and by lodge it is not even possible to say how many members of a particular profession are Freemasons. It cannot be overemphasised that provided a candidate has a belief in a Supreme Being neither Grand Lodge nor its individual lodges has any interest, or any reason to be interested, in an individual member's religious or political beliefs, or occupation or his membership of any other societies.

Freemasonry has always refused to express any opinion on religious, political or social matters simply because there is no collective opinion and none has ever been allowed to develop. From the diversity of its membership Freemasonry represents a wide spectrum of the society in which it exists and must therefore necessarily encompass a wide cross-section of beliefs and attitudes. These beliefs and attitudes, however, are personal to the individual who holds them and do not form any part of Freemasonry. For Freemasonry to express any opinion on such matters would offend against its basis of toleration, and would inevitably alienate sections of its membership. Freemasonry was born in a period of great intolerance when differences of view on politics and religion eventually led to civil war; in the final words of the first of the Ancient Charges, its purpose was to be a 'centre of union between good men and true, and the happy means of conciliating friendship amongst those who must otherwise have remained at a perpetual distance'.

If, then, Freemasonry is not a religion, a political force or a pressure group, and if its members do not receive any material gain from their membership, the questions might properly be asked why has it survived for so long, and why do so many seek initiation and continue their membership? The simple answer is that Freemasons enjoy their Freemasonry. That enjoyment arises, and continues for a number of different reasons. To some it is the pure enjoyment of fellowship in an atmosphere in which they can temporarily forget the problems of modern life. Others gain a real enjoyment and satisfaction from performing ritual and from seeing others perform it well. To many the principles of Freemasonry provide a framework to guide their lives, and in many cases lead those who have perhaps been only nominally members of their religion back to full membership of it. To some it provides the only opportunity they ever have, if they reach the Master's chair, of organising and running a meeting, and as such can be said to be character building. But above all it is the basic appeal of the principles of Freemasonry which motivate their continuing membership. It is often forgotten that membership of Freemasonry is voluntary. No one has to join, no one is coerced into joining and the candidate has to make the first approach. After initiation a member is at complete liberty to withdraw at any time. That so many remain in membership and derive enjoyment and satisfaction from it without any material gain is one of Freemasonry's strengths. So many other organisations with origins similar to or based on Freemasonry eventually failed because, unlike Freemasonry, they became partisan and materialistic, leading to their being fragmented by factions and ultimate collapse. By remaining true to its basic principles but having the capacity to adapt its practices to the changing society in which it exists, Freemasonry has not only survived but has done so on a scale which could not have been envisaged by those unknown men who came together to found it over four hundred years ago.

Appendix A

THE GRAND MASTERS OF ENGLAND

Premier Grand Lodge:

1717	Anthony Sayer
1718	George Payne
1719	John-Theophilus Desaguliers
1720	George Payne
1721	John, 2nd Duke of Montagu
1722	Philip, Duke of Wharton
1723	Francis, Earl of Dalkeith (later 2nd Duke of Buccleuch)
1724–5	Charles, 2nd Duke of Richmond and Lenox
1726	James, Lord Paisley (later 7th Earl of Abercorn)
1727	William, 4th Earl of Inchiquin
1727–8	Henry, 3rd Lord Coleraine
1729	James, 4th Lord Kingston
1730–31	Thomas, 8th Duke of Norfolk
1731	Thomas, Lord Lovel (later Earl of Leicester)
1732	Anthony, 6th Viscount Montagu
1733	James, 7th Earl of Strathmore and Kinghorn
1734	John, 20th Earl of Crawford
1735	Thomas, 2nd Viscount Weymouth
1736	John, 4th Earl of Loudoun
1737	Edward, 2nd Earl of Darnley
1738	Henry, Marquess of Carnarvon (later 2nd Duke of Chandos)
1739	Robert, 2nd Lord Raymond

1740	John, 3rd Earl of Kintore
1741	James, 14th Earl of Morton
1742–3	John, Baron Ward (later 1st Viscount Dudley and Ward)
1744	Thomas, 8th Earl of Strathmore and Kinghorn
1745–7	James, 6th Lord Cranstoun
1747–51	William, 5th Lord Byron
1752–3	John, 1st Lord Carysfort
1754–6	James, Marquess of Carnarvon (later 3rd Duke of Chandos)
1757–62	Sholto Charles, 15th Earl of Morton
1762–4	Washington, 5th Earl Ferrers
1764–6	Cadwallader, 9th Lord Blayney
1767–72	Henry, 5th Duke of Beaufort
1772–6	Robert Edward, 9th Lord Petre
1777–82	George, 4th Duke of Manchester
1782–90	HRH Henry Frederick, Duke of Cumberland
1790–1813	HRH George, Prince of Wales (later King George IV)
1813	HRH Augustus Frederick, Duke of Sussex

Antient Grand Lodge:

1753	Robert Turner
1754–6	Hon. Edward Vaughan
1756–60	William, 1st Earl of Blessinton
1760–5	Thomas Alexander, 6th Earl of Kellie
1766–70	Hon. Thomas Mathew
1771–4	John, 3rd Duke of Atholl
1775–81	John, 4th Duke of Atholl
1783–91	Randall William, 6th Earl & 2nd Marquess of Antrim
1791–1813	John, 4th Duke of Atholl
1813	HRH Edward, Duke of Kent

United Grand Lodge

1813–43	HRH Augustus Frederick, Duke of Sussex
1844–70	Thomas, 2nd Earl of Zetland
1870–4	George Frederick Samuel, Earl De Grey and Ripon (later 1st Marquess of Ripon)

1874–1901	HRH Albert Edward, Prince of Wales (later King Edward VII)
1901–39	HRH Arthur, Duke of Connaught and Strathearn
1939–42	HRH George, Duke of Kent
1942–7	Henry, 6th Earl of Harewood
1947–50	Edward William Spencer, 10th Duke of Devonshire
1951–67	Lawrence Roger, 11th Earl of Scarbrough
1967	HRH Edward, Duke of Kent

It was the practice of both the Premier and United Grand Lodge to elect Princes of the Blood and foreign royalty who were Masons to the rank of Past Grand Master:

Premier Grand Lodge

1767	HRH Edward Augustus, Duke of York
1767	HRH William Henry, Duke of Gloucester
1767	HRH Frederick, Duke of Cumberland
1787	HRH William Henry, Duke of Clarence (later King William IV)
1787	HRH Frederick, Duke of York
1790	HRH Edward, Duke of Kent
1796	HRH William Frederick, Duke of Gloucester
1796	HRH Ernest Augustus, Duke of Cumberland
1805	HRH Augustus Frederick, Duke of Sussex
1810	HE Mirza Abul Assam Khan

United Grand Lodge:

1869	HRH Albert Edward, Prince of Wales (later King Edward VII)
1888	HM Oscar II, King of Sweden
1890	HRH Arthur, Duke of Connaught and Strathearn
1897	HRH The Crown Prince of Denmark (later King Frederick VIII)
1936	HM King Edward VIII (later HRH Duke of Windsor)
1937	HM King George VI
1946	HM Christian X, King of Denmark

1947	HM Gustav V Adolf, King of Sweden
1966	HM Gustav VI Adolf, King of Sweden

With the election of HRH the Duke of Cumberland as Grand Master in 1782 the precedent of appointing an Acting Grand Master when a Royal Grand Master was elected was introduced. The holder is now styled Pro Grand Master.

Premier Grand Lodge:

1782–9	Thomas, 3rd Earl of Effingham
1790–1813	Francis, 2nd Earl of Moira (later 1st Marquess of Hastings)

United Grand Lodge:

1834–9	Lawrence, 1st Earl of Zetland
1839–40	John George, 1st Earl of Durham
1840–4	Thomas, 2nd Earl of Zetland
1874–90	Henry Howard Molyneux, 4th Earl of Carnarvon
1891–8	Edward, 1st Earl of Lathom
1899–1908	William Archer, 3rd Earl Amherst
1908–35	Arthur, 2nd Lord Ampthill
1935	Fiennes Stanley Wykeham, 1st Lord Cornwallis
1935–42	Henry, 6th Earl of Harewood
1967–9	Lawrence Roger, 11th Earl of Scarbrough
1969–82	William Gerald Charles, 7th Earl Cadogan
1982–91	Fiennes Neil Wykeham, 3rd Lord Cornwallis
1991–	Barry Owen Somerset Maxwell, 12th Baron Farnham

Appendix B

THE STRUCTURE OF THE CRAFT IN ENGLAND

Craft Freemasonry is governed by the *Book of Constitutions*, which is the codification of a body of rules and regulations that have evolved and been adapted as the Craft has developed. No alteration may be made to any of the rules without the consent of Grand Lodge itself, and this requires notice of motion to be given at one Quarterly Communication followed by a duly proposed and seconded resolution at the next Quarterly Communication. The *Book of Constitutions* defines the constituent parts of the Craft from the Grand Lodge itself to the basic unit: the lodge. It lays down the duties and prerogatives of constituent officers; the regulations governing the holding of Grand, Provincial and District Grand Lodges and individual lodges; it regulates all matters pertaining to the Craft.

The Grand Lodge consists of the Grand Officers for the year, past Grand Officers who remain subscribing members of English lodges, the Master and Wardens of all lodges under the Grand Lodge, and Past Masters who remain subscribing members of lodges under the Grand Lodge. It is the ultimate authority. It has the sole authority to enact new legislation, alter or repeal old, to erase or suspend lodges, and to expel members from the Craft. It sets and controls the finances of Grand Lodge, laying down minimum fees and dues and approving, or not, the annual accounts. Whilst it is the final arbiter in the most areas, in that of the ritual it chooses to recommend rather than legislate, believing that, provided the landmarks are observed, the manner of conducting the ceremonies is the prerogative of each individual lodge.

The Grand Master stands at the head of the Craft but is a constitutional rather than an autocratic ruler. He is subject to annual election by Grand

Lodge but the practice has evolved of re-electing the Grand Master till such time as he chooses to retire or is removed by death, thus providing a continuity of leadership lacking in many other Grand Lodges. It is his prerogative to appoint all Grand Officers with the exception of the Grand Treasurer, who has to be annually elected by Grand Lodge. Appointment to Grand Rank is an honour for services to the Craft and is made either to an active office or in the form of a *Past* or *brevet* rank, i.e. the appointee is honoured with a particular rank without actually serving in it. The Grand Master has the sole right to grant petitions to form new lodges, which have to be formally consecrated by the Grand Master or a suitable brother deputed to act on his behalf. If for any reason a lodge should fail, the warrant and lodge books have to be returned to the Grand Master. He has the sole authority to grant special warrants to mark centenaries and bicentenaries of lodges; to approve lodge by-laws, jewels, crests, badges and banners. He has the right to nominate eight members of the Board of General Purposes. He may suggest policy and request reports but has no authority to enact legislation or rule by edict.

The Board of General Purposes is the policy-making body. It is often compared to the Cabinet in British politics, but this is misleading as the Board has no authority to rule or enact legislation. It may report or make recommendatons but its reports and decisions have to be ratified at a meeting of the Grand Lodge. The Board comprises three types of members: eight appointed by the Grand Master, whose appointment lasts as long as the Grand Master wishes; twenty-four elected members, of whom twelve are elected by London lodges and twelve by the Provinces and must stand for re-election after three years of service; and *ex officio* members who serve as long as they hold their office in Grand Lodge. The Board is chaired by a President who is appointed by the Grand Master and a Vice-President who is chosen annually from among the members of the Board. To assist in its deliberations the Board has seven Committees covering Finance; Procedure; Premises; External Relations; Staff; Library, Art and Publications; and Information.

Masonically, England and Wales are divided into Provinces, based roughly on the old counties with the largest (Yorkshire, Lancashire and Kent) divided into two Provinces. Each Province is headed by a Provincial Grand Master who is appointed by the Grand Master and holds office until he retires, dies or reaches the age of 75. The Provincial Grand Master is the representative of the Grand Master in his Province and all lodges within its boundaries come under his rule. He has the right of recommending, or denying, petitions for new lodges and of consecrating lodges which result from successful petitions. He must call a meeting of his Provincial Grand Lodge at least once a year and is empowered to appoint Provincial Grand Officers, on a sliding scale according to the size of the Province, and to honour members of the Province with appointments to Past Provincial ranks. He is the ultimate authority within his Province and has the power to discipline lodges or brethren within the Province who have committed Masonic offences.

London, which for Masonic purposes is defined as an area within a radius of ten miles of Freemasons' Hall and which contains almost 1700 lodges, does not have Provincial or Metropolitan status. Its lodges come directly under the control of the Grand Master and are administered from Freemasons' Hall. Recognition of services to London Masonry is given by the Grand Master annually appointing recommended Past Masters of London lodges to London Grand Rank and promoting others to Senior London Grand Rank.

The United Lodge of England still has over 700 lodges working in various parts of the world outside England and Wales. Where there are sufficient lodges in a particular area they are formed into a District Grand Lodge, headed by a District Grand Master, which functions in the same way as a Provincial Grand Lodge. Where there are only two or three lodges an Inspectorate can be formed with a Grand Inspector appointed by the Grand Master. Lodges not coming under a District or Inspectorate come directly under the rule of the Grand Master and are administered from Freemasons' Hall. Members of lodges abroad not under Districts may be honoured by the Grand Master with appointment to Overseas Grand Rank.

The basic unit in the Craft is the lodge, ruled over by its Master. To be constitutional a lodge must have received a warrant from the Grand Master (the document must be present at every meeting for the proceedings to be regular) and have been formally constituted or consecrated. The Master of the lodge must have served as a Warden for twelve months and have been elected by a ballot of the members 'in open lodge assembled'. He is the ultimate authority in the lodge and has a duty to see that the *Book of Constitutions*, Grand Lodge Regulations, and by-laws are strictly complied with. He has the right to appoint all the lodge officers with the exception of the Treasurer (elected by ballot) and the Tyler (elected by a show of hands). The Master must be elected annually and may not serve for more than two years running without a special dispensation from the Grand Master. Such dispensations are rarely given. The principal work of the lodge is the working of the ceremonies of Initiation, Passing and Raising and the Installation of the Master. The remainder of the meeting is taken up with administrative matters necessary for the running of the lodge. A candidate for initiation must be proposed and seconded by two members of the lodge who have known him for some time. He is then proposed in open lodge, after which he is interviewed by a Committee of Members. If he and his reasons for wishing to join the Craft prove acceptable his details will appear on the summons for the next meeting, when a ballot will be held. Most lodges have some form of committee which has no authority in itself but can only make recommendations. Any proposed changes or resolution must be formally proposed and seconded in lodge and be subject to a vote of those present. In some matters, particularly financial, notice of motion is required before a formal proposition is made so that adequate time can be given to the members to consider the matter before a decision is taken.

Whilst all lodges have the right, conferred by their warrant, to make Masons, certain types of lodges choose not to exercise that right. Most Provinces have at least one Installed Masters' Lodge, the membership of which is made up of Masters and Past Masters of lodges in the Province, or a part of it. Similarly, many Provinces have a Provincial Grand Stewards' Lodge, membership of which is limited to those who hold or have held the office of Provincial Grand Steward. The 'work' at their meetings usually takes the form of a lecture on some aspect of Freemasonry or a demonstration of a particular 'working' of the ritual. In addition there are a number of Lodges of Research the members of which give and discuss papers on some aspect of Freemasonry.

Appendix C

CHRONOLOGY

c.1390	Regius MS Old Charges.
c.1420	Cooke MS Old Charges
1583	Grand Lodge No. 1 MS Old Charges.
1621	'Making of masons' in London Masons' Company.
1646	Elias Ashmole initiated at Warrington.
c.1672	Randle Holmes's lodge at Chester.
1676	Accepted Masons mentioned in *Poor Robin's Intelligence*.
1682	Ashmole summoned to a meeting at Masons' Hall, London.
1686	Society of Free Masons mentioned in Plot's *Natural History of Staffordshire* and Aubrey's *Natural History of Wiltshire*.
1688	Society of Freemasons mentioned in Randle Holme's *Academie of Armoury*.
1691	Aubrey's date for Sir Christopher Wren's initiation.
1693	York No. 4 MS Old Charges lists of lodge members.
1694	Anderson claims eight lodges working in London.
1698	Anti-masonic leaflet printed in London.
1705	Scarborough MS Old Charges list members of a lodge at Scarborough. First records of the lodge at York.
1709	Free Masons' modes of recognition mentioned in *The Tatler*.
1710	George Grey made a mason at Bedale.
1713	York lodge makes eighteen masons at Bradford.
1716	Members of London lodges resolve to form a Grand Lodge.
1717	Formation of the premier Grand Lodge of England by four London lodges and installation of Anthony Sayer as first Grand Master.

1721	2nd Duke of Montagu installed as the first 'noble Grand Master'.
1723	Andersons's *Constitutions* published.
	William Cowper appointed first Secretary to Grand Lodge.
	Grand Lodge Minutes begun.
	First registration of members.
	First extant minute book of a private lodge.
1725	First mention of the third degree.
	First Provincial Grand Masters appointed.
	Charity Committee established.
	Second registration of members.
1727	Nathaniel Blackerby appointed Treasurer of Grand Lodge.
1728	Lodges constituted in Gibraltar and India.
	First Grand Stewards appointed.
	Third registration of members
1730	Prichard's *Masonry Dissect'd* published.
1731	First Regulations concerning aprons and collars.
1737	Frederick Lewis, Prince of Wales, initiated, the first English royal Freemason.
1738	Anderson's second edition of the *Constitutions*.
	First Papal Bull against Freemasonry.
1741	Earliest record of the Royal Order of Scotland, in London.
1744	First undisputed printed reference to the Royal Arch.
1746	Laurence Dermott exalted in Dublin.
1747	Grand Lodge prohibits public processions for the Grand Feast.
1751	Antients Grand Lodge formed in London.
1753	First extant minute of the making of Royal Arch masons in the lodge at Fredericksburg, Virginia.
1754	Thomas Dunckerley exalted in his lodge at Portsmouth.
1761	Grand Lodge of all England revived at York.
1762	New printed exposures of the ritual begin to appear in England.
1766	Grand and Royal Arch Chapter formed by Charter of Compact.
1768	Premier Lodge begins registration of members.
1776	Freemasons' Hall dedicated in London.
1777	First English record of a masonic Knight Templar, at Portsmouth.

1779	Grand Lodge South of the River Trent formed in London.
1782	HRH Henry Frederick, Duke of Cumberland, installed as first Royal Grand Master.
1788	Royal Masonic Institution for Girls formed.
1790	HRH George, Prince of Wales, elected Grand Master. First record of conferal of Royal Ark Mariner, at Bath.
1791	Grand Conclave of Knights Templar formed by Dunckerley.
1798	Royal Masonic Institution for Boys founded.
1799	Freemasonry exempted from provision of the Unlawful Societies Act.
1809	Lodge of Promulgation warranted. Negotiations towards a Union of the two Grand Lodges opened.
1813	HRH Augustus Frederick, Duke of Sussex, installed as Grand Master of the premier Grand Lodge.
	HRH Edward, Duke of Kent installed as Grand Master of the Antients Grand Lodge.
	Union of the two Grand Lodges to form the United Grand Lodge.
1814	Standard patterns for regalia introduced.
1815	New Book of Constitutions issued for discussion.
1816	Grand Lodge agrees the new ritual devised by the Lodge of Reconciliation.
1817	Supreme Grand Chapter formed.
1818	HRH the Duke of Sussex receives a patent from France to form a Supreme Council of the Ancient and Accepted Rite.
1819	Liverpool Rebellion leading to the formation of the Wigan Grand Lodge.
1827	Craft Installation ceremony agreed.
1834	Special Committee formed to revise Royal Arch Ritual.
	Chapter of Promulgation chartered.
1837	Grand Lodge Library and Museum formed.
1842	Royal Masonic Benevolent Institution formed.
1845	Grand Conclave of Knights Templar revived. Supreme Council, Ancient and Accepted Rite formed.
1856	Grand Lodge of Mark Master Masons formed.
	Ontario lodges withdraw from Grand Lodge to form the first independent colonial Grand Lodge.

1865	Societas Rosicruciana in Anglia formed.
	Grand Council of the Red Cross of Constantine formed.
1869	New Freemasons' Hall building opened.
1872	Grand Council of Royal and Select Masters formed.
1874	Marquess of Ripon resigns as Grand Master on becoming a Roman Catholic.
	HRH Albert Edward, Prince of Wales, elected Grand Master.
1879	Grand Council of the Allied Masonic Degrees formed.
1887	Especial Grand Lodge to celebrate Golden Jubilee of Queen Victoria.
	Grand Council of the Order of the Secret Monitor formed.
1888	Centenary of the Royal Masonic Institution for Girls.
1897	Especial Grand Lodge to celebrate the Diamond Jubilee of Queen Victoria.
1898	Centenary of Royal Masonic Institution for Boys.
1901	Edward VII becomes Grand Protector of the Order. HRH Arthur, Duke of Connaught, installed as Grand Master.
1908	London Rank instituted.
1913	Worshipful Society of Free Masons, Wallers, Slaters, Paviours, Plaisterers and Bricklayers (the Operatives) formed.
1916	First Freemasons' War Hospital opened in London.
1917	Bicentenary of Grand Lodge celebrated.
1919	Masonic Million Memorial Fund opened.
1923	Grand Council of Knight Templar Priests formed.
1926	Overseas Rank instituted.
1933	Present Freemasons' Hall dedicated.
	Royal Masonic Hospital opened by King George V and Queen Mary.
1936	King Edward VIII (HRH Duke of Windsor) elected a Past Grand Master.
	King George VI elected a Past Grand Master.
1937	Brig. Gen. W. H. V. Darrell, CB, CMG, DSO, appointed first Assistant Grand Master.
1939	HRH Duke of Connaught resigns as Grand Master.
	HRH George, Duke of Kent installed as Grand Master by King George VI.
	Temporary suspension of meetings due to declaration of war.

1942	Earl of Harewood installed as Grand Master by King George VI.
1952	Earl of Scarbrough installed as Grand Master.
1964	Debate on the Penalties in the Obligations.
1966	Bi-centenary of Supreme Grand Chaper celebrated.
1967	250th Anniversary of Grand Lodge celebrated.
	HRH Edward, Duke of Kent installed as Grand Master.
	£594,850 Trust Fund set up, the income to be administered by the Royal College of Surgeons.
1974	Bagnall Report on the Charities published.
1979	Masonic Foundation for the Aged and Sick formed.
1981	Grand Charity formed.
1982	Masonic Trust for Girls and Boys formed.
1986	Removal of physical penalties from the obligations approved by Grand Lodge.
1989	Major revision of the Royal Arch ritual approved by Supreme Grand Chapter.
1990	New Masonic Samaritan Fund established.
	Annual Assembly of Royal Ark Mariners revived.
1991	Bi-centenary of Great Priory celebrated.
1992	275th Anniversary of Grand Lodge, 25th Anniversary as Grand Master of HRH The Duke of Kent and 40th Anniversary of the Accession of HM The Queen celebrated by 12,500 Freemasons and their guests at Earls Court, followed by a dinner for 4,000.

NOTES

[The abbreviation *AQC* refers to *Ars Quatuor Coronatorum*, the Transactions of Quatuor Coronati Lodge No. 2076]

1. Theories of Origin

1 James Anderson, *The Constitutions of the Free-Masons. Containing the history, charges, regulations &c. of that most Ancient and Right Worshipful Fraternity* (London, 1723).

2 For a discussion of the York Legend see Begemann *AQC* 6 (1893); Gould *AQC* 5 (1892); Oliver *AQC* 61 (1948); Speth *AQC* 6 (1893); and Alex Horne, *The York Legend in the Old Charges* (Shepperton A Lewis, 1978).

3 Anderson is the only source for the claim that the events of 1717 were a revival.

4 The pocket companions began to appear in 1735 and were a mixture of plagiarisms of Anderson's rules and history together with various Charges and Orations.

5 See Douglas Knoop, 'The Mason Word', *AQC* 51 (1938).

6 The most recent summing up of the operative-transitional-speculative theory is Harry Carr's *600 Years of Craft Ritual*, the last version of which appeared in his posthumous *Harry Carr's World of Freemasonry* (London: A Lewis, 1984).

7 See C. F. W. Dyer, 'Some thoughts on the Origin of Speculative Masonry', *AQC* 95 (1982).

8 Andrew Durr 'The origin of the Craft', *AQC* 96 (1983),

9 Henry Sadler, *Masonic facts and fictions* (London, 1887). Reprinted Wellingborough (Aquarian Press), 1984.

10 See J. S. M. Ward, *Freemasonry and the Antient Gods*, 2nd ed (London, 1926); A. E. Waite, *The secret tradition in Freemasonry*, (London, 1911).

11 Alfred Dodd, *Shakespeare: Creator of Freemasonry*, (London, *c.*1935) and *Was Shakespeare the Creator of the Rituals of Freemasonry?* (Liverpool, n.d.).

2. The Pre-1717 English Evidence

1 On Scottish operative masonry see H. Carr *AQC* 67 (1954); E. Macbean *ACQ* 7 (1894); R. J. Meekren *AQC* 53 (1940); D. Murray Lyon, *History of the Lodge of Edinburgh (Mary's Chapel) No. 1. Embracing an account of the rise and progress of Freemasonry in Scotland*, 2nd ed (Glasgow, 1900); R. F. Gould, *History of Freemasonry* Vol. 1, (London, 1882); David Stevenson, *The first Freemasons. Scotland's early Lodges and their members*, (Aberdeen University Press, 1988) and *The origins of Freemasonry; Scotland's century 1690–1710*, (Cambridge University Press, 1988).

2 See W. H. Rylands, 'The Alnwick Lodge Minutes, *AQC* 14 (1901) and William Waples, 'The Swalwell Lodge', *AQC* 62 (1949).

3 Eric Ward, 'The crisp English word Freemasonry', *AQC* 68 1955).

4 The most complete List of the Old Charges in print is to be found in Vol. 1 of Revd Poole's revision of Gould's *History of Freemasonry* (*c.*1952) which should be read in conjunction with Prof. Wallace McLeod's 'Additions to the List of Old Charges', *AQC* 96 (1983).

5 A comparison of the Cooke and Grand Lodge MSS is given in the appendix to C. F. W. Dyer's 'Some thoughts on the origins . . .' *AQC* 95 (1982).

6 C. F. W. Dyer, *op. cit.*

7 Harry Carr's comments appeared in his review of Dr. C. H. Josten's *Elias Ashmole 1617–1692* (Oxford University Press, 1966), in *AQC* 79 (1966),

8 The main source is Conder's *Hole Craft and Fellowship* and his papers in *AQC* 9 (1896) and 27 (1914).

9 Harry Carr, *600 Years of Craft Ritual, op. cit.*

10 See W. H. Rylands, 'Freemasonry in the 17th century: Chester 1650–1700', in The Masonic Magazine 103 (January) and 104 (February) 1882.

11 Andrew Durr, 'The origin of the Craft', *AQC* 96 (1983).

12 The Scarborough MS is now the property of the Grand Lodge of Canada in the Province of Ontario. A facsimile and transcript were published in *Quatuor Coronati Antihrapha* Vol. 5 (1984).

13 For the York Grand Lodge and its appendent bodies see G. Y. Johnson in *AQC* 52 (1939), 53 (1940), 57 (1944) and 58 (1945).

3. The Grand Lodge System

1 Anthony Sayer was the subject of T. Beck's Prestonian Lecture for 1975, which should be read in conjunction with the discussion of it in *AQC* 88 (1975).

2 For Desaguliers see J. Stokes, *AQC* 38 (1925) and for the Royal Society and Freemasonry see J. E. S. Tucket *AQC* 28 (1915) and J. R. Clarke *AQC* 80 (1967).

3 The revival theory is discussed in the various introductions to the Quatuor Coronati facsimile reprints of Anderson's 1738 *Constitutions*.

4 Henry Sadler, *Masonic facts and fictions* (London, 1887). Reprinted Wellingborough (Aquarian Press), 1984.

5 See L. Vibert *AQC* 36 (1923) and his introduction to the Quaritch 1923 facsimile reprint of Anderson's 1723 *Constitutions*.

6 Up to 1737 the Grand Secretary was simply Secretary to the Grand Lodge. Many of the early incumbents were lawyers and ran Grand Lodge affairs from their offices until the first Hall was built in 1776.

7 The first Minute Book of the premier Grand Lodge contains three lists of members of lodges dated 25 November 1723, 27 November 1725, and 1730. Thereafter there were no central registers until 1768.

8 The engraved *Lists of Lodges* first appeared in 1723 and continued to 1778, when they were superseded by the *Freemasons' Calendar*. All issues are exceedingly rare.

9 The first Provincial Grand Masters were Col. Francis Columbine for Cheshire (1725) and Gen. Hugh Warburton for Cheshire and North Wales (1727).

10 Whilst the Grand Lodge was establishing its authority there were regular complaints of Masons being made irregularly or clandestinely, i.e. being made in places other than a duly constituted lodge under the authority of the Grand Lodge.

11 Since Frederick Lewis was initiated in 1737 some twenty-two members of the Royal Family have involved themselves in Freemasonry.

12 The texts of the early exposures are printed in D. Knoop, G. P. Jones, and D. Hamer, *Early Masonic Catechisms*, edn. (London: Quatuor Coronati, 1963).

13 Samuel Prichard, *Masonry Dissect'd* (London, 1730). A facsimile, with an introduction by Harry Carr, was published by the Masonic Book Club (USA) in 1977.

14 Walpole was writing to a friend commenting upon the effects of the 1738 Papal Bull on Freemasonry in Europe and the complete lack of public reaction to it in England.

15 The premier Grand Lodge renumbered its lodges in 1729, 1740, 1755, 1770, 1780, 1781 (an error occurring in 1780), 1792. The Antients Grand Lodge did not renumber but regularly re-issued the numbers or documents of erased lodges. The United Grand Lodge had renumberings in 1814, 1832, 1863.

16 See W. I. Grantham on the Incorporation in *AQC* 46 (1933) and 47 (1934).

17 The standard work on Dunckerley is Henry Sadler's *Thomas Dunckerley, His Life, Labours and Letters* (London, 1891). More readable is R. Chudley's *Thomas Dunckerley. A Remarkable Freemason* (London: A. Lewis, 1982).

18 On Moira see J. M. Hamill in *AQC* 93 (1980); P. J Dawson in *Transactions*

Lodge of Research No. 2429, Leicester, for 1976 and 1978; H. V. Lorey in Grand Lodge of Scotland *Year Book* 1963.

19 Abbé Barruel, *Memoire, illustrating the History of Jacobinism*, 2nd edn. (London, 1798). J. Robison, *Proofs of a Conspiracy Against all Religions and Governments of Europe, carried on in secret meetings of Free Masons, Illuminati, and Reading Societies* (Edinburgh, 1797).

20 39 GEO.III, *c*.79. An Act for the more effectual suppression of Societies established for seditious and treasonable purposes . . . 12 July 1799.

21 C. N. Batham, 'The Grand Lodge of England according to the Old Institutions', The Prestonian Lecture for 1981. Reprinted, with discussion, in *AQC* 94 (1981).

22 L. Dermott, *Ahiman Rezon: or, a help to a brother* (London, 1756). As the *Constitutions* of the Antients Grand Lodge further editions were published in 1764, 1778, 1787, 1800, 1801, 1807 and 1813.

23 G. P. Hills, 'Brother William Preston', Prestonian Lecture for 1927. Reprinted in *Collected Prestonian Lectures Vol. 1* (London: A. Lewis, 1984). W. Preston, *Illustrations of Masonry*, reprinted with an introduction by C. F. W. Dyer, Wellingborough (Aquarian Press), 1985.

24 Henry Sadler, 'An Unrecorded Grand Lodge', *AQC* 18 (1905) and 22 (1909).

25 P. J. Dawson, 'Thomas Harper', in *Transactions*, Lodge of Research No. 2429, Leicester, 1982.

26 HRH Edward, Duke of Kent, had been initiated in La Loge l'Union des Coeurs, Geneva in 1789. He was elected a Past Grand Master in 1790 and appointed Provincial Grand Master for Gibraltar and Andalusia in the same year. In the Antients Grand Lodge he was appointed Provincial Grand Master for Lower Canada in 1792 and elected Grand Master in 1813. Augustus Frederick, Duke of Sussex, had been initiated in Lodge Victorious Truth, Berlin, in 1798. On returning to England he joined various English lodges; he was elected a Past Grand Master of the premier Grand Lodge in 1805, Deputy Grand Master in 1812 and Grand Master in 1813.

27 See T. O. Haunch, 'It is not in the power of any man'—A Study in Change', the Prestonian Lecture for 1972. Reprinted with discussion in *AQC* 85 (1972). Sir James Stubbs, 'The Government of the Craft', the Prestonian Lecture for 1982. Reprinted with discussion in *AQC* 95 (1982).

28 See M. J. Spurr, 'The Liverpool Rebellion', *AQC* 85 (1972).

29 E. B. Beesley, *The History of the Wigan Grand Lodge* (Manchester, 1920).

30 *The Masonic Observer and Grand Lodge Chronicle*, 1856–9.

31 P. R. James in *Grand Lodge 1717–1967*.

32 J. W. Stubbs, 'Building a Temple 1927–33', *AQC* 89 (1976).

33 The Prince of Wales (later King Edward VIII and Duke of Windsor) was

initiated in Household Brigade Lodge No. 2614 in 1919; Senior Grand Warden 1921; Provincial Grand Master for Surrey 1924–1936, and elected a Past Grand Master in 1936 on his accession to the throne. Albert, Duke of York (later King George VI), was initiated in Navy Lodge No. 2612 in 1919; Senior Grand Warden in 1923; Provincial Grand Master for Middlesex 1924–36; Grand Master of Scotland 1936; elected a Past Grand Master on his accession to the throne in 1936. George, Duke of Kent, was initiated in Navy Lodge No. 2612 in 1928, Senior Grand Warden in 1933; Provincial Grand Master for Wiltshire 1934–39; Grand Master 1939–42.

34 The penalties debate was opened by J. R. Rylands with his paper, and the subsequent discussion, in *AQC* 77 (1964). The official record of the debate is in the *Proceedings* of Grand Lodge for 10 June, 9 September, and 9 December 1964.

35 The relevant portion of the Grand Master's Address is reprinted herein on pp. 144–5.

4. The Development of the Lodge

1 The lodge was constituted on 2 February 1726 to meet at the Swan and Rummer, Finch Lane, London and lapsed in 1751. Its constitution and records were transferred to Stockton-on-Tees in 1755, where they were preserved. The Minute Book is now on permanent loan in the Grand Lodge Library.

2 T. O. Haunch, 'The Constitution and Consecration of Lodges', in *AQC* 83 (1970).

3 J. M. Hamill, 'English Grand Lodge Warrants', *AQC* 90 (1977).

4 T. O. Haunch, *op. cit.*

5 George Claret published the first Craft ritual, as opposed to an exposure, in 1838 and immediately came into conflict with the authorities. See R. A. Wells in *AQC* 87 (1974). Printed rituals did not become acceptable until the last quarter of the nineteenth century.

6 Knoop, Jones and Hamer, *The Early Masonic Catechisms*.

7 Ibid.

8 The minutes of the Philo Musicae Society are preserved in the British Museum, Add. MS No. 23202. They are reprinted in *Quatuor Coronati Antigrapha*, Vol. 9.

9 Preston's Lectures were printed in code. For transcripts see P. R. James in *AQC* 82 (1969), 83 (1970), 85 (1972). For details of Preston MSS see T. O. Haunch *AQC* 85 (1972) and for bibliographical details C. F. W. Dyer in *AQC* 89 (1976).

10 J. Browne, *The Master-Key of a Free-Mason's Lodge* (London, 1789); 2nd edn.

London, 1802. Originally printed in code there are typescript transcripts by E. H. Cartwright in the Grand Lodge Library.

11 William Finch began publishing his lectures of the Craft in 1801 and continued to issue them in print and manuscript up to 1814.

12 See W. B. Hextall's papers i n *AQC* 23 (1910), 24 (1911), 29 (1916).

13 See W. Wonnacott's paper in *AQC* 23 (1910).

14 C. F. W. Dyer, 'The Official 1816 Ritual?, *AQC* 88 (1976).

15 As a result of the lack of an officially controlled ritual there are over forty printed workings in the Grand Lodge Library, by no means a complete collection.

16 See W. Read in *AQC* 84 (1971).

17 R. A. Wells, 'The Tyler or Outer Guard', Prestonian Lecture for 1977. Printed with discussion in *AQC* 90 (1977).

18 See T. O. Haunch on Tracing Boards in *AQC* 75 (1962).

19 S. Bruce, 'Not only Ancient but useful and necessary . . . the Deacons', Prestonian Lecture 1985. Reprinted with discussion in *AQC* 98 (1985).

20 Grand Lodge's ruling on vocal music was agreed at the December 1916 meeting and re-confirmed in March 1963, *vide Proceedings*.

5. The Social Side

1 The definitive history of the Grand Stewards and their lodge was written by C. F. W. Dyer and published by the Grand Stewards' Lodge for their 250th Anniversary in 1985.

2 See W. Wonnacott in *AQC* 36 (1923) and J. M. Hamill in *AQC* 89 (1976).

3 N. Rogers produced various articles comprising humorous extracts from lodge minute books in various issues of *The Masonic Record* in 1949.

4 From the ritual changes of 1816 begins the development of local Masonic Halls and lodge rooms as permanent meeting places.

5 The songs in Anderson's 1723 *Constitutions* were The Master's Song, The Warden's Song, The Fellow Craft's Song, The Enter'd' Prentices Song, with music for all but the Fellow Craft's Song.

6 Serving brethren are admitted to all three degrees but pay no initiation fee or lodge dues and are not permitted to visit as Masons. Today the practice is usually reserved for those who are employed as caretakers for lodge buildings and generally act as Tyler for the lodges meeting there.

7 The List of Music in Oxford's history of Lodge No. 4 is impressive, containing a considerable amount of instrumental music, now regrettably lost.

8 Dr. Arne and Salomon (promoter of Haydn) regularly held concerts at Freemasons' Hall. In addition to concerts, play readings, and social events

the Hall was also used for meetings of learned societies and other organizations such as the Bible Society and the Anti-Slavery Society.

9 For Freemasonry and the theatre see H. W. Pedicord, 'White Gloves at Eight', *AQC* 93 (1980).

10 The earliest traced prologue and epilogue were for a performance sponsored by Grand Lodge on 30 December 1728 at the Theatre Royal, Drury Lane. The texts are in Knoop, Jones, and Hamer, *Early Masonic Pamphlets* (London: Quatuor Coronati, 1978).

6. English Freemasonry Abroad

The sources for this Chapter are the official archives and printed *Proceedings* of the United Grand Lodge of England and its predecessors.

7. The English Royal Arch

1 See W. J. Hughan, *Origins of the English Rite*; B. E. Jones *Freemasons' Book of the Royal Arch*, etc.

2 Vibert in an unpublished lecture attempted to show that the Royal Arch had developed from a split in the Installation ceremony, which did not then exist!

3 Harry Carr, 'The Relationship between the Craft and the Royal Arch', *In Harry Carr's World of Freemasonry* (London: A. Lewis, 1983).

4 The lodge was constituted at the Lord Blakeney's Head, Bristol, on 17 February 1757. It was meeting at the Crown in Christmas Street, Bristol, when the Royal Arch was worked but was erased by Grand Lodge in 1769.

5 J. R. Dashwood in *AQC* 64 (1951).

6 See A. R. Hewitt, 'The Supreme Grand Chapter of England. A brief history from Blayney to Sussex', reprinted in *AQC* 78 (1965) For the Minutes see J. R. Dashwood in *AQC* 62 (1949) and 72 (1959).

7 For Dermott see C. C. Adams *AQC* 46 (1933); J. H. Lepper *AQC* 44 (1931); G. W. Speth *AQC* 5 (1982). C. N. Batham's Prestonian Lecture in *AQC*.

8 On the Antients Grand Chapter see B. E. Jones, *Freemasons' Book of the Royal Arch*, Rev. edn. (London, 1969); A. R. Hewitt (see note 6 above); C. N. Batham, AQC 98 (1985).

9 A. R. Hewitt, *op. cit.*

10 Royal Arch ritual evidence pre-1780 is singularly lacking. There are some six French MSS, in brief skeleton form describing ceremonies with the title Royal Arch but no evidence to show how they relate to England.

11 For the Dovre Royal Arch ritual *see* N. Hackney in *AQC* 72 (1959) and for the Sheffield MS J. R. Clarke in *AQC* 93 (1980).

12 See J. M. Hamill in *AQC* 95 (1982).

13 *Proceedings*, Supreme Grand Chapter of England.

14 John Bunyan, *Solomon's Temple Spiritualised* (London, 1688). The work was regularly reprinted during the author's life and throughout the eighteenth century.

15 The first printed Royal Arch ritual, as opposed to an exposure, printed after the alterations of 1834–35 was George Claret's published in 1845.

16 See *Proceedings Supreme Grand Chapter of England* 1987–1989.

8. The Additional Degrees and Orders

1 The best general survey of the Additional Degrees is Keith Jackson, *Beyond the Craft* (Shepperton: A. Lewis, 1980).

2 See T. M. Greensill, *History of the SRIA*. London (SRIA), 1987. Westcott's writings on the SRIA are notoriously inaccurate, even when dealing with events in which he was concerned.

3 The Prince of Wales (later King Edward VII) and his successors the Dukes of Connaught and Kent were all Grand Masters of the Craft, Mark and Knights Templars, First Grand Principals in the Royal Arch, and Patrons of the Ancient and Accepted Rite.

4 Revd. Walton Hannah, *Christian by Degrees* (London, 1951). Hannah left his Ministry in the Anglican Church to devote his life to exposing Freemasonry. He later converted to Rome. He was apt to read, very unconvincingly, Christian liturgy and sacraments into decidely non-liturgical or theological Masonic rituals.

5 R. Le Forestier, *La Franc-Mąonnerie Templieṙe et Occultiste* (Paris, 1970).

6 Ellic Howe's 'Fringe Masonry', *AQC* 85 (1972), was the first serious study of the subject.

7 Ellic Howe *op. cit.* Yarker's journal *The Kneph* is the major source for the history of the Antient and Primitive Rite.

8 J. A. Grantham, An Introduction to Mark Masonry, 2nd edn. (Buxton, 1935). J. A. Grantham, *History of the Grand Lodge of Mark Master Masons* (London, 1960). R. M. Handfield-Jones, *A New and Comprehensive History of the Grand Lodge of Mark Master Masons* (London, 1969).

9 MS Minutes of the United Grand Lodge of England, 5 March and 4 June 1856. The correspondence columns of *The Masonic Magazine* are also an important source.

10 Keith Jackson, *op. cit.*

11 R. M. Handfield-Jones, *The Royal Ark Mariner Degree. Its History and Origins* (London, 1968).

12 Morton Edwards took over the so-called Grand Lodge of Royal Ark Mariners from the aged John Dorrington, who had been involved in it in the 1820s.

Edwards' Grand Lodge met on a number of occasions in 1871 (report in *The Freemason*) before he began negotiating with the Mark authorities. His machinations and eventual acceptance of cash for his interest in the Mariner degree led to his speedy disappearance from Masonic life.

13 R. L. Wilkinson, *The Cryptic Rite—An Historical Treatise* (London, 1968).

14 H. H. C. Prestige, *A Century of the Allied Masonic Degrees* (London, 1979).

15 R. L. Wilkinson, *History of the Order of the Secret Monitor 1887–1963* (London, 1964).

16 Frederick Smyth, *Brethren in Chivalry: A Celebration . . . 1791–1991*. London (A. Lewis), 1991. R. M. Handfield-Jones, *Origin and history of the Knights Templar and Knights of Malta*. (London, 1973).

17 R. Le Forestier, *op. cit.*

18 For Waller Rodwell Wright see D. Caywood in *AQC* 85 (1972).

19 A. C. F. Jackson, *Rose Croix. A History of the Antient and Accepted Rite,* 2nd edn. (London: A. Lewis, 1986).

9. Masonic Charity

The main sources for this chapter are the relevant files in the Grand Lodge Library, contemporary reports, official *Proceedings* and official histories of the individual Charities.

10. Attacks on the Craft

1 Stephen Knight, *The Brotherhood* (London, 1983).

2. *The Freemason* was published weekly from 1869–1941 and then intermittently to 1951. *The Freemasons' Chronicle* was published weekly from 1875–1959. *The Masonic Record* appeared monthly from 1920–77.

3. The full text of the Grand Master's Address was printed in the *Proceedings* of the United Grand Lodge for 25 April 1984.

4. The latest revised edition of the *Book of Constitutions* is that printed in 1989. There have been subsequent amendments, in particular dealing with disciplinary procedures, copies of which are issued with the book.

5. *City Limits*, 8 July 1983.

6. Alec Mellor, *Our Separated Brethren the Freemasons* (London, 1964) gives details of the various Papal pronouncements.

7. Extract from a circular to all Lodges issued by the Grand Secretary, February 1975.

8. The revised *Code of Canon Law* as published in 1983. An English translation was published in 1983 jointly by the Canon Law Society of America and Cassell & Co., London.

9. *Guidance to Methodists on Freemasonry.* Report of the Faith and Order Committee of the Methodist Conference, 1985.
10. The evidence from Freemasonry to the Synod Working Party was published by the United Grand Lodge in pamphlet form in 1987 as *Freemasonry and Christianity. Evidence on the compatability of Freemasonry and Christianity by the United Grand Lodge of England and other Masonic authorities.*
11. *Freemasonry and Christianity are they compatible? A contribution to discussion prepared by the Working Group established by the Standing Committee of the General Synod of the Church of England.* London: Church House Publishing, 1907.
12. The *Report* was printed as Appendix 2 to the World Church and Mission Department Section of the *Assembly Reports* presented to the 1986 General Assembly of the United Reformed Church held in Blackpool on 6–9 May 1986.
13. Full texts of the statements were printed in the *Proceedings* of the United Grand Lodge for 12 December 1962 and 9 December 1981, and were issued as a press release in June 1985.
14. The relevant part of the candidate's declaration states "I . . . do declare that, unbiased by the improper solicitation of friends, and uninfluenced by mercenary or other unworthy motive, do freely offer myself as a candidate for the mysteries of Freemasonry . . .". The full text of the declaration forms Rule 162 of the *Book of Constitutions.*
15. "Tuesday Call" was a BBC Radio 4 phone-in programme. The edition on 13 November 1984 was devoted to Freemasonry and had the present Grand Secretary, Cdr. M. B. S. Higham, RN, and Stephen Knight answering listeners' questions.
16. The theory has been largely disproved and had resulted largely from a confusion between Freemasonry and the Jacobin and other pseudo-Masonic clubs which met in private and demanded oaths of secrecy.
17. A number of publications produced during the celebrations for the bicentenary of the USA showed that not only was the American Revolution not a Masonic plot but that there were as many native Freemasons opposed to the split from Britain as there were amongst the rebels.
18. The legend of Masonic involvement in 19th century South American Revolutionary and freedom movements arose from the confusingly named Loggia Lautaro, a radical political society founded in Spain and Portugal in the first decade of the 19th century. Its aim was the political emancipation of the Iberian Peninsula. It spread to the Iberian colonies in South America where its aims became the liberation of those colonies from Portuguese and Spanish rule.
19. It has often been claimed, without foundation, that most of the Bolshevik leaders had secretly become Freemasons during their various periods of exile.

The legend later developed, particularly in Nazi hands, to a full blown Zionist-Masonic-Communist plot for world domination.

20. See note 20 to Chapter 3.
21. The latest additions to conspiracy theory is Stephen Knight's claim in *The Brotherhood* that English Freemasonry already has been or is ripe for infiltration by the KGB, a suggestion that Freemasons treated with great hilarity.
22. *Daily Mail*, 26 September 1984.

BIBLIOGRAPHY AND SOURCES

A. The primary source material is to be found in the official archives preserved at Freemasons' Hall as follows:

Premier Grand Lodge: MS Minutes 1723–1813; Registers 1768–1813; Committee of Charity Minutes 1761–1813; Hall Committee Minutes 1773–1813; Lists of Lodges 1723–1778; Freemasons' Calendars 1775–1813.

Antients Grand Lodge: MS Minutes 1751–1813; Registers 1751–1813; Steward's Lodge Minutes 1764–1813; Royal Arch Registers 1784–1813.

United Grand Lodge: MS Minutes 1813–1868; Printed Proceedings 1868–in progress; Registers 1814–in progress; Freemasons' Calendars 1814–1908; Grand Lodge Year Books 1909–in progress.

Grand and Royal Chapter: MS Minutes 1766–1817; Registers 1766–1817.

Supreme Grand Chapter: MS Minutes 1817–1868; Printed Proceedings 1868–in progress; Registers 1818–in progress.

B. Quatuor Coronati Lodge No. 2076 is the premier Lodge of Masonic Research and since its formation in 1866 it has published annual volumes of *Transactions* under the title *Ars Quatuor Coronatorum (AQC)*, which form a treasure house of Masonic knowledge. A *Concise Index* to the first eighty volumes of *AQC* was published by the Lodge in 1971.

C. *Books and Papers*

Adams, C. C. Ahiman Rezon, the book of Constitutions of the Antients. *AQC* 46 (1933).

Anderson, James. *The Constitutions of the Free Masons 1723* [and] *The new book of Constitutions . . . 1738*, facsimile reprints with introductions by Ward, Vibert and Hughan. (London: Quatuor Coronati, 1978).

Armitage, F. The story of the Craft as told in the *Gentleman's Magazine. AQC* 27 (1914).

Batham, C. N. The Grand Lodge of England According to the Old Institutions. Prestonian Lecture 1981. *AQC* 94 (1981).

——, The origin of Freemasonry, a new theory. *AQC* 106 (1993).

——, Some problems of the Grand Lodge of the Antients. *AQC* 98 (1985).

Beesley, Eustace. *The Wigan Grand Lodge.* (Manchester: privately printed 1920).

Brodsky, Michel. *English Freemasonry in Europe 1717–1919. Prestonian Lecture 1994.* (London, 1994).

——, The Regular Freemason. *AQC* 106 (1993).

——, Some reflections on the origins of the Royal Arch. *AQC* 102 (1989).

Bruce, Sinclair. Not only ancient but useful officers . . . the Deacons. Prestonian Lecture 1985. *AQC* 98 (1985).

Carr, Harry. A collection of early references to the Mason Word. *AQC* 85 (1972).

——, The conjoint theory. *AQC* 66 (1953).

——, *The Freemason at work, rev. ed.* (London: A. Lewis, 1983).

——, Grand Lodge and the significance of 1717. *AQC* 73 (1960).

——, *Harry Carr's World of Freemasonry.* (London: A. Lewis, 1984).

——, Masonic after proceedings. *AQC* 78 (1965).

——, 600 years of Craft ritual. *AQC* 81 (1968).

——, The transition from operative to speculative Masonry. *AQC* 69 (1956).

Cartwright, E. H. *Commentary on the Freemasonic ritual*, 3rd ed with introductions by Harry Carr and Colin Dyer. (London: A. Lewis, 1985).

Cerza, A. Anti-Masonry. *AQC* 80 (1967).

Chudley, R. *Thomas Dunckerley—remarkable Freemason.* (Shepperton: A. Lewis, 1982).

Clarke, J. R. The establishment of the premier Grand Lodge. *AQC* 81 (1968).

——, The Royal Society and early Grand Lodge Freemasonry. *AQC* 80 (1967).

——, Was Sir Christopher Wren a Freemason? *AQC* 78 (1965).

Collected Prestonian Lectures Vol. 1 1925–1960, ed. Harry Carr, 1965 (reprint London: A. Lewis, 1985).

Collected Prestonian Lectures Vol. 2 1961–1974, ed. Cyril Batham. (London: A. Lewis, 1984).

Collected Prestonian Lectures Vol. 3 1975–1987. (Shepperton: A. Lewis, 1988).

Crowe, F. J. Masonic clothing. *AQC* 5 (1892), 6 (1893), 7 (1894).

Cryer, N. B. The Church's concern with Freemasonry. *AQC* 95 (1982).

——, The de-Christianising of the Craft. *AQC* 97 (1984).

Daniel, James W. Pure-and-Ancient Masonry. The Craft and extra-Craft Degrees, 1843–1901. *AQC* 106 (1993).

Dashwood, J. R. Falsification of the Royal Arch Charter of Compact. *AQC* 64 (1961).

——, Notes on the first Minute Book of the Excellent Grand and Royal Arch Chapter. *AQC* 62 (1949).

——, The second and third Minute Books of Grand Chapter. *AQC* 72 (1959).

Durr, Andrew. The origin of the Craft. *AQC* 96 (1983).

——, Rituals of Association and the organizations of the common people. *AQC* 100 (1987).

Dyer, C. W. F. *Emulation a ritual to remember.* (London: A. Lewis, 1973).

——, *The Grand Stewards and their Lodge.* (London: privately printed, 1985).

——, Some thoughts on the origins of speculative Freemasonry. *AQC* 95 (1982).

——, *Symbolism in Craft Masonry.* (London: A. Lewis, 1976)

——, *William Preston and his work.* (Shepperton: A. Lewis, 1987).

Firminger, W. K. The romances of Robison and Barruel. *AQC* 50 (1937).

Frere, A. S. Organisation and administration of Grand Lodge. *AQC* 80 (1967).

Gillen, Mollie. *Royal Duke: Augustus Frederick, Duke of Sussex (1773–1843).* (London: Sidgewick, 1976).

Gould, R. F. *A concise history of Freemasonry.* (London: Gale and Polden, 1923).

——, *History and antiquities of Freemasonry.* 3 vols. (London: Caxton, 1882–87).

——, *History and antiquities of Freemasonry.* 3rd ed. revised by H. Poole. 4 vols. (London: Caxton, 1951).

——, *Military Lodges, 1723–1899.* (London: Gale and Polden, 1899).

Grantham, J. A. *An introduction to Mark Masonry.* 2nd ed. (Buxton: privately printed, 1935).

——, *History of the Grand Lodge of Mark Master Masons.* (London: privately printed, 1960).

Grantham, W. I. The attempted Incorporation of the Moderns. *AQC* 46 (1933), 47 (1934).

Greensill, T. M. *A history of the Societas Rosicruciana in Anglia.* (London: SRIA, 1987).

Haffner, C. *Craftsman unashamed . . .* (Shepperton: A. Lewis, 19??).

——, The eighteenth century lodge as a School of Architecture. *AQC* 101 (1988).

——, Regularity of Origin. *AQC* 96 (1983).

Hamill, John. The Country Stewards and their Feasts. *AQC* 89 (1976).

——, The Earl of Moira, Acting Grand Master 1790–1813. *AQC* 93 (1980).

——, Early Royal Arch MSS *c.*1780–*c.*1830. *AQC* 95 (1982).

——, *Masonic perspectives. Collected papers.* (Belmont, Victoria: privately printed, 1992).

——, The sins of our Masonic fathers. *AQC* 101 (1988).

——, Vocal music in Craft ceremonies. *AQC* 88 (1975).

Hamill, John *and* Gilbert, R. A. *Freemasonry. A celebration of the Craft* (London: MacKenzie, 1992).

——, *World Freemasonry. An illustrated history.* (London: Harper Collins, 1992).

Handfield-Jones, R. M. *The history and origin of the Masonic and Military Order of the Red Cross of Constantine.* (London: privately printed, 1971).

——, *History of the Royal Masonic Institution for Girls 1788–1974.* 5th rev. ed. (London: RMIG, 1974).

——, *New and comprehensive history of the Grand Lodge of Mark Master Masons 1856–1968.* (London: privately printed, 1968).

——, *Origin and history of the Knights Templar and Knights of Malta.* (London: privately printed, 1973).

——, *The Royal Ark Mariner Degree. Its origin and history.* (London: privately printed, 1968).

Haunch, T. O. The Constitution and Consecration of Lodges. *AQC* 83 (1970).

——, The dedication of Freemasons' Hall, 1776. *AQC* 88 (1975).

——, English Craft certificates. *AQC* 82 (1969).

——, Tracing Boards, their development and design. *AQC* 75 (1962).

Hewitt, A. R. Anderson's Constitutions as a source book for Masonic history. *AQC* 79 (1966).

——, Craftsmen in Captivity. *AQC* 77 (1964).

——, *Supreme Grand Chapter. A brief history from Lord Blayney to the Duke of Sussex.* (London: SGC, 1966).

Hextall, W. B. The special Lodge of Promulgation, 1809–1811. *AQC* 23 (1910), 24 (1911), 29 (1916).

Horne, Alex. *King Solomon's Temple in the Masonic tradition.* (Wellingborough: Aquarian Press, 1972).

——, *The York Legend in the Old Charges.* (Shepperton: A. Lewis, 1978).

Howe, Ellic. Fringe Masonry in England 1870–85. *AQC* 85 (1972).

Hughan, W. J. *The origin of the English Rite of Freemasonry.* 3rd ed. (Leicester: Lodge of Research, 1925).

Jackson, A. C. F. *English Masonic exposures 1760–1769.* (Shepperton: A. Lewis, 1986).

——, *Rose Croix. A history of the Ancient and Accepted Rite for England and Wales*, rev. and enlarged ed. (London: A. Lewis, 1987).

Jackson, Keith. *Beyond the Craft.* (Shepperton: A. Lewis, 1980).

James, P. R. The Grand Mastership of HRH The Duke of Sussex, 1813–1843. *AQC* 76 (1962).

Jones, B. E. *Freemasons' guide and compendium.* 2nd ed. (London: Harrap, 1956).

——, *Freemasons' book of the Royal Arch.* 2nd ed. rev. by Harry Carr and A. R. Hewitt. (London: Harrap, 1969).

Knoop, D. *and* Jones, G. P. *An introduction to Freemasonry.* (Manchester: University Press, 1937).

——, *The genesis of Freemasonry.* (1947, reprinted London: Quatuor Coronati, 1978).

——, *Handlist of Masonic documents.* 3rd rev. ed. (Manchester: University Press, 1967).

——, *The Medieval Mason.* 3rd ed. (Manchester: University Press, 1967).

——, *The Scottish Mason and the Mason word.* (Manchester: University Press, 1939).

Knoop, D., Jones, G. P. *and* Hamer, D. *Early Masonic catechisms.* 2nd ed. (1963; reprinted London: Quatuor Coronati, 1975).

——, *Early Masonic pamphlets.* (Manchester, 1945; reprinted London: Quatuor Coronati, 1978).

——, *The two earliest Masonic MSS.* (Manchester: University Press, 1938).

Lane, John. *Masonic records 1717–1894.* 2nd ed. (London, 1895).

Lenhoff, Eugen. *The Freemasons.* Translated by Einar Frame. (1936; reprinted Shepperton: A. Lewis, 1978).

Markham, G. H. Characteristics and origins in early Freemasonry. *AQC* 100 (1987).

——, Further views on the origins of Freemasonry in England. *AQC* 103 (1990).

——, The legendary history in the Old Charges. *AQC* 98 (1985).

McLeod, Wallace. The Old Charges. Prestonian Lecture 1986. *AQC* 99 (1986).

Mellor, Alec. *Our separated brethren the Freemasons.* (London: Harrap, 1969).

——, The Roman Catholic Church and the Craft. *AQC* 89 (1972).

Mendoza, H. *The ensigns of the Twelve Tribes of Israel.* (Shepperton: A. Lewis, 1989).

——, The penalties in the obligations. *AQC* 100 (1987).

Ogilvie, E. E. *Freemasons' Royal Arch Guide.* (Shepperton: A. Lewis, 1979).

Oliver, Bruce. The Assembly on the Hill. *AQC* 61 (1948).

Pace, M. de. *Introducing Freemasonry.* (London: A. Lewis, 1983).

Perrin, Dennis. *The sacking of the Masonic Temple in Jersey by the Nazis in 1941.* (Addlestone: Lewis Masonic, 1993).

Pick, F. L. *and* Knight, G. N. *Freemasons' pocket reference book.* 3rd ed. rev. by F. Smyth. (London: Muller, 1983).

——, *Pocket history of Freemasonry.* 8th ed. rev. by F. Smyth. (London: Muller, 1991).

Pedicord, H. W. White gloves at five. *AQC* 93 (1980).

Philips, A. L. *Freemasonry for beginners and others.* 2nd ed. (London: privately printed, 1976).

Poole, Herbert. Masonic songs and song-books of the 18th century. *AQC* 40 (1927).

——, *The Old Charges.* (London, 1924).

Prestige, H. H. C. *A century of the Allied Masonic degrees.* (London: privately printed, 1979).

Preston, William. *Illustrations of Masonry.* 11th ed., 1801, reprinted with an introduction by Colin Dyer. (Wellingborough: Aquarian Press, 1985).

Rogers, Norman. The Lodge of Elias Ashmole. *AQC* 65 (1962).

Rylands, J. A. The Alnwick Lodge Minutes. *AQC* 14 (1901).

——, The Masonic apron. *AQC* 5 (1892).

Rylands, J. R. The Masonic penalties. *AQC* 77 (1964).

Sadler, Henry. *Masonic facts and fictions,* 1887; reprinted with an introduction by John Hamill. (Wellingborough: Aquarian Press, 1985).

——, *Thomas Dunckerley, his life, labours and letters.* (London: Diprose, 1891).

——, An unrecorded Grand Lodge. *AQC* 18 (1905), 22 (1909).

Sandbach, R. S. E. *Priest and Freemason, the life of George Oliver.* 1988 (reprint London: Lewis Masonic, 1993).

——, *Understanding the Royal Arch.* (Addlestone: Lewis Masonic, 1992).

Seal Coon, F. W. The birth of Freemasonry. *AQC* 92 (1979).

——, Modern anti-Masonry at home and abroad. *AQC* 102 (1989).

——, Spanish American revolutionary Masonry. *AQC* 94 (1981).

Sharp, A. Masonic songs and song books of the late 18th century. *AQC* 65 (1952).

Smyth, Frederick. *Brethren in Chivalry* . . . (London: A. Lewis, 1991).

——, The Master Mason at Arms. Prestonian Lecture 1990. *AQC* 104 (1991).

Spurr, M. J. The Liverpool Rebellion. *AQC* 85 (1972).

Stokes, John. Life of John Theophilus Desaguliers. *AQC* 38 (1925).

——, *Royal Arch Masonry.* (London: Masonic Record, 1924).

Stevenson, David. *The first Freemasons. Scotland's early Lodges and their members.* (Aberdeen: University Press, 1988).

——, *The origins of Freemasonry. Scotland's century 1590–1710.* (Cambridge: University Press, 1988).

Stubbs, Sir James. Building a Temple 1927–33. *AQC* 89 (1976).

——, *The four corners.* (London: privately printed, 1983).

——, *Freemasonry in my life.* (London: A. Lewis, 1985).

——, The government of the Craft. Prestonian Lecture 1982. *AQC* 95 (1982).

Stubbs, Sir James *and* Haunch, T. O. *Freemasons' Hall. Home and heritage of the Craft.* (London: UGL of England, 1984).

Tunbridge, Paul. Field Marshall HRH the Duke of Kent as a Freemason. *AQC* 78 (1965).
United Grand Lodge of England. *Grand Lodge 1717–1967.* (London: UGL of England, 1967).
——, *Historical supplement to the Masonic Year Book*, 2nd ed. (London: UGL of England, 1969) *and Supplement 1969–76* (London: UGL of England, 1976).
Vibert, Lionel. *The story of the Craft.* (London: Spencer, 1925).
Vieler, D. As was seen—and as it was. *AQC* 96 (1983).
——, The power of persuasion. *AQC* 106 (1993).
——, The third man—a study of Browne's Master Keys. *AQC* 105 (1992).
——, William Finch—the positive view. *AQC* 102 (1989).
Waite, A. E. *A new Encyclopaedia of Freemasonry.* 2 vols. (London: Ryder, 1921).
——, *The secret tradition in Freemasonry.* 2 vols. (London: Redman, 1911).
Ward, Eric. The birth of Freemasonry. *AQC* 91 (1978).
——, The crisp English word Freemason. *AQC* 68 (1955).
——, Dassigny, Youghal and all that. *AQC* 88 (1975).
Ward, J. S. M. *Freemasonry and the Antient Gods.* (London: Simpkin, 1921).
——, *The higher degrees hand book.* (London: privately printed, 1924).
Wells, Roy A. *Freemasonry in London from 1785.* (London: A. Lewis, 1984).
——, An introduction to the structure of Freemasonry. *AQC* 86 (1973).
——, *Some Royal Arch Terms explained.* (Shepperton: A. Lewis, 1975).
——, *Royal Arch matters.* (London: A. Lewis, 1984).
Wilkinson, R. L. *The Cryptic Rite: an historical treatise.* (London: privately printed, 1968).
——, *History of the Order of the Secret Monitor 1887–1963.* (London: privately printed, 1964).
Wonnacott, W. Country Stewards and the Green Apron. *AQC* 36 (1923).
——, The Friendly Society of Free and Accepted Masons. *AQC* 29 (1916).
——, The Lodge of Reconciliation. *AQC* 23 (1910).
Yarker, John. *The arcane schools.* (Belfast: William Tait, 1909).

INDEX

NAMES